SHERIDAN MORLEY

TALES FROM THE HOLLYWOOD RAJ:
The British In California

'A well-informed, generously enthusiastic,
benignly mocking history of Britons in Hollywood
. . . entertaining'
Sunday Telegraph

'A proper and useful book'
Observer

'A good book, sparklingly written . . . quoting
generously and hilariously from dozens of
memoirists'
Standard

'A fascinating selection of pictures . . . his easily
readable style makes this a volume that cinema
addicts will welcome'
British Book News

'Morley at his witty, literate and informative best'
Publishers Weekly

DAVID NIVEN

THE OTHER SIDE OF THE MOON
by Sheridan Morley

'This excellent biography shows how uniquely
skilled its subject was in the use of a bonhomous
repair-kit'
Daily Telegraph

'Niven's greatest virtue was that he didn't take life
seriously . . . Sheridan Morley deals admirably
with the ghastly English colony in Hollywood'
John Mortimer, *The Sunday Times*

'Readably and exhaustively compiled . . . Rises
above the mere chronicle of an actor's not to say
chancer's life. The book offers new material and
insights into a life that had many shadows beneath
the light-hearted façade'
The Times

'It is devoid of sycophancy, without entering into
the unequal contest of trying to "top" Niven's
own brilliantly funny memoirs'
The Standard

DAVID NIVEN

THE OTHER SIDE OF THE MOON
by Sheridan Morley

'He was, when young, a great womanizer – he was, after all, a pal of Errol Flynn. There is something irresistible about the way Niven failed to take things seriously'

Punch

'Balanced, informative and factual . . . an efficient biography'

Daily Mail

'Admirably captures the more rueful, darker elements in Niven's life . . . touching'
Financial Times

'Skilfully and painstakingly researched by an author of outstanding ability. This must be the definitive version of the life and times of David Niven . . . He has done an excellent job'
Glasgow Herald

DAVID NIVEN

THE MOON'S A BALLOON

'This book is bloody marvellous. There must be *something* he cannot do'

Peter Sellers

'Miraculous autobiography . . . a commercial blockbuster . . . most engaging and delightfully funny'

Evening Standard

'The funniest volume of reminiscences for ages . . . forthright, bawdy and often hilarious . . . zany and zestful, his anecdotes should keep you entertained for hours'

Sunday Express

'A hilarious account . . . this is warm-hearted and self-revealing'

Daily Mail

'A first-rate, surprisingly frank, genuinely entertaining book'

Newsweek

'Niven writes with a zest for life that is catching'

Publishers Weekly

DAVID NIVEN

BRING ON THE EMPTY HORSES

'A masterful self-portrait. Might easily be the best
book ever written about Hollywood'
New York Times Book Review

'His charm and twinkling sense of humour are
rarely suppressed'
Sunday Express

'Niven reveals himself once again as entertaining
off the screen as on it and a very nice man'
Evening Standard

'A really glamorous autobiography'
Woman

'This time David Niven is riding a winner'
Irish Times

'Were David Niven not a brilliant actor, he would
be thought a brilliant writer. And after this book
he will surely be thought a brilliant writer'
J. K. Galbraith

About the Author

Sheridan Morley has been drama critic and arts editor of *Punch* since 1975. Born in Ascot in 1941, the elder son of Robert Morley, he started his career as a scriptwriter and newscaster with ITN, and in 1967 joined BBC2's *Late Night Line Up*. From 1973–5 he was deputy features editor of *The Times*, for which he still writes a fortnightly profile. He is also the London drama critic for the *International Herald Tribune*, and writes a column for the *Mail on Sunday*.

He is the author of the first biography of Sir Noël Coward (A TALENT TO AMUSE) as well as many other showbiz lives including his grandmother Gladys Cooper. He also wrote a history of the British in Hollywood, TALES FROM THE RAJ (published by Coronet) and co-edited THE NOËL COWARD DIARIES. On radio he regularly presents the *Kaleidoscope* and *Meridian* programmes about the arts. He lives in Berkshire with his wife, three children and a cat.

DAVID NIVEN

THE OTHER SIDE OF THE MOON

SHERIDAN MORLEY

CORONET BOOKS
Hodder and Stoughton

Copyright © by Sheridan Morley, 1985

First published in Great Britain in 1985
by George Weidenfeld & Nicholson Limited

Coronet edition 1986

British Library C.I.P.

Morley, Sheridan
[The other side of the moon] David Niven: the other side of the moon.
1. Niven, David   2. Moving-picture actors and actresses—
Great Britain—Biography
I. [The other side of the moon]   II. Title
791.43′028′0924   PN 2598.N5

Printed in Canada

Published in Canada under license by
General Paperbacks

ISBN 0-7736-8001-2

Hodder and Stoughton Paperbacks, a
division of Hodder and Stoughton Ltd.,
Mill Road, Dunton Green, Sevenoaks,
Kent (Editorial Office: 47 Bedford
Square, London WC1B 3DP)

Contents

Illustrations

ACKNOWLEDGEMENTS

When it was first suggested by my publisher, John Curtis, at Weidenfeld in 1983 that I should consider a biography of David Niven, I wrote rather tentatively to his elder son asking what he thought of the idea, because it seemed to me that without some sort of family co-operation it would be impossible to say more about David than he himself and countless journalists had already said. The younger David Niven and I are roughly of an age, and had last met in California soon after the war when we were both about five; he was, however, kind enough to look up some of my other biographies, including one of his godfather Noël Coward, and wrote back a remarkably enthusiastic go-ahead which included the two things that made me decide I wanted to write this book – an agreement to talk to me about his father without any request to see the manuscript before publication, and an invaluable list of the Hollywood telephone numbers of some of his father's oldest friends.

It is therefore to David Niven Jr that I owe my first debt of gratitude, and although at the time of writing I have no way of knowing whether he will like or even accept this portrait of his father, I hope he does, because without his initial enthusiasm and encouragement it would not exist.

Next I have to thank the three other members of Niven's immediate family who were all equally generous in their agreement to talk to me about a husband, brother and father, again without any demand for control or even sight of the final manuscript: David's widow Hjordis, his sole surviving sister Grizel, and his younger son James. The opinions expressed in this biography are only theirs when they appear as such in direct quotation; but it would certainly not have been possible to complete this jigsaw of the actor's life without them.

First among the non-relatives I would like to thank Barbra Paskin, who did a vast amount of Hollywood research without which I would still be somewhere in the middle of Chapter 6, while in this country I was greatly assisted by Sally Hibbin. In New York Sue Woodman did some valuable library checking, and in California Carol Epstein of the Academy of Motion Picture Arts and Sciences was, as usual, equally helpful.

There now follows an alphabetical list of the 130 people who, in Hollywood, New York, Monaco, Switzerland, France and England, were kind enough to talk about David Niven expressly for *The Other Side of the Moon*, or else to lead me toward those who would. To them all, my deep gratitude:

Sally Adams, Brian Aherne, Margo Albert, Lola Albright, David Rayvern Allen, June Allyson, Don Ameche, Dana Andrews, Ken Annakin, Jeffrey Archer, Lauren Bacall, Frith Banbury, Mary Hayley Bell, Scott Berg, Barry Bliss, David Bolton, Bernard Braden, Faith Brook, William F. Buckley, Judy Campbell, Capucine, John Carradine, Charles Champlin, Bob Cher, John Cockburn, Claudette Colbert, Theo Cowan, Janet Cowell, Cyril Cusack, Nigel Dempster, Susan Douglas, Lesley-Anne Down, Susan Dunford, Blake Edwards, Douglas Fairbanks Jr, Alice Faye, Christina Ferrare, Geraldine Fitzgerald, Alastair Forbes, Bryan Forbes, Sally Blane Foster, Eva Gabor, Greer Garson, Judy Geeson, Milton Goldman, Farley Granger, Stewart Granger, Cary Grant, Richard Greene, George Greenfield, Rosemary Hart, Doreen Hawkins, Richard Haydn, William Randolph Hearst Jr, Charlton Heston, Wendy Hiller, Bob Hope, Tom Hutchinson, Joe Hyams, John Ireland, Lionel Jeffries, Shirley Jones, Phil Kellogg, Gene Kelly, Deborah Kerr, Evelyn Keyes, Patric Knowles, Henry Koster, James Larcombe, Susan Leonard, Viveca Lindfors, Rich Little, Joanna Lumley, Patrick

MacNee, Joel McCrea, Cecil Madden, Henry Mancini, Delbert Mann, Roderick Mann, Raymond Massey, Katherine Matthewson, Patricia Medina, Alec Mellor, Jack Merivale, John Mills, Roger Moore, Jess Morgan, John Mortimer, Richard Mulligan, Robert Nathan, Ronald Neame, Barry Norman, Hedy Olden, Laurence Olivier, Pauline Page, Janis Paige, Joe Pasternak, John Patrick, Graham Payn, Anthony Quayle, HSH Prince Rainier of Monaco, James Reeves, Jeffrey Richards, Cesar Romero, Toby Rowland, Stewart Scheftel, Gus Schirmer, Dennis Selinger, Ken Sephton, Dinah Sheridan, Peter Sherwood, Don Siegel, Andrew Sinclair, Donald Sinden, Marc Sinden, Maggie Smith, John Standing, John Strauss, Shirley Temple, J. Lee Thompson, Deborah Thomson, Ann Todd, Neile McQueen Toffel, Wendy Toye, Ion Trewin, Michael Trubshawe, Christopher Turner, Peter Ustinov, Paul Vallely, Sam Vaughan, Peter Viertel, Robert Wagner, Eli Wallach, Hal Wallis, Al Weingand, Peter Willes, Teresa Wright, Michael and Patricia York.

I am also indebted to the headmaster and governors of Stowe School for permission to quote from the Niven files there, and to RMC Sandhurst for similar privileges. Express Newspapers have allowed me to quote from the columns Niven wrote for them from Hollywood after the war; and for permission to quote brief extracts from their published memoirs I am most grateful to Billy Milton, Lilli Palmer, Topol and the estate of the late Kenneth More as well as to their publishers. Philip Warner's history of the Phantom unit was a valuable source of reference, as was the official history of Stowe School, where both the headmaster and the housemaster of Grafton took considerable trouble in helping me to trace David's often rocky school career.

Graham Payn was kind enough to let me study the thirty-year correspondence between Noël Coward and David Niven, while Barry Norman was generous enough to let me read the uncut BBC transcripts of his interviews for the Niven programme in his *Film Greats* series. But above and beyond all the other help I have had from relatives, friends and fellow- journalists (both critics and interviewers in press, radio and television here and in the US), I would like to acknowledge one outstanding and overriding debt. This book is dedicated to the late Michael Trubshawe who, over one long and memorable weekend spent largely in a pub near his Sussex home a few months before he died, pointed me in most of the right directions and asked all the questions that needed to be raised about David as a man, as a fellow soldier and as an actor before giving me a good many of the answers. I do not believe that anybody knew David better in the first half of his life, nor that Niven ever had a more loving friend or more astute critic, and I am only sorry that Michael did not live to see *The Other Side of the Moon* in print.

I would also like to note here that, since 1974, this is the seventh book of mine to have been edited for John Curtis at Weidenfeld by his senior editor Alex MacCormick. In that time she has also worked with many more talented and distinguished authors; I, on the other hand, could never hope to work with a more talented or distinguished editor.

Copyright owners of photographs used in this book are gratefully acknowledged in the list of illustrations at the front.

For help with the transcription of tapes I am grateful to Jo Hayes and the staff of Tape Typing. I would also like to thank Lynda Poley for picture research, Mrs Evelyn Ford for the index, and Peter Carter-Ruck for legal advice.

Finally, but most importantly of all, I want to thank my editor at *Punch*, Alan Coren, for giving me the sabbatical leave during which I completed this jigsaw, and also my wife and children for putting up with me and a houseful of Niveniana across the two years that it took me to assemble all the pieces.

SHERIDAN MORLEY
March 1985

Chapter One

1985

'I don't like myself as I am, I suppose, so I've had to invent another person. It's not so harmful, really. We've all got daydreams. Mine have gone a step further than most people's – that's all. Quite often I've even managed to believe in them myself.' David Niven as the Major in the 1958 film of Separate Tables, *for which he won his only Oscar and in which he gave the best performance of his ninety-film career.*

When, at the time of his painful and tragic death in July 1983, I was asked to write this first biography of David Niven it seemed a curious suggestion. David had, after all, published within the last decade two of the best-selling autobiographies ever written by an actor (*The Moon's A Balloon* alone sold more than five million copies worldwide) and his life had already been covered by those and countless allied radio and television appearances. His career, though prolific, lacked the distinction of such English contemporaries as Cary Grant, Rex Harrison or James Mason. What, then, would there be to write about? And, if there was anything, would I be cast aright as Niven's biographer?

I was well aware that the project had already been turned down by at least one distinguished London film critic, presumably for the reasons already outlined. I am by trade a theatre critic, and Niven had made but one fleeting and two catastrophic stage appearances in a career of fifty years. So far as my publisher was concerned, all I had in my favour was the fact that I had written a number of other biographies ranging from Oscar Wilde to Gertrude Lawrence, and that my last book for him had been an account of the British actors who, in David's time, had colonized the California studios in much the same way that their parents and grandparents had colonized India and Africa.

But what I knew, as soon as I began to think about Niven's life, was that I had something else going for me: I had known him almost all of mine. We first met in Hollywood just after the war when I was a child living with my grandmother, Gladys Cooper, who was to work with him in both *The Bishop's Wife* and *Separate Tables*. When we arrived in Hollywood, Niven had just lost his first wife in a horrendous fall down a flight of cellar stairs, and their two small sons would sometimes come over to play in the house that Gladys owned just a few doors away from theirs in Pacific Palisades. Ten years later I met him again with Robert, my father, on the set of *Around the World in Eighty Days*. Twenty years later, when I was writing the first biography of Noël Coward, I used to meet David with Noël in Switzerland, where both men had chalets a few stations apart on the railway line that leads from Montreux to Gstaad. A few years later still, when David himself had begun turning his after-dinner stories into books, I began occasionally to write magazine and *Times* profiles of him. It was, however, by pure chance that I had written and narrated the BBC radio tribute on the night of his death (I happened to be working in the studio when the news came through) and I still had grave doubts about whether what I knew of him would make a book that could add anything much to what we all knew from his own writing and chatting over the years.

It was something said to me almost casually by David's elder son at the time of the memorial service a few months later that finally convinced me there was a book here: 'If you want to know about my father's life', said David Jr, 'you won't find it in his autobiographies. They're all about other people.' To some extent, of course, he was only stating the obvious, but I had long been intrigued by the great difference between the Niven of the films and autobiographies – the cheerfully grinning but stiff-upper-lipped storyteller – and the occasional glimpses I'd had of a much darker, more complex and intriguing figure behind the clenched mask of the grin and tonic man.

David traded in a kind of jovial good fortune: that of the untalented but happy-go-lucky adventurer who, after various military and romantic escapades, ends up as an extra in Hollywood, is plucked from the ranks almost by accident, becomes a star and then, when that stardom wanes, has the luck to fall into a whole new career as a best-selling author. This was the image, and out of it Niven carved a fortune estimated on his death at around $5 million; but if you look at the facts of his life, it rapidly becomes clear that he could as easily have written it in terms of tragedy rather than comedy.

The loss in the First World War of a father he had barely come to know, barbaric prep schools, a disappointing army career, the violent death of a first wife, an often deeply unhappy second marriage, the near-death of a beloved adopted daughter in a car crash and then the final loss of a two-year battle against a wasting motor-neurone disease do not exactly add up to what most of us would define as a carefree existence. If David's moon was a balloon, it got punctured very much more often than he cared to admit.

Yet to any journalist David was an utter and total joy. He had, after all, briefly been one of us, writing just after the war a good Hollywood column for the *Daily Express*, and it was another showbusiness journalist on the *Express*, Roderick Mann, who finally persuaded him to start writing *The Moon's A Balloon*. By the time I began interviewing David, this was just about to appear in print and he was genuinely convinced it would sell about fifty copies and that he'd have to give the rest of a remarkably small print run to his friends for Christmas. Before his book reached the bookstalls his stories were known only to an admittedly sizeable band of fellow workers in the entertainment business. I remember in Switzerland going with my wife and Noël Coward and his friend Graham Payn to lunch with David one Christmas in the late 1960s, and hearing him tell quite wonderfully ten of the best Hollywood anecdotes I had ever come across, and then hearing with even more amazement, on the train going back down the mountain to Noël's house, the Niven stories being scored out of ten by Noël and Graham for timing and delivery. Every one of those stories had been as familiar to them as the musical repertoire of such other Swiss neighbours as Yehudi Menuhin or Joan Sutherland, and it was simply a matter of how well David had run through them all that afternoon.

Those stories, rather than any kind of literal autobiographical truth, were at the heart of *The Moon's A Balloon* and *Bring on the Empty Horses*. David had rightly discerned that most actors' lives did not sell in hardback or paperback because they were depressing, portentous, over-confident or just plain unfunny. He also rightly discerned that if he reinvented himself as a kind of local boy made good in Hollywood, and then used himself as a narrator to pull together various time-honoured Californian travellers' tales, he would have a vastly more attractive and commercial text. David's autobiographies were the digest of his after-dinner stories, and his attitude to Hollywood was like that of Richard Gordon to medicine, Henry Cecil to the law or James Herriot to the veterinary business.

It is not that his stories were always exactly untrue, but that the truth in them was often rearranged to lead up to a better punchline. Hollywood historians were nonetheless appalled: one specialist US movie magazine once ran a contest to spot the factual errors in *Bring on the Empty Horses*, and the winner scored well over thirty.

Nor did David necessarily regard the purpose of his autobiographies as being to tell the true story of his own life. Some of the events that most affected him, such as the sudden loss of his beloved first wife, are dismissed in barely a page, and the people who most mattered to him hardly feature in his books at all. The four actresses who had most influence on him and his career on both sides of the Atlantic (Ann Todd, one of his first respectable girlfriends, who introduced him to the theatre; Merle Oberon, with whom and often on whom he lived in the early Hollywood days when he was by his own account a near-starving extra; Rita Hayworth, with whom he lived briefly after his first wife's death; and Deborah Kerr, who helped him towards his Oscar and through one of the many difficult patches in his second marriage) have seldom been publicly linked with him and rate only cursory references in his own writing, while fleeting affairs with actresses like Evelyn Keyes do not even make it to the index. Nor did David ever talk or write about his long and cheering affair during the 1970s when he was living, whenever in London, with the wife of a distinguished investigative journalist on *The Times*.

Even the best and most famous of the stories that do appear in his books tend to fall apart when double-checked: the celebrated Army-leaving telegram, 'REQUEST PERMISSION RESIGN COMMISSION', was in fact first sent not by David, but by his renegade elder brother, Max, when he too wanted out of uniform; later David would sometimes also claim to have been the recipient of the famous 'Streets full of water please advise' cable sent from Venice by Robert Benchley, though Douglas Fairbanks Jr remembers showing him that one in an old scrapbook of his father's. David was always a great borrower of other travellers' tales; he was also amazingly vague on such fundamental biographical details as his own place of birth. For decades he allowed all studio hand-outs and reference books to announce that he was born in 'Kirriemuir, Scotland', where he did indeed spend a short part of his early childhood. It was only after his death that a Somerset House certificate established his birth on 1 March 1910 at Belgrave Mansions in London, whereupon his sons discovered that their father had not been born in Scotland at all despite his frequent references to a tight purse. However, it is likely to be some time before his true birthplace is widely known, for at least one pictorial-tribute book published since his death is still firmly recording it as Kirriemuir.

There are other remarkable contradictions, even on internal evidence. Close observers of David's texts will note that he first meets his first wife at two or three totally different wartime locations. In the end, though, I'm not sure how much any of this really matters, and I certainly do not intend to spend the rest of this biography picking over his own writing for inconsistencies and inaccuracies; I merely think these need to be established in general by way of explaining the need now for a dispassionate biography.

When I started to write about Noël Coward twenty years ago (a man with whom David shared not only a close thirty-year friendship but also certain distinct characteristics of the quintessential Englishman abroad), he too had published a couple of autobiographies, and it occurred to me then that the function of the biographer was not to rewrite already existing memoirs in the light of further and external evidence, but rather to start out from the very beginning as if those often partial and partisan works did not exist. In David's case, this makes the truth a little easier to come by; the thing you have to remember about him is that he was first and last not an autobiographer, but a novelist, a journalist and a storyteller.

His first and last books (*Round the Rugged Rocks* in 1951 and *Go Slowly, Come Back Quickly* in 1981) were both novels and in them, paradoxically, you will find as much of the truth about David's life as you will in his own autobiographies; this was, I have long suspected, why he always refused to allow *Rugged Rocks* back into print, and why he often left it out of his list of past achievements. It was in *Rugged Rocks* that he first told the story of a young English Army officer reaching Hollywood fame by way of a series of adventures not so very different from his own; and it was in *Go Slowly* that he told the story of an English Army officer forced to select the names of men likely to go to certain death on a Dieppe bombing raid in the Second World War. None of that, David felt, could he tell in his own autobiographical voice, at least not while the relatives of those who were killed were still around to read it. For much the same reason, quite a lot of both *The Moon's A Balloon* and *Bring on the Empty Horses* is written in a kind of code. Nowhere in public did David ever admit that the character of 'Missie' whose total mental breakdown he describes in such graphic detail, climaxing in a final forced entry to a sanitarium reminiscent of the end of *A Streetcar Named Desire*, was in fact partly based on the star of that film Vivien Leigh.

Douglas Fairbanks once told me that Niven would sacrifice any friend to a good anecdote, but in fact there is evidence that, like most good journalists, he usually sacrificed only the ones he knew could take it; where he thought a story might do lasting harm, he tended to disguise the participants. All good raconteurs ornament the truth. David rearranged, reassembled, rewrote his life not (like the Major in *Separate Tables*) to hide the terrible truth that he liked attacking young girls in cinemas but simply because the truth was often too boring, too inconvenient, too predictable, too downbeat or just too dull to bear much retelling. David was an actor who gave some of his best performances at dinner parties and later on television talk shows. It is ironic but somehow typical that where a great actor like Irving had his final collapse on a stage during *The Bells*, David started his on a BBC television chat show with Michael Parkinson.

Writing early in 1985, the critic Auberon Waugh noted of a reprint of Niven's two autobiographies: 'They read like some joker in a saloon bar who has told the same

stories so often before to the same audience that they have
been improved beyond any resemblance to whatever truth
they originally contained.' But somewhere in them lay a
certain amount of truth, and David was something rather
more than a saloon-bar joker. For all his clubbable affa-
bility, he remained an outsider and a loner: the English
actors he first went out to join in Hollywood during the
1930s were at least a generation older and, like Ronald
Colman and C. Aubrey Smith, had all fought in the First
World War, which had ended when David was barely
eight. The ones who came after him, the generation of
Michael Caine and Roger Moore, were not English in
any sense that David would have recognized: they were
internationals who just happened to live in California and
come from England. Even among his own contemporaries,
David found precious few real friends: Michael Trubshawe, who was Best Man at both his weddings, found
himself cut off when he became a comic actor. James
Mason was never forgiven by David for his conscientious
objection to the Second World War. Stewart Granger he
had little time for as a man or an actor. Rex Harrison
was the only one of 150 relatives, friends and enemies I
approached who actually refused to talk to me about Niven
at all. The reason, Harrison later told me over a private
lunch in New York, was that he had always disliked (a)
Niven and (b) books about actors, and therefore saw no
reason to contribute to a project which would combine the
two.

It was only towards the end of David's life, with the
success and security that finally came to him after the move
back to Europe and the best-sellers, that he was able to
form enduring friendships with writers like William F.
Buckley and John Mortimer, and actors like Robert
Wagner and Roger Moore. Those last twenty years, away
from a dying Hollywood, were, I think, the best of David's
life, despite domestic difficulties and a film career that was
to lurch after *Guns of Navarone* into almost uninterrupted
mediocrity. These were the years when, quite rightly, he

thought of himself as a writer and a painter rather than an actor, though he was writing always about the past. Some of the best of the later stories sadly never made it into print, though they have a kind of 'ageing Englishman abroad' quality of considerable and hilarious charm, like the night at a grand Malibu gathering when he was apparently asked by a glamorous hostess if he would like a blow. Unable to believe his luck, David whispers that he would and is told to follow his hostess into an upstairs bathroom. Finding her there with her back to the door and standing by the bathroom cupboard, David removes his trousers in delighted expectation, only to have her turn and scream in horror and surprise at his nudity. In her hand is a glass phial containing an exotic powdered drug – and I know of no better generation-gap story than that.

The major requirements of a Niven story were that it should be funny and involve famous people: indeed if they were not famous enough, or if their fame had started to slip, he would have no hesitation in recasting. Thus Cirrhosis-by-the-Sea was in fact the name first given to a California beach house he shared with an excellent English character actor called Robert Coote. Niven remained loyal to Coote, making sure that he worked regularly in his one major television series *The Rogues*, but from the storytelling point of view Coote lacked adequate alcoholic celebrity, and therefore in retrospect the co-tenant of Cirrhosis was always said by David to be Errol Flynn, an actor with whom he only later and briefly shared that residence.

By the time I got to know David well in the late 1960s, those stories were already embedded in his party repertoire and they were to turn up intact in the memoirs. Niven was by then only in his late fifties, but already he was summoning up words that one had thought long dead: clubbable, debonair, impeccable, jaunty. His prose style was that of an elegant gossip, poised somewhere half-way between Harold Nicolson and Hedda Hopper, and, though he had risen well above the ranks of the George Sanders/

Nigel Bruce/Basil Rathbone school of expatriate English gentlemen players, he had never risen far enough to be, like Cary Grant or Ronald Colman, the kind of star on whom alone you could hang a picture. There remained something mysterious and contradictory about him: when he looked in his shaving mirror each morning, did he have any real idea who looked back at him? Friends certainly were often puzzled.

Niven was a devoted father and husband who went through the female population of Hollywood like a mechanical digger; he was a patriotic Englishman who passed for a Scot and spent two-thirds of his life abroad; he was an expert and professional soldier who was yet appalled when one of his sons suggested that he might do military service; he was a rich man who went to his grave convinced that he couldn't afford to pay a nurse to look after him; he was a serious man desperately keen to be taken for a joker; he was a film star whose name alone above a title couldn't sell a ticket, so that even for such a long and epic performance as Phileas Fogg in *Around the World in Eighty Days* he had to share top billing with a Mexican comedian (Cantinflas), a Broadway dancer in her third film (Shirley MacLaine), and an old English actor on a short alcoholic run to the grave (Robert Newton). Even for his Oscar-winning *Separate Tables*, Niven was only billed third in a quartet comprising Burt Lancaster, Rita Hayworth and Deborah Kerr.

David was a veneer actor capable of a few remarkable performances but haunted by a feeling of professional inadequacy: of the ninety movies he made, only *The Charge of the Light Brigade* (1936), *The Prisoner of Zenda* (1937), *Wuthering Heights* (1939) and the three that he made in wartime England (*The First of the Few*, *The Way Ahead* and *A Matter of Life and Death*) have any real claim to lasting distinction before *Separate Tables* (where he was a replacement for Laurence Olivier) and then *The Guns of Navarone* (where the original casting had been Kenneth More).

It is hard to think of any leading actor who made as many bad films as Niven (no less than thirty in the 1960s and 1970s alone) or whose career suffered quite so many missed opportunities. The *Raffles* that might at last have made him a solo star came just at the outbreak of a war he felt bound to leave Hollywood to fight; the James Bond he was surely born to play reached the screen when he was already too old, so that instead of *Dr No* he ended up in the appalling *Casino Royale; The Pink Panther* was stolen from under him by Peter Sellers as the manic Inspector Clouseau; the triumphs he had enjoyed on home territory during the war were rapidly destroyed by the fiasco of *Bonnie Prince Charlie* in 1948, and his film career ended in a plethora of rubbish (*Escape to Athena*; *A Nightingale Sang in Berkeley Square*; *Rough Cut*; *Better Late Than Never*; *The Trail of the Pink Panther*) from which even David might have found it hard to rise again had his health permitted.

Yet, as Burt Reynolds once noted, 'If you want sophistication, go have lunch with David Niven.' Until the very last few months of his life, when he could neither speak nor eat, he insisted on dictating jokey letters to the friends who wrote their condolences, but to the really close ones he wrote something altogether more chilling: 'Dear old chum,' reads his last hand-written note to Deborah Kerr, 'don't stretch the elastic too far, because it snaps.'

A few weeks before the death that came as a kind of relief to those who had loved him after the physical agony of his last eighteen months, David Niven moved out of his home in the South of France to die in the Swiss Alps, where many of his happiest hours had been spent skiing. He died peacefully at seventy-three, after a long and commercially triumphant career, but it was to some extent a refugee's end, not the one that might have been expected of that apparently most debonair and carefree man. Niven was the last of his kind. To be a screen Englishman is nowadays a contradiction in terms as well as a professional impossibility – there is simply no such thing. But his conjuring act has proved a curiously difficult one to follow, as has been discovered by the countless actors who rushed into print hoping to profit from the fair wind that blew *The Moon's A Balloon* into the booksellers' charts.

It was once said of Rex Harrison by Noël Coward that if he hadn't been just about the best light comedian in the business, he'd have been fit only for selling secondhand cars in Great Portland Street; by the same token I have always thought of Niven ending up, had it not been for the ciné camera and for the fountain-pen he always used to write his books, as the commodore of a minor yacht club somewhere like Bembridge on the Isle of Wight, one of his many childhood homes. The jovial storytelling talent required would not, after all, have been so very different; nor would the ever-open bottle of Scotch (David laid off the gin after his sons complained of the temper it put him in) and the remarkable hospitality. One of the best things about being a journalist interviewing David was that he not only gave you the lunch and all the stories needed for your article, but he also ritually presented you with the paid bill so that you could claim it on your expenses. Not surprisingly he was loved probably more than any other actor by Fleet Street and, towards the end, when he had more right than most to play for sympathy, he still played for nothing more than entertainment.

David's life was essentially a pageant with himself at its head. When he wrote about it, the lighting and the dialogue were much improved and the extras had become an all-star cast. Like Coward and Mountbatten, Englishmen of Niven's own generation whom he much resembled in often exiled Englishness, David was his own best impresario, invention and contribution to the twentieth century. Like them, he stood, often before foreigners, as the symbol of an already lost England; like them, he understood the crucial importance of showbusiness; and, like them, he knew that everybody loves a parade. In the forty years or so that separated *The Prisoner of Zenda* from *The Moon's A Balloon*, David had managed to rise through the ranks to the head of a Hollywood parade of which he was by the end not only a leader but also the most successful chronicler.

The 5,000 people who turned up at his memorial service in St Martin-in-the-Fields were mourning a man who never seemed to have a care in the world. In fact, he had rather more than many, but to discuss them we had better go back to the beginning.

Chapter Two

1910–1925

'I don't believe my mother was actually taking in washing, but she was sure as hell sending precious little out.'

James David Graham Niven was born on 1 March 1910 in London, and by the time his father (listed as William Edward Graham Niven) got around to registering his birth six weeks later the family appear to have been living at Carswell Manor near Farringdon in Berkshire. Neither this address nor that of his birth in Belgrave Mansions is ever referred to by David in his autobiographies, which pick up around the time of his father's death five years later. His father is described on the birth certificate as a 'landed proprietor' and his mother as Henrietta Julia Niven, formerly de Gacher. David was the last of their four children: first had come Joyce, then Max, and then Grizel, who after a brief theatrical career became a sculptor in Chelsea and was the only sibling to outlive David. In their early childhood, with Max and Joyce considerably older, it was Grizel who found herself closest to 'the baby of the family', though her recollections are of a reversed relationship: 'I was always the fool who dropped everything and lost everything, and it was always David who came to my rescue. He called me "the silly gump", and that's still how I'm known to his children – Aunt Gump.'

Born on St David's Day (hence the Christian name) to

a mother who was three-quarters French and a Scots father who had spent much of his own early life on a farm in Patagonia, David had a distinctly unsettled early childhood, one on which his father seems to have made remarkably little impression; indeed, in the 550 pages that comprise David's two autobiographies, his father rates only two passing references.

However, when interviewed in the pre-war Hollywood years, David does seem to have had rather better recollections of the father he hardly knew: 'The late William G. Niven was a very rich man, and when I appeared on the scene we lived in a large country house staffed with footmen, butlers and gamekeepers. We also had our own private bookmaker. My father devoted hours to the scientific study of thoroughbred horses, but he must have been reading the wrong reference books, because by the time I was two years old the horses had all our money and we had to give up the great estate.'

The estate appears to have been in Scotland, though there were also the homes in London and Berkshire, and David talked of an estate in Gloucestershire too – all this between 1910 and the outbreak of the First World War four years later. Clearly there had been money on the father's side of the family, and just as clearly he went through it pretty rapidly, though there was still enough for Niven *père* to set off to war with a valet, an under-gardener and two grooms. Grizel remembers him standing with David on his back outside their London house waiting for the taxi that would take him off to fight, the last time they saw him. As Grizel recalled, 'David was four and I was seven, and I think that afternoon was probably the clearest recollection either of us ever had of him. He wasn't really a military man at all. He'd done all sorts of things in his life, none of them for very long.'

So with their father, aged only twenty-five, now a lieutenant in the Berkshire Yeomanry the four young children were left in the care of assorted nursemaids and a mother whom Grizel remembers as 'utterly charming, if a little vague'. David, eager in his memoirs to press on to the sexual delights of his youth, seemed to recall that with his father's disappearance into the army the Nivens' life changed virtually overnight from landed wealth to genteel poverty. In fact it was not quite as simple as that. When his father was killed over a year later, he left rather more than £5,000, which for the period was a respectable sum. Yet life did change fairly drastically, for David now had no father and no one to replace him until eventually, at Stowe almost a decade later, he found the headmaster whom he was always to think of with strong filial affection.

For the time being, as Grizel remembers, Mrs Niven and her four children were perpetually on the move: 'From Scotland and Gloucestershire we moved to Cirencester, then back to London, where we lived in Cadogan Place and then Sloane Street and then Cheyne Walk, before finishing up on the Isle of Wight at Rose Cottage in Bembridge. I think all the moves were to do with money or the lack of it, but somehow they never seemed to matter terribly to us because we were all sent away to boarding schools very early, and so it was just a question of having somewhere new to live in the holidays.'

Long after their mother died, Grizel came upon a trunk of family letters indicating the strain that she had endured during that first year of the war. With virtually no news of her husband, who never returned from the front, she would scour the 'Missing' lists until, at the very end of 1917, she received a formal note of regret from the War Office that her husband had been killed in action on 21 August 1915 during the doomed attack on the Gallipoli peninsula. Lieutenant Niven's war had been a brief and distinguished one, and he was referred to by his men as 'a fine leader and a marvellous man': not quite distinguished enough, however, for the Goldwyn Studio publicity office, which posthumously promoted him to the rank of general in many of David's early publicity hand-outs.

By the time she learned of her husband's death in action, Mrs Niven had already met the man who was to be her second husband: Sir Thomas Comyn-Platt was, by David's reckoning, 'a second-line politician who did not fight in the war' and was later to be known as the mystery man of the Conservative Party, largely as a result of contesting Portsmouth Central in the 1929 election. As a stepfather, he seems to have left a good deal to be desired. Though he married David's mother in March 1919 he had no particular desire also to take on her children except in the financial sense, and indeed took to staying up at his club in London whenever they threatened to return home for the holidays.

'None of us liked him at all,' recalls Grizel Niven, 'though he used to stay well away from Bembridge in the summers. When he did appear he used to denigrate us all the time. I remember the first time I was given a knife to use instead of a spoon, and all he said was, "Oh, how stupid the girl looks." I don't think he really ever understood about children, and of course it wasn't as though we were his own. Because of that, David and I were thrown together more and more in the school holidays – we even started to look rather like each other. The rest of the family was dark and rather French-looking after our mother, but David and I were both fair with bright blue eyes.'

David took the view that the family's frequent change of address marked a steep social decline and that Bembridge was rock bottom. Rose Cottage he found an altogether unsuitable address with which to impress fellow prep-school pupils, especially as the very few who did ever venture there found the house in a state of some disrepair. Bembridge residents were, however, then as now a grand lot with their own yacht club, and would doubtless not have been delighted to learn that David regarded the area as a come-down from Chelsea. The problem, indeed, that one finds with almost all his childhood memories is that there was always another side to the story. When he first published (in *The Moon's A Balloon*) a graphic account of the Dickensian horrors of one particular prep school near Worthing where the headmaster apparently gave David's ears their curious shape by half-pulling them out of his head, a lady wrote more in sorrow than in anger to point out that her late father, the headmaster in question, had laboured long and hard to get some sort of education into a Niven head that seemed to respond only to brute force at that time.

Certainly David's home life was now less than happy, and this doubtless contributed to his determination to be a less than ideal pupil at the many prep schools to which his despairing stepfather committed him. What little David saw of Sir Thomas Comyn-Platt he disliked, and the feeling was undoubtedly mutual. Seldom can so many theories of stepfather–stepson anguish have been so neatly proved as by Mrs Niven's remarriage. Accordingly David was parcelled off first to Worthing and then to Heatherdown, a vastly more gentle prep school in Ascot. There, however, he disgraced himself, as Grizel recalls: 'All the pupils at Heatherdown were supposed to cultivate their own little garden plots and on speech day they were to be filled with marvellous flowers and vegetables and things like that, only one term mother forgot to send David any of the seeds so the night before speech day he decided to climb over the wall that separated Heatherdown from Heathfield, the girls' school next door, and steal a prize marrow to exhibit in the midst of his plot next morning. There was a hell of a lot of trouble about that.'

So much, in fact, that David was summarily expelled at the end of that term for stealing. It had not been his only escapade (sending a box of dogshit to a friend at a neighbouring school had been another), and the staff of Heatherdown decided that they could get along rather better without him. Sir Thomas Comyn-Platt, predictably, was not pleased: the only thing more troublesome than a stepson was an expelled stepson, and David began to acquire the 'naughty schoolboy' qualities that were to condition so much of his later attitude to army discipline, Hollywood studios and almost anyone or anything in any kind of authority over him. A psychiatrist could probably be found to argue that a deep sense of school behaviour – its loyalties to fellow pupils, its delight at 'putting one over' on the teachers, its fear of being 'found out' – was central to the rest of David's life. In his sixties he was still talking about a fear that critics would 'find him out', discover that perhaps he wasn't a real actor at all, but a likely lad who had somehow managed to creep into the wrong class and stay there undiscovered by the authorities. David's screen characteristics, and the language in which he wrote his memoirs, were all rooted in English prep- and public-school ethics of the 1920s. Behind the blazer and the old school tie I believe there grew up a vastly more cynical, complex and contradictory man, but David was careful to leave the everlasting schoolboy up front – it was a lovable, simplistic image that easily crossed the Atlantic and the divide between audience and screen. David's predecessors in Hollywood, from C. Aubrey Smith to Ronald Colman, had mostly been father figures; Niven intelligently recognized the gap that could be filled by a son figure who was essentially naughty but decent, somewhere half-way between George Arliss and George Sanders.

After the comparative comfort of Heatherdown, life went rapidly downhill again. Eton, for which he had been entered along with many other Heatherdown boys, suddenly found its entrance list mysteriously full for the next two or three years, and David returned somewhat sheepishly to Bembridge, where neighbours, John Cockburn and Alec Mellor, remember him in that summer of 1920 as 'just great fun to be with and up to every prank you could think of. His mother was a fine, tall, woman and he was obviously very fond of her, but there wasn't much discipline and every night he'd be off to the local Garland Club which was the centre of adult activity. We of course weren't allowed in, but there was old David trying to climb over an iron fence and running a spike through his thigh. We got him back to Rose Cottage and then his mother came rushing in, about eleven at night and dressed as a nun so there must have been some sort of fancy-dress party going on, and there was David with a bath towel wrapped around his thigh and blood everywhere. A few years later we somehow got hold of a car and used to drive over to Shanklin in search of the night life, but David was always also fascinated by the harbour and the yacht club where they allowed children to keep dinghies. Bembridge was where that love of sailing really started, and he never lost it. In California and France he always had to live near the water's edge, and he took his sailing very seriously indeed. He was a very good boyhood friend to have, cheerful and not especially sensitive although he was being chucked about from pillar to post, especially after he was expelled from Heatherdown, and he was a bit mixed-up and worried about his school career and the fact that he didn't really have a father. But he was not one to brood on that. In public he was always the greatest fun on earth.'

That Bembridge summer came to an end, however, and now that he could no longer return to Heatherdown David was sent across the Solent to a kind of reformatory in Southsea which specialized in treating expelled children, the treatment being apparently more often physical than educational. After a bruising month there he was moved on again, this time to a somewhat more congenial crammer in Buckinghamshire (run by a clergyman grandson of Robert Browning) where he was supposed to sit the entrance examination to Dartmouth, it having been decided by David's mother and stepfather that he should attempt to follow his brother Max into the Royal Navy.

David's terms at the crammer in Penn were uneventful, except for what he was later to call the 'dreary experience' of a homosexual encounter with a large ex-Etonian willing to pay ten shillings for his favours. This seems not to have been an encounter that radically changed Niven's sexual orientation.

David failed the entrance examination to Dartmouth, and by now there was a kind of desperation in Comyn-Platt's attempts to get his stepson educated. Niven could not hang around the Bembridge yacht club forever – at

least, not in term time – and both Eton and Dartmouth
had indicated even before his twelfth birthday their determination not to have him darken their desks. A boy of
thirteen who had already been expelled from one school
for stealing and who showed no marked academic talents
of any kind was not easy to place academically even in
1923; and it was therefore with more optimism than confidence that Sir Thomas considered a radical new alternative. That year a large number of prep-school headmasters
from all over England had met to consider the problem
facing them: more pupils about to leave than there were
places available at the established public schools. The First
World War had led to a breakdown in the old system of
entering a boy for public school at birth, and there was
suddenly a large number of thirteen-year-olds with no
place to go. Few of them had been in the kind of academic
or disciplinary trouble that David had known, but all of
them had to be found somewhere to study. The answer
was clearly the founding of a new public school. Stowe
House near Buckingham had just come on the market,
and its first headmaster, a remarkable housemaster from
Lancing College called J. F. Roxburgh, made it clear that
this was to be no ordinary public school: 'If we do not
fail wholly in our purpose, every boy who goes out from
Stowe will know beauty when he sees it all the rest of his
life.'

These were fighting words in 1923. Indeed, the headmaster of Eton was swift to complain that what the British
public-school world needed were more establishments like
his instead of new-fangled beauty-training camps. Nevertheless it was clear that Stowe would be seeking a rather
different kind of pupil, and David's name was rapidly
submitted. There followed a brief interview with Roxburgh, in whom David seems instantly to have found the
father he had never really had, and you can almost hear
the sigh of relief in the letter written to Roxburgh from
the Carlton Club by Sir Thomas on 2 July 1923:

Sir, I have received a letter from Mr Browning, with whom my stepson David Niven has been for this last year or so, stating that you would be prepared to have the boy at Stowe. That I am sure would be greatly to his advantage, for I have heard the very best accounts of your school from many of my friends. Would it be asking too much if I brought my wife down to see the school?

David's mother duly inspected the premises, approved them, and David started at Stowe in the September which marked the beginning of the school's second term. That early Stoic intake also included the stage director Frith Banbury and the future Conservative minister Lord Boyd-Carpenter (with whom David also went to Sandhurst) and the 9th Earl of Glasgow, but the fellow pupil who seems to have retained the clearest memories of David as a teenage schoolboy is Peter Sherwood.

'Niven was always getting into scrapes, as I gather he had at his prep schools, but he found in Roxburgh a wonderful and clever mentor who knew exactly how to handle him. He would only have to say, "My dear David, I don't think that is very helpful," and David would say, "I suppose not, Sir, I'm awfully sorry," and that would be more or less the end of that. It was indeed true that David introduced a young tart [Nessie] into the school on one of the parents' days, and that Roxburgh had a long chat to her on the grass as if she had been the grandest of the mothers, but then that would have been exactly the kind of thing Roxburgh took in his stride. His influence on David was incalculable: he taught him grace, elegance, the kind of behaviour that became the Niven manner on screen and off. David had no pretensions to being a scholar, but he was very quick and if he took the trouble to apply himself he could pick things up easily enough. The trouble was that he seldom bothered to apply himself, at least in the classroom.

'We spent a year together in a science class taken by an absurd and ineffectual master who had a missionary box

which he used to make us put a penny into instead of being
given lines or any other punishment. I need hardly tell you
that this was a challenge which David couldn't possibly
resist. He got one kind of big old penny you could drill a
hole through, threaded it with cotton and would then drop
the coin loudly into the box. Having done that he'd return
to his seat, put up his hand and say, "Well, Sir, I know
you think I am a most frightful fool and I expect I am, but
I really do think that if you could explain that theorem on
the blackboard just one more time even I might get the
hang of it." So the gullible man would turn back to the
board, and David would pull the thread and get the coin
back into his pocket.

'His jokes and pranks were always much the same; they
were repetitive but somehow he always made them work
and got the laughs, and I suppose that was where it all
started. He also used to do a lot of impersonations, men
who'd eaten mothballs thinking they were peppermint
lumps, gracious ladies having to be polite about ghastly
Christmas gifts, that kind of thing. His face would become
contorted with grotesque smiles and he'd keep the routine
going for five or ten minutes.'

At this stage it was still widely believed that David was
going into the Navy, despite his early failure to get into
Dartmouth. Indeed, on his entry form to Stowe his stepfather boldly crossed out the options 'University', 'Army'
and 'Medical Profession' but underlined the one word
'Navy' twice, as if such emphasis might make up for academic failures. By the start of his second Stoic year, however, David had discovered another interest apart from
yachts and making fun of science masters, and this was
largely the result of a decision by Peter Sherwood.

'I had always been incurably stagestruck,' recalls Peter,
'and so, rather precociously, in my first term I formed a
drama group called the Bruce Players after the name of
our house. David was also very keen to start acting, so we
did a number of one-act plays and then, when we used to
have to go off for officer training camps in dreary places

on Salisbury Plain, we would stage camp concerts and I was always persuading David to go on and do one of his impressions. These became an annual event at the camps, and were so popular that the audience used to chant "We want Niven!" whenever any other poor schoolboy got up to do a turn . . . all except the pianist from Charterhouse who was also very good.'

At this period in his school life David was far from being the svelte figure he was to become: 'I was known as Podger Niven,' he told me years later, 'because I was terribly fat with this great round face and I couldn't run very fast, and in the shower after football I used to turn bright pink. I was so gross for a while that I actually sent off for some shilling tubes of stuff I'd seen advertised as a fat dissolvent. Fearful-smelling stuff it was – I can remember it to this day – and every night I'd rub it on my stomach, but as I kept eating chocolate whirls during the daytime it really didn't have much effect.'

The Stowe school records in these years show David making steady progress through its sporting and even academic ranks. 'Niven must use his voice even more to encourage his side,' reported the rugger master. 'Niven put up a stout fight against Montague-Scott,' read his fencing report, 'but after 2–all the Captain of Fencing got the final point.' The squash-racquets finals were equally depressing ('Niven easily beaten'), but by the next term he had won the hundred yards relay race and by the summer term he had become a Lance-Corporal in the school Corps. That term he also took three wickets off Eton, thereby gaining his Second Eleven cricket colours, and slept out 'on the roof to inspect the total eclipse of the sun of June 29th. Unfortunately', continues the house-master's report, 'it was a wet and cloudy morning.' That term Niven was also voted 'best all-round competitor' in the school Life-Saving contests and 'prominent in the dramatic side of the school concert'. He also seems to have formed his own Niven XI, which made 69 against the Colts 143, and by the time he was ready to leave the school his

record was looking good: 'Monitor 6 terms. Sergeant in
OTC. School colours: 2nd xi cricket, 2nd xv rugger. House
colours: rugger, cricket, tennis, swimming.'

Ten years after the death of his father and five after his
ignominious expulsion from Heatherdown, David was at
last coming into his own – much helped by Roxburgh, of
whom Evelyn Waugh once noted, 'Most good schoolmas-
ters are homosexual by inclination – how else could they
endure their work – but their interest is diffuse and un-
acknowledged. J.F.'s passions ran deep, though I do not
think he ever gave them physical release with any of his
pupils.' David would in any case have been an unlikely
candidate for advances of that nature, because by the time
he was fourteen he had already met the Soho prostitute
he called Nessie, and though she may well have been
a composite portrait of several ladies of dubious virtue
encountered during his teenage wandering around London's less salubrious streets, there is no doubt that a
detailed and precocious interest in the opposite sex was
the main feature of David's later schooldays.

Fifty years afterwards, writing of all that teenage groping
around Soho, David took a novelist's interest in Nessie's
fate and announced that, when he was about twenty, she
had written him a tender note of farewell, had married well
and become a housewife in Seattle. From then onwards, he
was seldom able to do a television show in the United
States without dozens of studio phones ringing as elderly
English matrons called in claiming to be the long-lost love
of his early youth.

Chapter Three

1925–1930

'It is with grief and great disappointment that I have to tell you a boy representing Stowe in the School Certificate has been caught cheating.'

For a while, David seemed to be leading a charmed life at Stowe. A favourite pupil of Roxburgh's whose classroom pranks in the presence of minor masters were generally overlooked on account of his attractive personality and undoubted good nature, he moved through the school with apparently effortless ease. At the end of the 1926 summer term, when David was just sixteen, Roxburgh even thought the time had come to give him a little responsibility. 'I am asking David', he wrote to Lady Comyn-Platt in Bembridge, 'to go over next term to the New House which I am launching and to be a monitor there. I don't think his prospects of promotion are very good in his own House, as so many of the senior boys are all of the same age, and in Grafton he will have a chance of taking responsibility at once. It will do him a world of good to have something to run, and the feeling that something really depends on him.'

By now school excursions were getting more adventurous. As well as the summer OTC camps on Salisbury Plain there was a camping trip to Switzerland, of which the school magazine reported, 'Niven temporarily but alarmingly lost at Boulogne: he reappeared, however, and evening sing-songs produced some unexpected and hitherto hidden talents including Niven in the role of a muddled army recruit.' This was in March 1925, at the time of his fifteenth birthday. In that same school year he began also to develop a considerable interest in writing, as the poet James Reeves recalls: 'We collaborated in starting the first unofficial Stowe magazine, *The Chandosian.* David was a born entertainer. One could never be bored in his presence. He treated us to dozens of very funny sketches based on the Aldwych farces of the day and other London amusements. I must claim the honour of being one of his first stage directors, for at my last end-of-term concert I produced him in a little play by A. A. Milne. But the memory of David which I recall with greatest vividness and affection was an episode which may seem tepid enough today, but which at the time was irresistibly funny, a touch of creative comic genius. As we went into hall for lunch one day, we noticed the pudding for the meal: a huge, hemispherical, flesh-coloured blancmange on a dish, one for each table, on the trolleys which lined one wall of the long state dining room. Swiftly David walked along the line of blancmanges, administering with the flat of his right hand a neat smack to each one in turn. Is it not of such trivial fond records that much of one's personal past is composed?'

David's role at Stowe was thus that of the school joker. A deep desire to be liked by his fellow schoolboys, coupled with the hope that popularity might just make up for a distinct lack of academic success, kept him larking about. Yet there was, as Frith Banbury recalls, a sharp difference between the performer and the actor: 'I was a couple of years younger than David at Stowe, but I remember that he seemed to me even then a curiously old-fashioned figure of fun. The big stage hit of the time was a musical in which Leslie Henson had a famous drunk scene and David was forever imitating that, so even in his teens one thought of him ending up as an entertainer, maybe a comic song-and-dance man, rather than a legitimate actor and I think the short and relatively undistinguished stage career he had later bears that out. Acting seemed to inhibit him, whereas performing, being himself on a slightly broader canvas and doing turns rather than plays, was always what suited him best. He was always assing about, and I rather thought he'd end up in the West End revues that were so popular at that time, doing comic sketches and then maybe a musical number in top hat and tails – a broader comic version of Jack Buchanan, perhaps. There was no doubting his interest in showbusiness, but I always rather doubted his interest in pure theatre.'

In any case, David had by now discovered the other interest that was to occupy him for most of the rest of his life, until in his last twelve years it became the main source of his income and fame: he had begun to write. Niven's first published work appeared in the Stowe school magazine for April 1926. Entitled 'A Tailing Party At The Swiss Camp', it was an account of the school outing to the ski slopes in the previous winter, one on which they were joined by boys from other British public schools including Eton, Rugby and Repton. David's debut in print, bylined J.D.G. Niven, has not been republished in almost sixty years, but it is not too hard to see in this some early traces of that curious journalistic mix of gossip-column reporting, fairly plausible anecdotage and high-society (or at any rate high-school-society) name dropping which, half a century later, was to sell those three million copies of Niven's memoirs:

The procession prepared to start in the following order: first, a couple of sinister-looking horses; second, Antoine, or 'The Last Bandit', or 'Why - cause - a - lot - of - trouble - by - pushing - your - rich - uncle - over - the - cliff - when - you - can - have - him - quietly - stabbed - for - one - franc-fifty'; third, a sleigh full of lunch; and fourth, the cream of the Hotel Valbella on luges, reading from left to right – an Etonian, a Rugbe-ian, Hartland-Swann, a Reptonian, me, a Cantab, and Reptonian II

While Antoine put the finishing knots to the luges, we all stood round admiring the Etonian's apricot ski-ing suit. 'Take your seats, please!' from the Rugbeian. We sat down. The Rugbeian took Hartland-Swann's feet on his lap; Reptonian I took mine; Cantab took Reptonian II's; the Etonian, alone in front, nursed a guide book.

'*En avant!*' cried the Etonian, in his best taught-in-twelve-lessons accent. Antoine muttered an oath to his animals. They pulled bravely. The rope snapped – and they trotted gaily down the hill with Antoine.

We hurried after them with the luges.

'It's a good joke,' said the Cantab when this happened the third time, 'but personally I'm fed up with it.' Antoine, who seemed full of rope, produced a fourth piece and tied a knot that would have made even Major Haworth envious. We settled down again.

Once more Antoine cursed his horses, and once more they pulled bravely . . . and this time we went with them. 'The idea all along,' I explained to Hartland-Swann.

We fell to discussing why we should enjoy the journey more in our present position than we had done coming up from the station a few days before in a comfortable sleigh, feeling bitterly cold and extremely bored.

'It's the possibility of an accident,' explained the Rugbeian. 'At any moment somebody may fall off.'

'My dear chap,' said the Etonian, turning round to take part in the conversation, 'why anybody should fall off –' We went suddenly round a corner, and quietly the Etonian left his luge and rolled onto the track.

As soon as we had recovered our powers of speech, we called upon Antoine to stop. He indicated with the back of his neck that it was dangerous to stop just then; and it was not until we were at the bottom of the hill, almost a mile from the place where the Etonian had left us, that the procession halted and gave itself up to laughter.

Ten minutes later a brilliant sunset was observed approaching from the North. A little later it was seen to be a large dish of apricots and cream – or shall we say the Etonian? When he had arrived and told us all about our lineage and our future, he lapsed into a gloomy silence.

'Let's get on, then,' said the Rugbeian. We resumed our seats once more. The Etonian clung tight to his seat with both hands.

'Right!' said the Cantab. Antoine swore at the horses. They pulled bravely. The rope snapped, and they trotted gaily up the hill with Antoine. We hurried after them with the luges.

The empty horses had been brought on for the first time, and if Niven was reading very much around the time of his sixteenth birthday apart from the occasional text book, one might guess from the tone of that piece that it was either Jerome K. Jerome or P.G. Wodehouse – possibly both.

A few weeks later, however, David was back in real trouble. On 23 July 1926 his headmaster wrote to his mother: 'I would very much rather not have to send you this letter, but I'm afraid it can't be helped and you must know some time or other. David has been disqualified in the School Certificate examination for making use of another boy's work. I am thankful for the sake of the school that I found out what happened before the papers were sent to the examiners. I wish David would think rather more carefully before he does these impulsive things, which are so entirely below his proper level and which cannot help lowering him in the estimation of us all.'

What had happened was straightforward enough. David, whose stepfather had by this time decided that the Army rather than the Navy would be a suitable career for him, was sitting the School Certificate examination that was supposed to lead him in due course to Sandhurst. He was doing so early, on the reasonable grounds that if he failed he would still have the time for no less than three further attempts at it before leaving Stowe. This first time, finding that he'd already failed the maths paper by being unable to answer more than a couple of questions, he saw no point in wasting any time on the Latin, especially as it was set on a Saturday when the sex-educational delights of Nessie were awaiting him if he could manage to meet her off the London train. Accordingly he copied out the answers of a boy at the next desk, thereby completing the work in about half the usual time as the friend was a rapid scribbler. David was then off to Buckingham station to meet Nessie, leaving his Latin master to locate the deception and report it to the headmaster.

It was one thing to be expelled from his prep school at ten for having stolen a prize marrow; it was quite another, six years later, to destroy the considerable faith that Roxburgh had put in him by an act of such wanton idiocy, and it is considerably to Stowe's credit that instead of throwing him out they merely beat him severely, stripped him of his job as monitor in the new house, and told him never again to be so silly. David appears to have taken the advice to heart. Though he was to remain the naughty schoolboy right through his relationship with Sam Goldwyn, whom he regarded as a headmaster somewhere fairly far down the Roxburgh scale, he took care never again to get caught quite so red-handed. Academically, however, he did not much improve. A few months after that first debacle with the School Certificate examinations, Roxburgh was again in touch with Lady Comyn-Platt to inform her of David's failure at the second attempt.

'I too am most grieved about your son,' he wrote, 'who failed with extraordinary completeness on this occasion. He did not get a credit in any single subject. I had a talk with him and we have together come to the conclusion that he and we must make a terrific effort to pass him through in July . . . I really do not think that there is anything to be gained by sending him to a crammer for the summer term. David has all the brains required to get a Certificate, but he has always lacked real application.

However, he did begin to work properly last term, and the feeling that he is now really up against it should provide the necessary spur. With reasonable luck he will pass in July, I feel pretty sure.'

Even now, with one attempt at the exam aborted through cheating and one totally failed, Roxburgh did not lose much of his considerable and, some might think, surprising faith in David's future. Unlike Comyn-Platt, to whom his stepson was still more of a hazard than a happiness, the headmaster took a fatherly interest in Niven best expressed in a letter he wrote by hand to the examiners at Sandhurst, urging them to accept David into the Royal Military College in 1928: 'This is an excellent type of boy, enormously improved since he came here. Not clever, but useful to have around. He will be popular wherever he goes unless he gets into bad company, which ought to be avoided because he does get on with everybody. Recommended.'

Few reviews that David was to receive in his later career, indeed few obituaries, so concisely summed up the essential Niven characteristics and, together with his eventual success in the third of his attempts at a School Certificate, it was enough to get him into Sandhurst greatly to the delight of his mother, who bought him a £12 sailing dinghy to celebrate, and the relief of his stepfather. By now he had also managed to lose some of the weight that had worried him at Stowe, and it was thus a thin, eager, lusty eighteen-year-old Sandhurst recruit who wrote from Bembridge on 12 August 1928 to thank Roxburgh for all his faith and trouble:

'I can now tell you that I have been accepted for Sandhurst and I want to thank you very, very much for all you did in connection with getting me in . . . I had to appear before a bevy of Generals and one clergyman who seemed to be very impressed that I had been at Stowe almost from the very beginning, and I had to tell them the history of the place from that very beginning. I was very fortunate in one respect, because I recognized the face of the clergyman, though I couldn't recall his name. He'd come down to preach at Stowe about a year ago, and I reminded him of it. That went very well . . . The weather has been quite good for sailing down here in Bembridge, and Cowes Week went off with a swing. I have had something that I have been wanting to say to you for a long time, and I decided to say it to you at the end of term but when the time came I'm afraid my heart failed me. You may think it is a colossal piece of cheek, and indeed it is, but please forgive me for certainly it is sincere. I want to congratulate you, Sir, on your wonderful achievement in bringing Stowe to what it is. I think it's marvellous and so, I know, does everyone and I always wish I could have done something to help. Once again many thanks for your help in getting me into Sandhurst.'

Looking back on the Niven he had known at Stowe, and then the Niven he was occasionally to meet again in adult life, Peter Sherwood saw one tremendous difference: 'David was always like champagne, though I think in later life the fizz rather went out of him. At school he was there with all the fizz, bubbling all the time. He was a great natural comedian, though oddly enough if they actually put him in a comedy then he sometimes lost some of the sparkle which came to him naturally when he wasn't acting. And he was a great joker, though some of his pranks could be oddly cruel and thoughtless. I remember him once when we were teenagers rushing out of Waterloo Station into the back of a cab and saying to the driver, "King's Cross, and drive like hell!" and then slipping out again through the other door so that the cab would arrive totally empty at the other station. But the root of his popularity was that, for most of the time, he was an extremely kind and tolerant person, who took tremendous trouble always to know your name and ask after your family. Stowe was lucky to have him, because he was a natural sort of fit. I don't think he'd have flourished in the same way if he had gone to Eton or one of the more conventional schools of those days, where life could be a lot tougher. Stowe was a new concept, and Roxburgh almost encouraged you to be a rebel, as long as you were never anti-social. He hated corporal punishment, and only used it in such very last resorts as when David cheated at the exam, though I should think Roxburgh was violently sick afterwards, whereas David was just unable to lie on his back for a day or two. We all envied David his sexual precocity. In those days boys grew up a lot more slowly, and for David at fifteen to have this lady who came down from London was highly enviable. He had trodden paths few of us had the opportunity to tread for at least another couple of years, but there was always something faintly reserved behind all that charm. You felt that if you could really strip it off, which of course you never could, a quite different David might emerge.'

The David that emerged from Sandhurst a couple of years later was, however, not much removed from the Roxburgh Stoic: indeed his devotion to the old school and to Roxburgh was such that from now on, through Sandhurst and Hollywood and right into the war, Niven would regularly write to his old headmaster with news of his activities, letters couched still in jocular self-deprecation but also revealing an odd kind of yearning for Stoic approval of his chosen if still somewhat suspect film career. It was as though, having let Roxburgh down once by cheating in the exam, he was determined never to do so again but was unsure whether a Hollywood career counted as a let-down or not. Until he died in 1954 (by which time Niven had entered both his sons at birth for Stowe, though in the event neither ever went there) Roxburgh remained for David a distant father substitute and the man he most wanted to impress. Whether Roxburgh ever found it in his academic soul to be impressed by a film star remains unclear, though his replies to David's domestic and professional reports from home and abroad were always warm and generally encouraging, if somewhat vague. If Roxburgh ever saw a Niven film, he appears not to have told David about it.

Sandhurst in the late 1920s gave Niven a brisk and tough initiation into the British Army, yet for David it seems to have resembled a kind of extended sixth-form life – a lot of marching around in uniform as per the old OTC weekends, a lot of bruising rugger matches, mercifully not too much academic work, and a chance to beetle off to London and the ever-open arms of Nessie rather more frequently than had been possible at Stowe. David's life revolved around three centres: Bembridge where he still spent his holiday summers sailing with some old prep- and public-school friends; London where there was Nessie; and Camberley where there was Sandhurst. His late teenage years were spent, as he later had the grace to acknowledge, in reasonably cloistered surroundings. Money may still have been tight, as indeed often was Niven, but by and large this was an existence whole worlds removed from the hunger marches, general strikes and mass unemployment that characterized the late 1920s for so many millions of his fellow countrymen. David had managed to clamber, albeit shakily, on to the bottom rungs of a ladder which led to fast cars and late-night parties and high-society escapades. He was not by any standards rich but he was good-looking, public-school mannered, prematurely sexy and willing to try almost anything at least once. If, in the immortal social definition of the time, it was true that a well-bred young Englishman should always give the impression of being good at a hunt ball and invaluable in a shipwreck, then this was precisely the impression that David managed to convey. My mother, an exact contemporary who met him occasionally at London gatherings in the late 1920s and who had been at Heathfield around the time that David stole that school's prize marrow, remembers him still as one of the more entertaining and eligible young men of the period. At a time when most of his Sandhurst and Stowe contemporaries viewed the opposite sex with embarrassed terror or naked lust, David had acquired some invaluable social graces – he was a good mimic, a good dancer and blessed with an ability to make people laugh, and on that alone he managed to travel a fair way around the party circuit.

It was also while at Sandhurst that Niven discovered what he was going to do for a living, though it took a while for the implications to sink into a brain that was by now conditioned to a life in the Army. During the first of his two winters there as a gentleman cadet under Major 'Boy' Browning, who later married Daphne du Maurier and commanded British airborne troops in the Second World War, a theatrical notice appeared in the local Camberley paper for 12 October 1928: 'The first entertainment of the season to be held at the Royal Military College took place on Thursday and Friday evenings last week when a talented company consisting mainly of Gentlemen Cadets presented an excellent programme to large and appreciative audiences . . . the star turns were a syncopated group of singers who rendered several of the latest hit numbers including "How long has this been going on?" and "The best things in life are free", but the duologue "Searching for the Supernatural" by Mr R.E. Osborne-Smith and Mr D. Niven proved a most amusing and extremely popular item.'

D. Niven (he had already dropped the James and the J.D.G. prefixes by which he'd been known at school) had made his first appearance in front of the paying public, and though it was only in one of his beloved concert-party routines it was rapidly followed by more legitimate stage work – by Christmas 1928 he had also appeared as 'John Cutting, a Reporter' in a drama called *The Creaking Chair* (the Camberley drama critic did not specifically mention his performance, but merely listed David among those 'also appearing') and then took the lead opposite his company commander's wife in a revival of *It Pays to Advertise* which the Camberley critic seems to have managed to miss altogether.

A letter written to Roxburgh at Stowe by David reported his theatrical progress: 'Niven has had some amazing pieces of luck. As a matter of fact, Sir, I have been very lucky. It started at a concert where I made my debut. I made one of those blathering speeches and brought in some topical bits about the RMC. My Company Commander must have thought I treated life here in the right way, because I am not really super-efficient but I was given one of the much coveted stripes off the square. Only four juniors in each Company are promoted off the square [and therefore spared a good deal of the more turgid marching around which Sandhurst cadets were then required to spend their days doing] so you can see it'll be very useful. My next effort was when I met the RMC champion heavyweight in the Boxing Competition. Altogether eight blows were struck. I struck the first two, he struck the next six. I went down six times. I've been given my Rugger blue and played yesterday for the College versus Woolwich. I don't expect I was much of a success, but Niven (Stowe) looked grand in the papers and on the programme . . . My riding is frightfully funny. My first ride was a classic. They gave me a completely mad horse, no leather on it anywhere, and told me to mount. Well, I couldn't get on it for a long time until all the sergeants in the place helped me up. Then they said "Trot": well, it didn't do anything at first but then the brute understood and away I went, bump bump bump, until I finally bumped off but it's all very amusing and keeps me fit. When the King and Queen come down to Stowe for the opening of the chapel, do you think our Sandhurst contingent could form an extra guard of honour? Everyone here has a very high opinion of Stowe, as of course they should, and we will see that it is kept up.'

David's career at Sandhurst was uneventful and, allowing for the usual schoolboy pranks, reasonably distinguished. He became a commandant's orderly, managed to master the empty horses and keep up with the acting. By his last term there in 1930 he had been promoted to under-officer, gained his rugger blue for the second year running and starred in a college production of *The Speckled Band*. Although the affair with Nessie was drifting to a close, London now held many other delights for him on weekend leaves. His interest in the theatre, coupled with that of his sister Grizel who was shortly to go to the Royal

Academy of Dramatic Art in the same generation as my
father, meant that David was now increasingly to be found
around stage doors in hot pursuit of such actresses as Zoe
Gail and Ann Todd.

But the stage was still a romantic rather than a professional interest. David's life, as he and Sandhurst saw it,
was to be in the Army and specifically in the Argyll and
Sutherland Highlanders where there were still family connexions, thanks to his late father's Scottish ancestry. That
is where David would have ended up, probably happily
enough, had he not once again blown it all for a joke.

Chapter Four

1930–1932

'Malta is a sod of a place.'

There are certain people who should never be asked or allowed to fill in forms, the kind of person who answers 'Yes, please' to the question 'Sex?' and puts 'Assassination of the President' when asked on American visa forms to outline their reasons for visiting the United States. David was one such: asked, shortly before leaving Sandhurst, to list in order of preference those regiments he would be happy to join, he started well enough with the Argyll and Sutherland at number one and the Black Watch at number two, it having been decided that he was to revert to his father's Scots affiliations. Then, however, running out of ideas and unable to come up with a third choice, he simply wrote in 'Anything but the Highland Light Infantry'.

That was not, in 1930, the kind of levity they cared for much at Army headquarters, and David was accordingly despatched into the Highland Light Infantry as a junior officer and a sharp lesson. That in itself might not have mattered, had the HLI not then been stationed as far afield as Malta. David's idea of army life exactly half-way between the two world wars was that it should happen somewhere conveniently close to London's West End, be compatible with a good night-life, and preferably also the occasional country house-party for weekends. Malta did not look likely to meet those requirements; nor, given that we were not actually at war with the place, did military glory look very likely there.

On the other hand, there didn't seem to be much alternative. At home, relations with 'Uncle Tommy' Comyn-Platt were no better than they had been when his mother had married him a decade earlier, though the two men had reached a sort of compromise whereby only one of them ever went home for Christmas. His mother's health had started, alarmingly and inexplicably, to deteriorate and though David was more and more drawn to her there was no way that he could make a living at the Bembridge Sailing Club.

Nor was he really trained for any other kind of life but the Army: his academic qualifications were still shaky, he had no interest in the City or business, was bleakly unenthusiastic about the political life represented by his loathed stepfather, and was really most impressed by his elder brother Max who seemed to be having a good time drinking and fornicating his way through the Army and later the Navy.

Whatever else Stowe and Sandhurst had given him, it certainly was not a definable ambition beyond the enjoyment of life wherever and whenever possible, and Malta constituted a grave threat to that ambition. There being no reasonable alternative, however (a theatrical life was not regarded at that time even by David as reasonable), he bade a stiff-upper-lipped farewell to mother and Nessie and set sail on the *Kaisar-i-Hind* in January 1929, two months before his nineteenth birthday if you believe his reckoning in *The Moon's A Balloon*, or alternatively in January 1930, two months before his twentieth if you believe mine which is based on Stowe evidence that he only went up to Sandhurst in the autumn of 1928 and is therefore unlikely to have completed his time there in less than six months.

It was shortly after Niven's arrival in Malta that he met the man who was to become his adult lifelong friend and Best Man at both his weddings, Michael Trubshawe: 'We were playing cricket at the time, and Niven came across the ground with the adjutant who said, "Here's your eleventh man," because we were one short. And so we naturally enough started talking about cricket and that night in the mess he asked me what the form was about parade the next day and what time was breakfast, and I remember an elderly major looking up from his paper in front of the fire and saying, "Breakfast? Officers of the Highland Light Infantry never have breakfast. They are generally sick around eleven."

'I suppose we came from the same sort of background, which is why we hit it off so well from the very beginning. I'd already been flung out of Cambridge because my tutor there told my mother that, as I seemed to attend all my lectures on the hunting field, there was really no point in wasting my time and her money and the college energy on my further education. So I left in a closed cab with the blinds drawn after two years and one term.

'I was about three years older than David; like him I'd lost my father early in life, and like him I was really in the Highland Light Infantry by accident, having nothing better to do at the time. David endeared himself greatly to his brother subalterns as soon as he arrived in Malta, because we had a rather fiery second-in-command who introduced fencing periods every evening at about six. He resented sitting on his bum in front of the mess fire seeing all us bright young sparks pissing off to cocktail parties while he couldn't even find enough friends to make a four at bridge. He therefore started the compulsory fencing, and people began getting cut into ribbons, so at the end of about a week David came over to me and muttered, "I say, old bean, oughtn't something to be done about this waste of good drinking time?" and I said I couldn't agree more, but what did he propose doing? David just gave me one of those looks that meant leave it to him; what he didn't tell me was that he'd done some after-hours fencing at Sandhurst with one of the staff sergeants, who had taught him some of the dirtiest tricks in the history of sabres. So

David set about the fencing tutor in Malta like Douglas Fairbanks in an early film, and from that night onward there were no more fencing parades. I think that was when he really made his name in Malta, at least among his brother officers.'

Trubshawe remembered 'this wonderful smile, flashing white teeth, very blue eyes and a blue-and-white polka-dot scarf tied around the neck'. He also remembered a deeply disillusioned and unhappy man: 'The sad thing about Niven and the Army is that he really could have been a very good soldier. Unlike me he took the whole thing very seriously, but he'd been desperate to get into the Argylls where he had a few Sandhurst and school friends. Being sent into the Highland Light Infantry where he knew no one depressed him, and like the rest of us he rapidly got fed up with Malta. There was really nothing at all to do there except the four Ps (Polo, Piss-ups, Parade and Poking) and it wasn't even as though we were fighting; we were regarded as a Home Service station, domestic duties, whereas if he'd got into the 2nd Battalion instead of ours he'd have been sent out to India which would have been a lot more exciting.'

As it was, all the skills and training and even the dedication that Niven had acquired at Sandhurst rapidly faded in the torpor of life on Malta, and he soon began to wonder what not just he but indeed the entire battalion was doing there. Finding no answer, he and Trubshawe contented themselves with the invention of the Husbandometer, an early-warning device which could be signalled from the entrance to the Grand Harbour to indicate that the Navy, or at least some of it, was returning to Malta after a ritual spring or summer cruise. As it was both Niven's and Trubshawe's habit to spend much time during these naval absences in bed with the wives of the officers who were at sea, this early-warning system was (though never perfected) much discussed, it being thought that, on the first whistle, doors of houses all around the harbour could be flung open as streams of brutal and licentious soldiers belted back to barracks doing up their trousers *en route*.

Trubshawe and Niven spent two long years on Malta, and by the time they got their release from the island at the end of 1931 David was no longer at all sure that he wanted to spend the rest of his life as a soldier. Behind the dashing young officer in the well-cut uniform larking about with the jocks there was an altogether different Niven whom Trubshawe was probably the only one on Malta to recognize: 'Something about him just didn't fit: in the mess, on parade, you'd always think he was one of the regulars, but then if you went into his room in the Malta Barracks late at night you'd find him leafing through old theatre magazines or the society pages of the *Tatler*. Still, the sex life was excellent and David really learnt out there how to be a good soldier. It's not difficult to be popular in the Army, but to be respected by your men is an entirely different matter and David always managed to command respect. He really did have the makings of a very fine officer indeed, though we were always in trouble, mainly I think out of boredom and frustration. One night there was a fancy-dress ball at the Opera House in Valetta and David and I decided to go as goats, so we got the skins over our heads and crawled in on all fours; to make the thing look realistic we got a couple of football bladders and hung them beneath us, and then we had our privates walking along behind sprinkling olives all over the floor.

'Unfortunately, nobody bothered to tell us that in Malta the goat is a sacred animal, and we ended up being pursued down the main street of Valetta by not just the privates but most of the local police and fire brigades too. Not a good night.'

During his time overseas David did manage to get one brief home leave, but life in Rose Cottage proved not a lot rosier than life in Malta. His beloved mother was now having more and more of what the family called 'Mum's pains', his stepfather had retreated to a kind of elderly bachelor life in London, and Grizel, the only one of his immediate generation he really warmed to (though he was

in later years to be more than generous to Joyce in times
of financial distress), had started at RADA where Niven
increasingly began to feel that he too should have gone.

Worse still, old friends he met in Bembridge and London
all seemed to be doing rather better than him. Fellow
cadets from Sandhurst were being given glamorous or at
any rate intriguing assignments to China (where the Argylls
had now gone, much to David's chagrin), and those who
had opted for university or business careers had all started
to make good while he was messing about on Malta. The
only mystery was what had become of his ever-errant elder
brother, and that was soon resolved on Niven's return to
Malta, as Trubshawe recalled:. 'David got a cable from
him saying that he would be passing through on the P&O
liner *Empress of India*, so we laid on the full treatment.
We checked the time of the arrival of the boat at Malta,
dressed in our best blue patrols, got hold of a piper, went
down the Custom House steps and rowed out to this bloody
great ship. David finds the purser, and asks to be directed
to the cabin of Mr Max Niven. The purser goes through
the passenger list. Nobody of that name on board. So we
go to the bar, have a couple of drinks rather dejectedly,
and are making our way back to our little boat when there's
a sudden scream and we look down into the foredeck and
there, coming up from the holds, are all the stokers going
off duty. And this pitch-black character with a sweatband
round his head is Max. So we fell about, gave him time
to get cleaned up, went ashore and had a monumental
twenty-four-hour piss-up before we had to deliver him
back on board. But that was Max all right.'

Eventually, and not a moment too soon for Niven,
the 1st Battalion Highland Light Infantry was recalled to
Dover at the end of 1931. By now he had lost not only
his faith in the Army but also the undivided loyalty of
Trubshawe, who had fallen in love with the woman who
was to become his first wife and had decided to leave the
Army altogether. This was for David a considerable blow.
There was nobody else in the battalion he particularly

cared for, certainly nobody as finely tuned as was Michael
to Niven's character and sense of humour. There appeared
to be no major wars on the horizon, little chance therefore
of promotion through active service, and not much point
in soldiering around Dover where the natives were as
friendly as they had been in Malta. Still, it was a few
months before Trubshawe could actually gain his freedom,
and in the meantime Dover was accessible to London
theatres.

'David and I would frequently go belting up to the West
End to take girls to plays or else parties,' recalled Michael,
'but we always had to be back in Dover for the 7am parade.
On one occasion we were going to a nightclub party at the
Coconut Grove which I knew wouldn't end until about
five in the morning, so in order to make it back to Dover
we chartered an ambulance which could go very fast indeed, and we had our two batmen inside it with our Army
uniforms at the ready. My plan was that about 20 miles
short of Dover we'd pull into a layby, change into uniform
and arrive in plenty of time for the parade. Unfortunately
we got a puncture, and that made us pretty late because
we had to wait for a passing car in order to borrow a
wheelbrace and in those days there were very few passing
cars on the Dover road at six in the morning. Anyway,
we eventually got the wheel changed and drove like the
clappers, thinking we'd made a mess of the whole affair.
As we drove on to the parade ground there were the 800
men of the battalion already marshalled, but we had two
things on our side. One, nobody knew what was inside the
ambulance and two, if we could lie doggo until we'd got
past the senior officers, we might have a chance of not
being spotted until we'd rejoined the ranks. So as the
adjutant shouted, "March off the Officers," the ambulance
doors were opened and Niven and Trubshawe marched
out with swords raised to join the others. We got the most
imperial rocket and one month's detention for that, but I
reckon it was worth every minute, because during our
confinement to barracks a couple of lovely girls drove

down from London to see us with a magnum of the Widow: very kind and charming of them. It was the little events like that which kept one going; otherwise peacetime soldiering was really very boring.'

Except, of course, for the little matter of the King's 1932 Levee. 'We were all on parade at St James's Palace,' Trubshawe remembered, 'full dress with scarlet tunics and crossbelts and tartan trousers, all smelling of mothballs and borrowed for the occasion from brother officers. You march along and eventually you get inside the palace, down long corridors, and then you form up on the huge staircase where there is the Honourable Corps of Gentlemen at Arms, all very senior generals and that sort of thing with great plumes coming out of their helmets, and very slowly you ascend the stairs until you get into the throne room and then you appear in front of the monarch, in our case King George v, and you give your nod and march off. Only while we were waiting our turn on the stairs, David prodded one of the Gentlemen at Arms and said, "Christ, Trubshawe, he's alive!" I thought then that our army careers really were ended at last.'

Trubshawe's career indeed was; the freedom he had so long desired from military uniform finally came through and he went off to marry Margie MacDougall, leaving David more alone than ever. Not only had Michael shared his theatrical interests (he too was to become an actor in later life, and had formed with David a breakaway group of amateur players in Malta after both had been turned down by the resident dramatic society for a revival of *The Last Mrs Cheyney*), but the double act they had formed on the parade ground as well as in countless pubs had been abruptly ended. 'I knew', said Trubshawe, 'at the time I left the Army that Niven was also getting very itchy, but he didn't seem to know what else he was going to do with himself if he left. He was really best, even then, at just telling stories. I'd seen him, at some pompous dinner party given by the C-in-C on board ship in Malta, with perhaps twenty-four other guests, gradually manipulate the conversation around until in time everybody was listening to this young man with just one pip on his shoulder. He had this astonishing capacity for anecdote and the trick was that he hoisted in situations, ideas, anything that amused him as he went through life and then he'd take out these little incidents from time to time, polish and embellish them so that in due course he'd built up a store of stories which would then be brought out at precisely the right moment to sound as if they were spontaneous.'

Yet the loss of Trubshawe was by no means the worst that David was to suffer in 1932. Late that November, while he was on an Army training course at Aldershot, he had a telephone call from the stepfather he'd not seen for three years. Comyn-Platt was phoning with the news that David's mother was in a Queen's Gate nursing home dying of cancer.

That, of course, is what 'Mum's pains' in Bembridge had all been about, and as David went to see her for the last time (she died without recognizing her adored younger son) he had time to reflect on the kind of relationship they'd shared. It had not been especially close, but as Ann Todd recollects, 'He was the baby of the family and she really loved him. I remember once her telling me that, when I had my own children (she always hoped that David and I would marry), I was not to be hurt if they spent their school holidays going off to shoot with friends in Scotland or to parties in London instead of staying at home, and that was clearly something she'd had to learn from him. He took me to see her in hospital just before she died, and I think at that time David was getting very serious about me, though in an odd way we never seemed to be alone together much. He liked crowds, and I didn't; also I didn't much care for that terribly jovial Army life that he and Trubshawe seemed to share. He was always very keen to impress me, I think partly because I was already an actress and he was getting more and more interested in the business.

'One evening, just around the time that his mother died,

he came to see me and he said he wanted to ask my advice about leaving the Army and becoming an actor. I told him he couldn't possibly be an actor. I'd only ever seen him doing sketches in Army concerts and although he was very funny it was always a turn, usually imitating somebody or pretending to skate. I didn't see much sign of him being an actor, so I told him that in my view he was a "ha-ha-ho-ho" sort of person and that he should stick to the Army because nobody would ever believe him on a stage. Even if he said, "I love you," they would just laugh. I think that rather depressed him.'

It did not, however, stop David deciding that he wanted to be an actor, or indeed almost anything so long as it was no longer a soldier.

Chapter Five

1932–1934

'Request Permission Resign Commission.'

The early 1930s to which David had returned from the timeless world of Malta were not his best period. The cocktail-party life he had left at the end of the 1920s seemed to be disappearing into a cold wind of 1930s reality, and an overgrown schoolboy of no fixed abode with a talent for mimicry but not much else was in danger of becoming an embarrassment rather than a continuing delight. 'The thing you have to understand about David,' says Janet Cowell, whose husband was stationed on Malta at the same time as Niven and Trubshawe, 'is that mentally he had never really left school. Whether he had a tough colonel or a tough headmaster made very little difference; David's attitude was still that of the prankster who wanted to see what he could get away with. He believed that charm, and an ability to make even his superiors fall about with laughter, would probably see him through.'

But through what? Judged as an extension of public-school life, the Army had suited him well enough so long as there was Trubshawe to giggle with. Now that Trubshawe had gone out into the real world of marriage and professional employment, David was left hanging around the Dover barracks like a sixth-former who keeps going back to his old school because he has nowhere else to settle. With the death of his mother, Bembridge could no longer really be called home. Max was still stoking somewhere in the Mediterranean, Grizel was occupied with her acting and the start of a long and successful career as a sculptor, Joyce was married, and the stepfather to whom he had hardly spoken in his mother's lifetime was not likely to become a close friend after her death.

David thus started the 1930s without family, without many friends and without the faintest idea what he was going to do for a living, even supposing he could find the courage to leave an increasingly turgid Army life and strike out on his own. The prospects for a young man who could do passable impersonations of a skater on dry land were not at the time especially good, and increasingly it was Ann Todd who tried to instil in him some sense of reality.

'David used to hang around the stage doors a lot,' she recalls. 'I suppose a generation earlier he'd have been called a stage-door Johnnie. Once, when I was on tour in an Ian Hay comedy, he used to come to the theatre in Portsmouth every night and draw little hearts against my name in the programme to indicate his love. I got very uptight about that because it seemed so childish, and on the last night I knew the author was coming round so I was desperately keen to keep David away, but when Ian Hay came into my dressing room the first thing he said was, "I'd like you to meet David Niven, I knew his father." David always knew everybody.'

The affair with Ann Todd never really developed in the way that David hoped it would, but for years afterwards he used to carry her photograph around in his wallet as a kind of insurance policy. 'Whenever any girl in New York or Hollywood threatened to take him too seriously, he would suddenly say, "Oh, by the way, I ought to tell you that I'm engaged to this girl back in England and here's her picture," and out from his wallet would come this ghastly old sepia snapshot of me.'

By now David's cabaret turns, notably the one concerning the skater without ice, were becoming so well known around town that on one occasion the then Prince of Wales demanded to have him perform it at Quaglino's. A useful nightclub act was still not a living, however, and although the theatre was at this time beginning to change from a classical retreat of Shakespearians to a West End filled with likely young men in moustaches leaping through French windows on to tennis courts, David had been effectively deterred by Ann Todd from continuing to think of himself as any sort of actor. Along Shaftesbury Avenue could be seen the first stirrings of that generation of actors from Olivier through Hugh Williams to Rex Harrison, most of whom were later to join the Hollywood Raj of expatriate English gentlemen players led by Niven; but for now he was not of their ranks, and while they began to appear on stage as officers and gentlemen, he merely appeared in those roles at the Dover barracks.

There were occasional escapes from guard duty. At a dinner party some time in the summer of 1932 David had found himself sitting next to Barbara Hutton, the Woolworth heiress so devoted to jokey and good-looking Englishmen that she later married Cary Grant in a wartime partnership uncharitably known as Cash and Cary. At this time she was starting an affair with the first of her seven husbands, Alexis Mdivani, but David still caught her fancy and she lightly invited him to spend Christmas with the family in the Woolworth apartments at the Pierre Hotel in New York. Quite how much of Christmas she meant was unclear, but this was certainly not an invitation to be ignored by someone as restless and travel-eager as was David. His grandmother had recently left him a couple of hundred pounds in her will, and armed with that plus the proceeds from the sale of a second-hand car and a small loan from Grizel, he set sail early in December 1932 for the country that was soon to become his principal home for the next three decades.

On arrival in New York, after a stormy ten-day crossing from Southampton, he found Miss Hutton understandably preoccupied with her Russian prince ('hung like a bear', her advisers had reassuringly informed her) but still happy to supply David with a few days in the Pierre and some of the best Christmas presents of his entire life. For the next few weeks (he'd obtained an extension to his month's leave from the Army by wiring his colonel with the unlikely news that he was going big-game hunting in Florida) David enjoyed for the first time the hospitality of a nation that was always to have a soft spot for his particular brand of recklessly charming Englishness.

Parties at the Central Park Casino, parties at Jack and Charlie's 21 Club which in these Prohibition years was generally considered the best speakeasy in town, parties in Florida and Richmond, Virginia, through which David moved like a debs' delight at a succession of hunt balls only in a rather better climate, parties where his still-unusual English accent was both a passport and an open invitation to the next social gathering on the calendar, parties up and down the East Coast, parties offering a bed and a hot meal and a girl for the night or perhaps even the weekend, parties just about everywhere within a few hundred miles of New York, all saw David happily and alcoholically into the New Year of 1933.

Then it was time to return reluctantly and gloomily to an English Army that still seemed to have not the remotest idea what to do with him. Now, however, there was one major difference: David knew that his soldiering days were numbered, and that if the theatre was not a reasonable alternative then at least he had somewhere else that he desperately wanted to go – America. Like Noël Coward a decade earlier, Niven had found there an energy, a warmth, an excitement and a hospitality totally lacking in London, and he began to think more and more about starting a life across the Atlantic, conveniently forgetting of course that a Christmas visiting with the Woolworths was something rather less than the start of an American career.

On the other hand there didn't seem to be a lot going for him back in England – not unless you count Priscilla Weigall, débutante of the year 1933 and a new friend of

David's with a family who took the view that his future undoubtedly lay in Australia, possibly as an ADC to the governor. Priscilla herself had other ideas. She also, luckily enough, happened to know Douglas Fairbanks, who had taken a house in England for that summer. Yet when they were introduced, David's courage failed him and it was only in California a couple of years later that he could bring himself to mention the possibility of a movie career to the great swashbuckler and founding father of Hollywood. In the meantime Priscilla narrowed her horizons and introduced Niven to Bunty Watts, an English film producer who thus became the first man ever to put him on film.

The film in question was *All The Winners*, a racing saga with Allan Jeayes, released early in 1934 and technically David's first movie, though he didn't bother to list it in the reference books and is indeed only to be glimpsed in a crowd scene at a racecourse looking cheerfully nonchalant, as though he'd really meant to be somewhere else that day. It was a screen look that Niven was to perfect over the next quarter-century; here it merely earned him £5 for a Sunday's work and left him and his producer with the impression that he was unlikely to become the next Rudolf Valentino, or even the next John Gilbert. English screen heroes tended at that time to be, if the picture was made at home, young West End stars recreating stage successes and, if the picture was made in America, elderly character men able, like George Arliss, to do passable impersonations of Wellington. David clearly belonged in neither category, and therefore returned to barracks only to find that they proposed to send him to a machine-gun school.

It was there, on Salisbury Plain one hot afternoon in the summer of 1933, that Niven's five-year career in the British Army came to an abrupt halt. He had accepted a dinner invitation in London, and found to his horror that it was being endangered by a major-general whose lecture on the technicalities of machine-gunning was badly overrunning. Finally, it reached an end and questions were called for.

'I wonder, Sir, if you happen to have the time?' asked
Niven. 'I have a train to catch.' It was not a good question
in the circumstances, and for it he was confined under
close arrest to a barracks from which he escaped in time
to drive to town after all. Once there, he sought the advice
of Philip Astley, a high-society figure of the time who had
himself been asked to resign his commission after an affair
with Gertrude Lawrence and a marriage to Madeleine
Carroll. Astley took the view that an Army which could
dispense with his services so lightly could also dispense
with Niven's, especially as he had been adjutant of the
Life Guards and Niven a mere lieutenant in the Highland
Light Infantry. As Astley saw it, a return to barracks would
undoubtedly result in court-martial for having escaped
while under close arrest for asking daft questions during
training; why should Niven go through all that, when he
was planning to leave the Army as soon as possible anyway? There was no time like the present.

Fortified by the dinner, the advice and a certain amount
of Cockburn's Port, Niven recalled the telegram that his
brother Max had sent to a commanding officer when he
too wanted a rapid escape from the Army. The words
'DEAR COLONEL REQUEST PERMISSION RESIGN COMMISSION
LOVE NIVEN' were once again sent by wire, and Niven was
no longer a soldier – at least, not for the next six years.

But what to do next? It was unlikely that Barbara
Hutton, now the Princess Mdivani (though not for long),
would send him another invitation to stay at the Pierre in
New York, and certainly not in the steamy Manhattan
midsummer when she herself would be elsewhere, probably on a yacht. On the other hand David had no immediate job prospects in London, and no particular reason
for staying there. For once he was comparatively free of
romantic attachments, and still at the back of his mind
was the feeling that America was a land of some sort of
opportunity; or, if not America, perhaps Canada. Another
man at dinner the night Astley told him to break with the
Army had been Victor Gordon-Lennox, an ex-Grenadier

Guardsman who had become a journalist on the *Daily Telegraph* and was just going out to Quebec (since he had a Canadian wife) *en route* to an assignment in Washington. If Niven would give him his car, Gordon-Lennox agreed that he would hand over in return a ticket to Quebec.

Quite what David thought he was going to do there is uncertain; but he was just twenty-three and Canada seemed as good a place as any to start out on a new life. As things turned out, it was very nearly the place where he ended his life. After spending a few happy days with the in-laws of Gordon-Lennox, he developed infected tonsils and woke up in an Ottawa hotel bed almost drowning in his own blood since the tonsils had caused a throat haemorrhage. Recovering from that, and eager to pay his hotel bill, he introduced himself to the craft of journalism by copying several chapters out of a Canadian fox-hunting manual and selling them to a local newspaper.

Once totally recovered, he travelled south to New York, which was now into the beginning of a cold October, checked into the reasonably cheap Montclair Hotel on Lexington Avenue, a far cry from the luxuries of his last Manhattan sojourn at the Pierre nine months earlier, and began to wonder what he was supposed to be doing next. Lacking the money for the journey back to England, or any real idea of what he would do if and when he got there, he began phoning around some of the New York friends he had made over the previous Christmas, only to make the discovery that an attractive young British Army officer staying briefly with the Woolworths was a considerably more interesting proposition than an out-of-work drifter recovering from poisoned tonsils and staying at a vastly less glamorous address.

One or two of his new-found friends did remain loyal, however, most notably yet another of the journalists who seemed most often to come to David's rescue in his many hours of minor distress. John McClain, later one of Broadway's best drama critics, was in 1933 a street reporter on the *New York Sun* and it was he who first brought David

the news that, with the imminent repeal of Prohibition, the
Jack and Charlie who had run the great speakeasy at the
21 Club were having to rethink their own futures and were
therefore going into the subsidiary business of being wine
merchants. This in turn would mean that they required
salesmen, and who better than a handsome young English
ex-Army officer to go around flogging their whisky?

Niven duly applied for the job and, as there were few
other applicants and Jack and Charlie already had a soft
spot for him as one of their former clients (in later years
they took to hanging a portrait of Niven in the club bar
above the fond legend 'Our First and Worst Salesman'),
he started on the day that New York drinking once again
became legal, 4 December 1933. His first American employment was remarkably unsuccessful. Though Jack and
Charlie were kind enough to keep him at it for several
months, David was surprisingly unable to shift their crates
of whisky into other bars or even people's homes. He
himself took to blaming the Mafia, competition from older
established wine merchants, or simply a kind of well-bred
English reticence which prevented him from flogging the
Ballantynes to his friends or occasional weekend house-
party hosts. The qualities required of a perfect romantic
suitor or dinner-party guest (all of which David possessed
in abundance) were not precisely the same as those required to sell cases of Scotch to the owners of the seedier
bars that ran down the midtown streets east of Lexington
towards the river, and David was thus deeply relieved
when, early in the New Year, Elsa Maxwell came up with
a rather better idea for him.

Miss Maxwell was one of the legendary gossips, fixers,
procurers and party-givers of the period, and it was at her
apartment high in the Waldorf Towers (to which Niven
had been taken for tea by some old English friends) that
she lectured him severely on the shape of his future career.
Whisky selling was, she reckoned, a dead loss. On her
travels around America she had noticed that in Hollywood,
with the recent arrival of talking pictures, there was a

considerable demand for handsome young Englishmen who could look, sound and act at least vaguely like Ronald Colman. Surprisingly few others had as yet made the long journey out to Hollywood from London, and Miss Maxwell took the view that, having already got half-way there, Niven should complete the trek westwards and try his luck as an actor.

Elsa was also the kind of woman who, having had an idea, liked to do something about it; a few days after their first meeting she summoned David back to the Waldorf Towers and into the presence of a small dark German who proved to be Ernst Lubitsch, the director who had already made *Trouble in Paradise* and *The Love Parade* and was generally reckoned to be the best spotter and filmer of light comedians in the movie business. Like Ann Todd, he was, however, unimpressed by the likelihood of Niven becoming any kind of actor, let alone a film star.

Elsa's next idea was that David should marry a rich American wife, a practice not unknown in the 1930s among indigent Englishmen in New York. Accordingly she sent him up for a charity auction at which the brightest and richest of New York's eligible young ladies were supposed to bid for the best-looking young men about town. David scored barely $100 to the several thousand notched up by Jock Whitney, and took the defeat as an indication that once again perhaps it was time to start packing. Hanging around the Waldorf lobby (he much preferred it to the lobby of his own hotel across the street, which consisted only of a small night-porter's desk and the start of a sleazy staircase) he had however encountered a reasonable cross-section of New York society, while in the bars which he had to frequent as Jack's and Charlie's travelling whisky salesman he had also encountered a reasonable cross-section of the rest of American society including Douglas Hertz and Lefty Flynn, a couple of promoters whose plan it was to start up an indoor pony-racing track in Atlantic City.

'For reasons which have never been entirely clear to

me,' says Stewart Scheftel, husband of Geraldine Fitzgerald, with whom Niven was later to star in *Wuthering
Heights*, and himself a friend of David's from the earliest
Manhattan days, 'he joined a syndicate with these two
other guys and they went off to Atlantic City, and when
inevitably they got into trouble David wired me, "Send
$500 or I go to jail." I thought about that for a while. Five
hundred dollars was a lot of money in 1934, and I had
really in those days only met David at a few parties. So I
wired back, "Go to jail," and that was the last I saw of
him until he began the film with Geraldine four years
later.'

The trouble had started almost as soon as Niven, Hertz
and Flynn arrived in Atlantic City, and for those who think
that this whole pony-gambling escapade had many of the
qualities of a Damon Runyon short story, there is a kind
of literary or at any rate historical satisfaction in discovering that Runyon was in fact one of its original backers.

The plan was simple enough. The American Pony Express Racing Association, as the three men were now
calling themselves, was to purchase large numbers of over-
the-hill polo ponies and organize them into short relay
races for betting purposes at night in a large covered
auditorium. All went according to plan on the first night,
and the event even attracted good reviews in the next
morning's Atlantic City papers, which was when the luck
ran out.

Some local gentlemen in extremely large and bulky black
overcoats began to think that they did not especially want
three promoters from New York setting up a pony-racing
racket on their home territory, at least not without a
sizeable share of the profits being handed over to the
Atlantic City branch of their Sicilian organization. David
and his partners decided loftily enough that they were
going to be no part of a Mafia shakedown, and summoned
the local police who unfortunately signally failed to prevent
all the lights fusing on the second night of racing. By the
third night the jockeys had disappeared, and by the fourth

the food for the horses had also mysteriously vanished. By the fifth night, when the lights went out yet again, Niven, Hertz and Flynn decided they could take a hint. The horses and remaining saddles were sold off to pay a few debts, urgent if unsuccessful entreaties were sent out to friends, and the local police were eventually inclined to the belief that if all three men left town quietly no actual charges would be pressed.

So by the end of April David was back in New York sadder, fractionally wiser and considerably poorer in that he had given up a guaranteed $40 a week from Jack and Charlie to start racing the ponies. This time it was Grizel who came to his rescue, via an airmail letter. Now that their mother's will had been proved, £300 had been left to each of her children in case of immediate need. The rest of her estate was to go to them only after the death of Comyn-Platt. Deciding that his was a case of immediate need, David wired Grizel for the money and ended up at the current exchange rates with a fortune of just over $800, enough to get himself a small but sensible apartment and start seriously job hunting around Manhattan – or, in Niven's case, enough to get himself on a boat to Bermuda, where one of his pony-racing partners had now rented a cottage on Devonshire Bay.

Chapter Six

1934–1935

*'I often told myself that if all else failed, I could
always go to Hollywood. So when all else did fail,
I did go to Hollywood. And only then found out
how wrong I had been.'*

Bermuda in the early summer of 1934 suited David down
to the ground, as well it might. Anyone nurturing, as he
did, fond memories of an Isle of Wight childhood could
only have been thrilled by the vastly better climate and
sailing conditions within what was otherwise a remarkably
similar gin-belt community. Moreover, there was a promising sex life and free accommodation in the beach cottage
rented by Lefty Flynn with what little was left of the
Atlantic City capital. Compared to selling Scotch off Lexington Avenue, beach life in Bermuda had to be an improvement. The only trouble was that it looked unlikely
to lead anywhere, and David did not relish the thought of
returning to Grizel in London with the news that while in
America he had achieved precisely nothing.

Besides that, he was now twenty-four and there was a
limit to the length of time that he could go on drifting
around the New World on little more than Stoic charm.
He really would have to start thinking, however reluctantly, about some sort of a career. At least he now knew
what he didn't want to be: he didn't want to be a soldier,
or a whisky salesman, or anything much that he had seen

his friends doing back in England except possibly acting, and he now had not only Ann Todd but also Ernst Lubitsch telling him not to do that.

On the other hand, various travellers' tales had started to reach him about life in California. Several school and Army friends had been out there on visits and spoke well of the climate and the sex life and even the job opportunities. Some took the Todd/Lubitsch view that David was no actor, and one even unkindly suggested that his legs were too big for movie stardom, but California still seemed like a better idea than a sheepish return to London, and besides it was possible to get there remarkably economically from Bermuda on a tramp steamer via Havana, Cuba.

Quite what happened to David in Cuba that late summer of 1934 is still a matter of some academic conjecture. According to one of his own later accounts, he was approached in a dockside bar by an anti-Batista freedom fighter with the suggestion that he might like to become a soldier of fortune. Deciding this was a less than sensible proposition, even for someone with his exotic sense of career opportunities, David rapidly boarded the ss *President Pierce* and sailed on to Los Angeles. Like his later friend and mentor Noël Coward, Niven was always at his best on board ship. He liked the life of an extended cocktail party, and could be relied upon to end up in the first-class staterooms, regardless of what it actually said on his ticket, with those passengers likely to do him the most good. Few men in the social history of the Western world can have refused a smaller number of invitations than the young Niven.

On this occasion the invitation to try his luck in California had actually come from Dennis Smith-Bingham, an old Army friend who had been one of the original investors in the Atlantic City ponies, but had generously not let that end his friendship with David. On arrival in Los Angeles it was decided by Dennis and his then girlfriend, the actress Sally Blane, that David would need some sort of story for the local papers. His first Californian press cutting thus comes from the *Los Angeles Examiner* where, over a ritually grinning Niven photograph, there is the announcement 'British Sportsman Arrives to Buy Over a Hundred Head of Polo Ponies'.

Quite what he proposed to do with over a hundred polo ponies, or how he proposed to pay for even one of them, was never made clear; but the all-important image (England, sportsman, good-looking, polo, money) had been successfully established within hours of Niven's first arrival in Hollywood. All he had to do now was live up to it – that and find somewhere to live, and perhaps a job, apart from which he was all set.

Finding a place to live proved unexpectedly easy. Sally Blane turned out, by the great good fortune which so often accompanied David's travels, to have a large, starry and accommodating family, as she now recalls: 'Dennis called me one morning and said he had this friend arriving off the boat and could we go and meet him, as I was the one with the car. So we go down to the pier and there is this man waving at us over the rail and shouting, "I don't have $25 to get my baggage off the boat." So I gave the captain a cheque and they released him.'

As they drove back to the house David was like a happy child, staring out of the car window in amazement at his first sight of California. Sally's family were out of town that week but she was in the middle of a film, so she had the house to herself. She had promised her mother that she would not let anyone stay while the family was away, but there was a poolside changing room with its own bathroom, and as David didn't have anywhere to sleep she reckoned it would be all right for him to spend the night there since it wasn't exactly in the house. When Mrs Blane came back to find David's luggage all over the hall, because he seemed to have brought everything he ever owned over from England, 'we figured it was going to be quite a long stay', and sure enough he slept in the pool house for about six weeks.

'He was the nicest boy, and I suppose we all kind of adopted him. Certainly he always said we were his first American family, and when he finally left us he said it was like leaving home. We took him around with us, especially up to the Goldwyns when they were having tennis parties. I used to tell David, "Go play tennis with Mrs Goldwyn, go to all the dinner parties up there, get liked by Frances and she'll push you towards Sam," and that was really how it all started. David never offered to pay the rent or anything like that; I guess he just knew we didn't need it, but he'd often run errands or bring Mum flowers and he was just so courteous, such fun to have around. He always knew how to bolster the ladies.'

It was Sally Blane's sister, also an actress but one who had by now taken the screen name of Loretta Young, who gave David his first introduction to the studios. Like most of the Blane family she had been in the movie business since childhood, and was now under contract to Warner's where she had just starred as James Cagney's wife in *Taxi*. Even in the random history of Hollywood fortunes, few actors can ever have equalled David's brilliant choice of landladies.

The Hollywood to which Niven got that marvellous introduction in the late summer of 1934 was still in a state of transition. Films had been made there since about 1907 (in which year a local census revealed that there were already more than a hundred English residents) and the talking picture had been a reality for five years, but there was still considerable uncertainty as to precisely what pictures should be talking about. The coming of sound had meant an initial rush towards musicals, but that was now slowing down and instead there was a headlong flight back to literary classics – accepted and familiar masterworks from which chunks of ready-made dialogue could be lifted wholesale. This was the Hollywood year of *The Barretts of Wimpole Street* and *The House of Rothschild*: the first starred Charles Laughton who had won an Oscar in the

previous year for his *Henry VIII*, and the second starred
George Arliss who had won an Oscar three years earlier
for his *Disraeli*. The English were thus looking good. They
could speak the language, appeared plausible in robes and
uniforms at a time when American actors really only made
it as singers, cowboys or gangsters, and they had already
set up a California colony that much resembled the heyday
of the Raj. English actors were nothing new in California.
Sybil Thorndike had played on stage there as early as 1905,
Chaplin and Stan Laurel arrived as refugees from Victorian
music hall five years later, and by 1916 Sir Herbert Beer-
bohm Tree had been filming his *Macbeth* for D. W.
Griffith.

In the 1920s these pioneers had been followed by the
formidable romantic novelist Elinor Glyn who, besides
discovering Clara Bow, Gary Cooper and John Gilbert,
volunteered to teach such backwoods Californian natives
as Gloria Swanson the correct manner in which to pour
a cup of tea. Actors, too, with failed, unpromising or
cold-starting careers in the English provincial theatre
would often find themselves in Los Angeles at the end of
some long stage tour and suddenly discover this magical
place in the sun where an English accent was still rare
enough to guarantee immediate employment. Such an
accent was of course not much use before the coming of
sound; nevertheless Ronald Colman had been taken on a
five-year contract by Sam Goldwyn as early as 1925, and
he and Chaplin had soon been joined in Hollywood by
Ivor Novello, Reginald Denny, Cedric Hardwicke, Victor
McLaglen, Clive Brook and Nigel Bruce among many
others – enough, in fact, to populate the Hollywood hills
as their fathers and grandfathers had once populated the
hills of India and Africa. True, not every Briton found real
happiness there. The actor Sir Guy Standing died a painful
death after being poisoned by a snake, the director William
Desmond Taylor was murdered in the first of the great
'Hollywood Babylon' scandals, and Edgar Wallace was
also taken home in a coffin after contracting a fatal bout

of pneumonia in the unexpectedly cold winter of 1932.

However, for those who survived in Hollywood – and they were a motley crew ranging from P. G. Wodehouse to Leslie Howard – the fame and the money and the sunshine and the money and the oranges and the money were attraction enough. Certain rules did have to be clearly observed by those who wished to join the city's British colony, for it was not until a decade later, after the war, that anybody went to California just to make a film. In the 1930s you went to California to stay; it was in those days a ten-day trek from England by boat and train, and unless you were ignominiously sacked (as the young Laurence Olivier had been by Garbo from the set of *Queen Christina* a year before Niven's arrival) you generally settled. The colony was still professionally an exclusively male preserve, but wives, children and nannies were brought out from England, furniture was solemnly shipped across the Atlantic, and C. Aubrey Smith refused to believe any news until he had seen it printed in the three-week-old copy of *The Times* which used to be posted out to him from London.

The colony was always ready to welcome distinguished transient visitors, especially as Hollywood badly lacked a night or social life outside the studios. When Lord and Lady Mountbatten passed through on their honeymoon in 1922, Chaplin even shot an entire film around them, and anybody with a passably English accent was guaranteed at least one invitation to the two social castles of the time, William Randolph Hearst's San Simeon and Douglas Fairbanks's Pickfair.

But David wasn't a distinguished transient visitor from home. He was a penniless ex-whisky salesman from the wrong side of Lexington Avenue, and therefore to the settlers his very Englishness was either going to be an embarrassment or a threat: an embarrassment because he would, if unsuccessful, doubtless wish to touch his compatriots for a ticket home or a loan, and a threat because he would, if successful, doubtless be taking from

them film jobs that they might very well want for themselves.

Because of this catch–22, which David with his usual
finely tuned social sense was among the first to appreciate,
he decided to try an altogether different approach to the
movie capital: he would go native. Whereas the average
young Englishman arriving out there paid ritual calls on
C. Aubrey Smith, in whose Beverly Hills garden the raised
Union Jack denoted some sort of semi-ambassadorial
status, and stayed close to Colman, Hardwicke and Willy
(Nigel) Bruce, especially on cricketing afternoons, David
chose to avail himself of the altogether greater and warmer
hospitality being offered by the Blane family down on
Sunset Boulevard.

He would in any case have been an uneasy fit into the
British colony as it was then constituted and ruled over by
Ronald Colman, for the simple reason that, although many
people think of David as belonging to that screen generation (since by the late 1930s they were all filming together
in such classics as *The Prisoner of Zenda*), most of the
others from Karloff to Bruce tended to recall a First World
War in which they had been wounded when David was
barely into his prep school. While David was now in
his middle twenties, Colman and his contemporaries had
already reached their early forties, members of an
altogether different generation who had been both battle-
scarred and theatre-trained while Niven was still in short
trousers. As a result, even those who did bother to make
his acquaintance found him a creature from another world.

The Americans, however, had no such problems with
him and, used as they were to the English in Hollywood
being a cliquey and clubby lot, preferring to take tea only
on each other's imitation-English lawns when not actually
working, David came as a new and unexpected delight.
An Englishman who would talk to them, mix with them,
even stay with them was still a rarity – and one exploited
by David to the full.

Within a day or two of his arrival in the Blane household

he had confessed his new-found ambition to be an actor and persuaded Loretta Young to take him on to the set of a hospital picture called *The White Parade* for which she had been loaned to Fox. At that first glimpse of studio life he instantly fell in love with the film world and duly reported to Central Casting in the hopes of becoming an extra. It was only there that a kind clerk gently explained the rules to this apparently imbecilic young man. In order even to apply for a job as a film extra ('For every one we employ we turn away a thousand' read a legend over her desk) you had first to present a work permit. David had no work permit. It wasn't the kind of thing they asked you for in bars off Lexington Avenue or at pony-tracks in Atlantic City.

He also didn't possess any money, having spent his last $80 on a much-needed second-hand car since the public transport system in Los Angeles was no better then than now. Besides those minor problems, he also had nowhere to live, since even he had decided, after his first six weeks in Hollywood, that the generous Mrs Blane might quite like her poolside changing room back. Accordingly he began scouring the district round Sunset Boulevard for a cheap hotel, preferably one so desperately in need of guests that they wouldn't mind waiting a few months to have the bill paid. What David then found was another remarkable bit of good fortune known as Alvin C. Weingand, later a California state senator but at this time manager of the Hollywood Roosevelt Hotel on Hollywood Boulevard.

'One afternoon I looked up from the desk and confronted this very attractive, jolly Englishman,' Weingand remembers. 'I asked him what he was doing in Hollywood, and he said he'd never been there before but he had a lot of friends who told him to come visit, but that unfortunately he seemed to have no money. However, he impressed me as a very bright, engaging gentleman so I said I would give him credit for one month and see what happened from there on. We had a lot of empty rooms at the time and I figured he wouldn't do us any harm: a room in those days was only $65 per month anyway. But he didn't seem to have a lot to do, or anywhere very much to go, so most mornings he'd come down to my office and then we'd go out to lunch across the road.'

After Weingand's, the next helping hands for Niven in California came from some old Malta friends in the Royal Navy. Staying one weekend up at Montecito, David happened to discover HMS *Norfolk* putting into Santa Barbara on one of the goodwill missions that His Majesty's Navy could then still afford. As the *Norfolk* had put into Malta during David's army service there three years earlier, he reckoned he might find some friends aboard; and as long as they hadn't been the ones for whom Trubshawe's Husbandometer had been devised all should go well, if Niven could just get to see them and remind them who he was.

This worked well enough, so well in fact that after a long and alcoholic evening recapturing memories of Malta, David fell into a deep sleep on board the cruiser. When he awoke, it was to see through the porthole an eighteenth-century warship steaming straight towards them. This was of course the *Bounty*, or rather a replica thereof which had been sent out to meet the *Norfolk* as a publicity stunt for the Clark Gable–Charles Laughton film which was then about to go into production at MGM.

Niven's naval mates, ever a practical lot, decided that if he was really going to succeed as a film star, then the sooner he met a few film people the better. They therefore lowered him, still in evening dress, on to the *Bounty* where the director, Frank Lloyd, regretted politely that there was no actual work available, but agreed to introduce him to another Metro director of the time, Edmund Goulding. Goulding was, Chaplin apart, the first British film director to have made it to the top in a Hollywood studio, largely as a result of the Garbo film *Grand Hotel*, and he was known to be sympathetic towards his fellow countrymen.

Sure enough, he agreed to test Niven for the small role of Ruth Chatterton's drunken younger brother (one which eventually went to another hopeful young expatriate of the period, Louis Hayward, a South African who had established himself in the London theatre and then moved to Hollywood at the same time as Niven) in a film entitled *The Flame Within*, of which Goulding was not only director but also writer and producer. The test was a fair old disaster, with a frozen David desperately reciting off-colour limericks and telling some of his old cocktail-party anecdotes in an effort to cover up a total lack of acting experience; yet Goulding saw something in it which made him think that just possibly, with a great deal of work and help, Niven might have some sort of screen future. His intuition was not shared by Louis B. Mayer or anyone else around the MGM lot in 1934; nevertheless, Goulding was then quick enough and clever enough to remember somebody else in Hollywood with a known liking for handsome young Englishmen – Mae West, who had given Cary Grant a handsome screen start the year before in *She Done Him Wrong*.

Like Grant, Niven was, in Katharine Hepburn's intelligent distinction, 'not so much an actor acting as a personality functioning on camera', and that clearly appealed to Mae West. What else appealed to her about Niven is perhaps best left to the imagination, but he was given a rapid screen test and told of a role available in her forthcoming *Going To Town*. It was at this point that several gentlemen from the US Immigration Service turned up at Paramount asking to see David's work permit.

When it was not forthcoming, and they further discovered that Niven had in fact entered California on a ten-day visitor's visa which was now several weeks out of date, they gave him twenty-four hours to leave the country. In some despair, he went back to the Roosevelt Hotel and Al Weingand for advice. It transpired that this was routine behaviour for the Immigration Service: the recognized procedure was to cross the Mexican border, wait a few days on the other side, and then re-enter the United States on a resident alien visa, which would bring with it the right to a work permit. Indeed, so many English, Swedish and German actors and directors were at that time pouring into the border town of Mexicali for the same purpose that any halfway intelligent Mexican should have opened a movie studio and a repertory theatre there.

What David did in Mexico during those few days around Christmas 1934 is open to much the same kind of doubt as what he did in Cuba a few months earlier – probably not a lot, though he himself later claimed to have been working in a bar-room polishing guns. Occasionally the claims ran a bit further. The English actor and pianist Billy Milton recalls that back in Hollywood a few months later, 'sitting by a hotel pool one day a stranger got into conversation with me. He said he had just arrived from Mexico where he had been instructing both sides of the revolutionary war in the use of firearms and had then had to get out . . . Wanting to be helpful and perhaps a little boastful, I said I would be happy to introduce him to some of my Hollywood friends. He thanked me, then casually re-marked that he was playing tennis with Charlie Chaplin later in the day and then having tea with Mr and Mrs Ronald Colman.'

By the time he got back to Hollywood it was to find that Paul Cavanagh had won the Mae West film part in much the same way that Louis Hayward had beaten Niven to the role in the Goulding movie. Good-looking young Eng-lishmen were getting ominously thick on the California ground, and David went to the back of the queue at Central Casting, where he was at least now able to flourish a legal work permit.

In his own books and many interviews, David always described himself as 'Anglo-Saxon Type No 2008' on the books of Central Casting, though intriguingly in his pre-war interviews he used to describe himself as 'Type No 4008' – presumably until he realized that the likelihood of there being 4,000 look-alike Anglo-Saxon types seeking work as extras in Hollywood even in 1935 was perhaps a little slim. He did, however, definitely apply for and get work as an extra, but because nobody has ever managed to trace any of the films in which he appeared (often, by his own account, heavily disguised as a Mexican bandit) it is hard to estimate precisely how many of these exist. In 1958, before he had himself begun to copyright his memoirs in print, he told an interviewer from the *Saturday Evening Post*: 'My first twenty-seven pictures were bang-bang westerns in which I played a variety of non-speaking barflies, coach passengers or poker players. I even got into some of the early *Hopalong Cassidy* pictures at Paramount.' 'Twenty-seven' sounds like a number plucked out of fairly thin air, especially as the period in question lasted only about three months before he got his first credited speaking role. Even supposing we settled on, say, half a dozen movies, that was still more than enough to acquaint him with the $2–a-day life of the Hollywood extra and to convince him that he didn't want to lead it for long, even if he had, as he later claimed, got into the Cecil B. de Mille *Cleopatra*.

Breaking out was a matter of getting a good agent, and that might take a little time; but it needs to be recalled constantly that David was no ordinary starving extra. With Al Weingand still willing to delay presenting him with a bill at the Roosevelt, Loretta Young and Edmund Goulding going in to bat for him whenever studio conversation turned to new talent, and budding friendships with not only the anglophile Fairbanks Sr (whom David had first met back in England a couple of years earlier, at the time of his abortive screen debut in *All The Winners*) but also Chaplin and the Ronald Colmans, to whom he had been introduced by Weingand, who appears to have known everybody who was anybody in what was still a very small town, Niven could now consider himself rather better connected both socially and professionally than at any previous time in an admittedly undistinguished and unstructured career.

Sure enough, the agent didn't take long in coming around. Goulding found him one called Bill Hawks who instantly got him a test with Claudette Colbert for a film called *The Gilded Lily*. Two other actors were tested with him, and both were given long contracts at Paramount. David was always a little hazy about who his immediate contemporaries really were, announcing at one moment in *The Moon's A Balloon* that when he first went to work as an extra at Metro, Elizabeth Taylor was already there as a child star. This being 1935, Miss Taylor was all of three and almost a decade away from her arrival in California. It seems highly possible, however, that the two men tested successfully with him were Ray Milland and Fred Mac-Murray, and it was understandably depressing for David that while they got full studio contracts, he didn't even get the role for which they were testing.

One of Niven's problems now was, oddly enough, his very Englishness. Whereas Herbert Marshall, Ronald Colman, Clive Brook and even Milland had all arrived in Hollywood as identifiable characters, created through either stage or previous British film work, Niven had been seen on screen by precisely nobody. An Englishman was only useful if you knew he was going to be an Englishman in a specific role, preferably uniformed. Where a Fred MacMurray could play almost any local script that came along, Niven was severely limited by what he hoped would be his greatest asset – his nationality.

At least his social life was now looking up, as he later told an American radio reporter: 'I went one morning to a Turkish Bath, invited by Doug Fairbanks's father whom I'd met in England when I was a miserable officer in a regiment. I'd played golf with him, and he found me on the street in Hollywood Boulevard wandering about. So he asked what I was doing, and I said trying to be an actor. And he said, "Please, please don't ask me to help you because I simply can't; but come to the house whenever you like, eat, drink, do whatever you want to do, but please don't ask me to help you become an actor." In the meantime, he said, why didn't I come down to his studio and have what he called "a steam", which was a Turkish

Bath. What I really needed right then was a nice hot lunch, but he took me down to the steam and sat me on a marble slab between Darryl Zanuck and Joe Schenck who were then forming Twentieth Century-Fox. Sid Grauman, who owned all the big cinemas in Los Angeles, was on another slab and so too was Sam Goldwyn, and I sat there thinking this was my big chance – not that I thought being naked would help much, but I sat there waiting for my big moment and then Fairbanks, who had a wild and idiotic sense of humour but knew that I was stoney broke suddenly said, thinking it would help my image, "Oh, Niven, what are you going to do this winter, play polo or bring the yacht around?" I said, "Polo, polo, polo," and then did actually faint from the heat and lack of food. I was carried out and put in a nice cold plunge; I came to a few minutes later to find Zanuck, who played polo and had his own team with a lot of internationals on it, bending over me and saying to Fairbanks, "Does he really play polo?" and Fairbanks, still thinking to help me get on in Hollywood, said, "He played for the British Army," which of course was an exaggeration because all I'd done was to play a couple of times in Malta on some ghastly old animal. Then Zanuck said, "Come and play for me on Saturday."

'So I turned up on the Saturday at the Riviera Country Club, determined that this was my way into Twentieth Century-Fox, and Zanuck put me on this terrible horse called St George, a stallion that bit like a dog. And I had this hat which didn't fit, and tight trousers and also hundreds of people staring at me as well as all these internationals playing. And I was told to mark Zanuck, so I thought this was my big moment – I knew enough about polo to know that I had to ride at him and stop him hitting the ball. So every time Zanuck got near the ball I charged at him: he was Back in his team, and I was the Number One in ours. And there came a moment when Zanuck was galloping with the ball, so I charged at him from the back, whereupon St George reached out and bit him in the arse – got him right in the bum through his muzzle, and Zanuck was shrieking with the pain. Then we galloped over the ball which got trodden into the turf, so I took a vague swing at it with my stick, which passed right underneath Zanuck's pony's tail. And the pony, being extremely randy, clamped his tail to his behind and imprisoned the head of my stick. So I'm holding on to one end of the stick by its leather thong, and the other end is up the pony's bum, and Zanuck is shrieking, and this ghastly triangle gallops past the stand where Fairbanks is laughing so hard that he falls out of his chair. I didn't work at Twentieth Century-Fox for many, many years.'

Edmund Goulding, however, still remained loyal and, though now clutching at some very short straws indeed, decided the time had come to remind his boy-wonder boss at Metro, Irving Thalberg, that David had made one of his first entries into Hollywood aboard the mock-up of the *Bounty*. That film was now at an advanced stage of production, and Thalberg reckoned that he might as well, for the sake of a couple of gossip-column paragraphs, have David play one of the minor mutineers.

The news that the great Thalberg was thinking of signing Niven finally provoked some of the action that Goulding had been trying to start up on David's behalf for months. By the following Monday morning, Samuel Goldwyn had decided that his studio, too, could perhaps do with the young man's talents – whatever they might turn out to be.

Chapter Seven

1935–1936

'This actor is tall, dark and not the slightest bit handsome.'

Like most Middle European movie moguls of the Hollywood 1930s, Samuel Goldwyn was small (Philip French once estimated that you could have swung a scythe 5 feet 6 inches above the ground all around California at that time and not done lasting harm to the head of any major motion-picture company) and anglophile. He had also just lost Ronald Colman from his roster of long-term contract employees, and was thus in the market for another presentable Englishman who knew how to stand around in uniform; and if David had precious little acting experience at this time, the Army had at least managed to teach him how to dress for battles.

Nor was Goldwyn really running much of a risk with his new acquisition. Though the contract was to be for seven years, the starting salary for the first two was to be a minimal $100 a week and during that time Niven could not expect the honour of working in any Goldwyn pictures. He was instead to hack around the other studios, learning his craft as a film actor until such time as Goldwyn deemed him ready to work in one of his own productions; moreover, at any time in those two years the contract could be dropped by Goldwyn, but not by David. As the man who is now writing Goldwyn's biography, Scott Berg, reflects:

'I don't think Goldwyn ever really understood what David could be in the movies, and he only really once used Niven as a leading man, years after the war in *The Bishop's Wife*, by which time their relationship was almost at an end. Goldwyn knew right from the start that Niven could never be another great solo star like Colman, but he believed in grooming, and each time he used Niven he gave him just a little more to do. You have to remember also that he was making a lot more money out of Niven than Niven was out of him.' Goldwyn at this time was by himself: he was not with MGM or Paramount, he was a one-man band, and by farming Niven out to the other studios he realized he was going to win two ways. They would be paying him more for Niven than the $100 a week he was paying under Niven's contract, and if Niven were going to fail, then better he should fail in a Paramount movie or an MGM movie rather than a Goldwyn movie.

The Goldwyn–Niven relationship was thus going to be very different from the Goldwyn–Colman relationship: where that had grown over ten years and eighteen films to the point where Colman was now earning $6,000 a week as the tenth highest-paid player in Hollywood, Niven was merely to be regarded as a useful loan-out property. It could perhaps be argued at this point that if Goldwyn in 1935 had chosen to set about shaping and building Niven's studio career with the energy and single-minded devotion he had shown in 1925 when setting about the building and shaping of Colman's, Niven too might have turned out to be the great solo star that Colman undoubtedly was. On the other hand, it could also be argued that Colman had arrived at the Goldwyn studios with seven years of European stage and screen experience already behind him. He had come to Hollywood as an actor, and was turned fairly rapidly into a star; Niven had reached Hollywood as a travelling adventurer, and would have to be turned first of all into some kind of an actor.

That process was soon begun. A day or two after signing his Goldwyn contract David was sent over to Paramount to play his first speaking role in which the speaking amounted to three words ('Goodbye, my dear,' addressed to Elissa Landi on a station platform). The film was *Without Regret*, based on a Broadway and London stage hit of the period called *Interference*. Advance publicity announced that it would make a star of a hitherto unknown English player; unfortunately, the player was not David but Paul Cavanagh, who had already beaten him to Mae West's capacious bosom in *Going To Town*. In fact, however, *Without Regret* ('Jennifer Gage learns to regret her marriage to a dashing, dissolute aviator in China, especially after he comes back from the dead,' read one plot synopsis) did nobody much good, unless you count Sam Goldwyn, who was able to pocket Niven's Paramount fee and show a small profit on his first month's contract salary.

Yet for David, Hollywood life had suddenly taken a distinct turn for the better. He was now a Goldwyn contract artist, able at last to check out of the Roosevelt and begin to repay Al Weingand for his considerable hospitality. He had even taken a small house on North Vista, not that he saw a great deal of it as he had now cheerfully begun to sleep around some of the best beds in Hollywood where his reviews were considerably better than any he was to get as an actor for the foreseeable future. The actress Evelyn Keyes, who married directors Charles Vidor and John Huston and made her screen name as Scarlett O'Hara's younger sister in *Gone With The Wind*, was to recall 'a marvellous sense of humour, a delightful storyteller, delicious as French pastry, single then and ripe for plucking'.

Thus plucked, Niven was to go on to one of the most prolific and discreet sexual careers in the whole history of Hollywood. He lived briefly not only with Evelyn Keyes and several others but also rather less briefly with Merle Oberon, managing with considerable and rare dexterity to keep his bachelor and later extra-marital affairs quite secret, omitting any mention of them even in his own memoirs. While it could be reckoned that many of these

were fleeting film-set encounters which would not radically
have altered those memoirs, the long 1935–7 affair with
Merle Oberon does actually have considerable importance
in his life and career in that it drastically alters the picture
David himself painted of his early California years.

True, he does in his own writing refer anonymously to
a 'Great Big Star' with whom he was 'very much involved',
and as Miss Oberon was still alive at the first publication
of *The Moon's A Balloon* it could be argued that in
preserving her secrecy he was merely doing the decent
thing that any gentleman would. This was, however, forty
years on, and in the interim Miss Oberon had been much
married, not least to Alexander Korda; it would not perhaps be too uncharitable to reflect that David's romantic
image of himself as a young and penniless adventurer
banging on studio gates was in some ways rather more
attractive than the truth of a young actor living off a much
bigger star and using her if not to get jobs (they were
together only in *Wuthering Heights* and *Beloved Enemy*),
then at least to gain invitations to the kind of parties where
jobs might be on offer.

Merle Oberon was then (like Charles Laughton and
because of the same film, Korda's *Private Life of Henry
VIII*) one of the most bankable and sought-after of the
Hollywood English. An Anglo-Indian from the wrong side
of the Calcutta tracks – a secret she had taken some trouble
to hide and one which, when he discovered it, may well
have affected David's decision not to marry and start a
family with her at a later time, when that was very much
her wish – Oberon was one of the most intriguing of all
movie stars and also one of the most secretive, which
perhaps explains why even David at his most gossipy wrote
so little about her. It was, therefore, only years after her
death that her nephew by marriage, Michael Korda, turned
that exotic life into a steamy best-selling novel entitled
Queenie, wherein certain elements of David's character
along with those of Olivier can be discerned in the actor
who finally delivers the eulogy at her funeral.

Oberon had first met David in London in the early thirties when she was a hostess at the Café de Paris, living with Hutch, the great cabaret pianist, and David was on his nightclub rounds. A couple of years later, Laurence Olivier (who was, of course, to join them in *Wuthering Heights*) recalled a meeting at Korda's Denham Studios where Merle was then filming: 'She had this young man with her, who kept putting on silly voices and seemed terribly ill at ease with people who were already making their names as actors, but she was very sweet with him and then by the time we all got to Hollywood she was the love of his life. I don't think he was ever the most faithful of lovers, even to her, but she was very good with him and I do think she helped him a lot, both socially and professionally. He was never going to be a dedicated actor – he couldn't have done a stage classic to save his life – but he had a lot of charm and was very good at sport, and Merley loved all that about him.'

By 1935 she herself was just coming out of an unhappy affair with the introvert, intellectual Leslie Howard, and David thus came as a welcome change. An outdoor man with an uncomplicated attitude to sex and work, he proved an ideal partner on the tennis courts and in bed while, in return, Merle took him to some of the grander social gatherings and worked with him on some of the many screen tests that he was having to undergo.

At weekends they would head up to a ranch near Santa Barbara, which Ronald Colman and Al Weingand had acquired as a kind of country retreat for their friends – not that they were ever in danger of being alone there, as Weingand recalls: 'We had a lot of romances up at San Ysidro: Gloria Swanson and Herbert Marshall, Bill Powell and a gorgeous young actress, but I want it distinctly understood that we always provided two-roomed cottages. Neither David nor Merle was married at that time, but we weren't running a brothel, you understand. Ronnie Colman was highly respectable, and David really looked up to him as a father figure, so I'm sure he and Merle were always very discreet. They used to go sailing and play tennis with the Colmans; it was a very outdoor life and I think David made Merle very happy, taught her not to take anything too seriously.'

In return, she taught him how to read scripts in front of a camera with rather less of the usual stiff Niven embarrassment, and as a result of that he soon got his second speaking role in a film. While they were staying up at San Ysidro (where Olivier was later to marry Vivien Leigh, where the Kennedys often stayed in some seclusion, and where Niven was once to entertain the not entirely daft idea of opening a summer theatre for out-of-work Hollywood actors), Merle coached him to the point where even Goldwyn agreed he could be used by his own studio for another one-line appearance. This was in Howard Hawks's *Barbary Coast*, for which he was billed as 'A Sailor' and achieved a moment of glory, or at any rate attention, by being flung through the window of a San Francisco brothel during a riot. Unfortunately, his line was spoken on the way down, and was almost lost in the general hubbub. Still, it was progress of a kind.

Niven's third film of 1935 was another loan-out, this one to Columbia. *A Feather in Her Hat* starred Pauline Lord and Louis Hayward, yet another of the young English officer-and-gentleman types whose careers seemed to be moving so much faster and more purposefully in Hollywood than Niven's at this time. There was, however, not a lot to be said for starring in what the *New York Times* described as 'a shy and fragile little drama of mother love striving with minor success to make itself heard above the clatter of the plot', and David was far enough down the castlist as 'Leo Cartwright' to escape any blame for the proceedings. The film is noteworthy for containing his first actual scene: as a witty young poet, he has to make a flamboyant entrance at a party, one which was only achieved after several early takes during which the director tactfully refrained from putting any film in his camera. David managed to obliterate the entire movie from accurate memory, so that when he came to write *The Moon's A Balloon* he got both its star and its year wrong.

The experience had shown that he was still badly in need of acting lessons. Though large numbers of actresses from Hedy Lamarr to Lana Turner were being offered studio contracts by virtue of their other attributes, usually in sweaters, it was still comparatively rare for a male actor, especially one from London, to arrive in Hollywood with no Thespian experience of any kind and David's patent inability to act (which hadn't much mattered when he was still camping around as a dress extra in minor westerns) threatened to become something of an embarrassment. So, at the urging of both Merle Oberon and Sam Goldwyn, he considered the revolutionary idea of going on the stage – something he had not done since the days of Army concerts in Malta and was only to do again on two other occasions in his life, one of them catastrophic. Near enough to Hollywood was the Pasadena Playhouse, a theatre where 'resting' Hollywood stars would occasionally go to work and where young and promising players could sometimes be sent to polish up their craft, or in David's case to start learning it.

Niven's professional stage début in the 1935 production of a play called *Wedding* was not what one might call a success; while he had begun greatly to enjoy the comparatively relaxed air of a film set, with its gossiping extras and endless waits for action, he found the theatre far too intense and homosexual for his liking. The players at Pasadena seemed to be taking themselves too seriously and, worse, to be regarding their work as a kind of holy calling instead of the fortunate accident that David reckoned his was. His reaction was to make fun of them, while telling his new-found friends at the Colman and Fairbanks Sunday afternoon parties that he was 'starring at Pasadena' when in fact he was merely walking on in the third act.

Came the first night and, having already had a few stiff ones in the dressing room to enliven what promised to be a remarkably boring evening, Niven went on to see lined up in the front row a galaxy of stars from Herbert Marshall and Gloria Swanson to Charles Laughton via the great Goldwyn himself, all of whom had travelled out to see Niven in his starring role. So as not to disappoint them, he told half a dirty story during his walk-on and made an exit of sorts into a piece of scenery. The result was a sharp lecture from Goldwyn and a decision not to act again on stage, a resolution which he was not to break until 1951.

Once he'd recovered his temper and after heavy pressure from Merle Oberon (who was now starring in his *Dark Angel*), Goldwyn at last made Niven a reasonable offer on behalf of his own studio. The film concerned was Rachel Crothers's *Splendour*, and humiliatingly its leading man was a young actor who had been taken under contract by Goldwyn on the same day as David but had since been used by him to much better advantage – Joel McCrea. There was a role for 'a wastrel son' and in that David did manage to attract one or two non-committal reviews, the first he had ever had. So at least a couple of observant film critics were now aware of his existence, and had even stopped spelling his name Nevins as it appeared on some early press handouts, the same ones which announced that his late father had been a general.

He also managed on this picture to establish an early friendship with Joel McCrea: 'We were starting out together, and David was of course living with Merle whom I had just played with in *These Three*; he seemed so desperate for work that Merle and I had a word with the director of *Splendour* and that was how that happened. His was only a very small part, but he was terribly nervous and kept coming over to me and reading out his lines and saying, "Do you think that's all right, old boy?" He kept repeating his most difficult line, which was when he was trying to persuade me to marry some girl I wasn't in love with and he had to say, "I'd marry her twenty millions if she had two heads and a club foot." But by the time we got around to shooting that scene, he'd said it so often and was so nervous of the camera that it came out, "I'd marry her club foot." The curious thing about David at that time was that he had great confidence in himself as a person, always kidding around with Merle and furious if people called him "Mr Oberon" which they sometimes did, but absolutely no confidence in himself as an actor at all.'

Yet by the end of 1935 Niven had made four films, all admittedly undistinguished but all featuring him as something more than an extra. Goldwyn, however, remained unimpressed by his screen appearances, and made it clear that while his contract would not actually be terminated, David would continue to be hired out to any studio that could find a use for him rather than having, like McCrea, a career built for him at Sam's home base.

A more ambitious or dedicated actor might have taken this news badly. Niven went cheerfully back to the beach, to Merle, to the weekend parties with the Colmans up at San Ysidro, to cricket matches umpired by C. Aubrey Smith himself and to the increasingly good life that he had now begun to carve out for himself around Hollywood. In that sense, California was fast becoming to the twenty-five-year-old Niven an acceptable mirror-image of Malta. Instead of the Army barracks there were the film studios where a little generally undemanding work had occasionally to be done, but the climate and the sexual and social opportunities were if anything rather better. All that he really lacked was a Trubshawe, some close friend with whom to share the jokes and the larking about and the general good fortune of landing up in the film capital of the world. In Michael's absence, David began writing him the letters that were the origin of all his later published anecdotage about Hollywood: long, rambling, hand-written, jocular accounts of bad films made, good parties attended and starry women bedded, all intercut with cricket and tennis scores and the feeling that he had somehow blundered into an over-the-rainbow existence from which there would one day come a rude awakening. Yet 1939 was still three years away, and 1936 opened uneventfully enough with another batch of loan-outs.

First David was sent by Goldwyn over to MGM to do his already familiar wealthy wastrel playboy routine in a Nelson Eddy– Jeanette MacDonald rendering of *Rose Marie* which was notable mainly for getting through the five acts of Gounod's *Romeo and Juliet* in roughly one minute per act, and for establishing James Stewart in his first sizeable screen role. But with MacDonald and Eddy warbling away at some length, there really wasn't much for the non-musical actors to do and David was soon off to Paramount for a bit in another romantic musical, this one entitled *Palm Springs Affair*. It only ran one hour ten minutes, and David's fleeting appearance as 'George Brittel, a young millionaire tied to his aunt's apron strings' seems to have passed unnoticed.

His next loan-out was an even tackier affair at Twentieth Century-Fox, though ironically, if any time, money or enthusiasm had been put into it, *Thank You, Jeeves* might conceivably have lifted Niven's career off the ground at last. This was conceived as a fifty-minute B-to-Z programme filler with David (as the ineffable Bertie Wooster) taking third billing to Arthur Treacher as the butler Jeeves and Virginia Fields as the mysterious Lady Marjorie. Whether the producer, Sol M. Wurtzel, himself a character who seemed to have stepped from a minor Wodehouse comic novel of American social life, was hoping that David would make his name and Wurtzel's fortune in an inexpensive series of the *Sherlock Holmes* kind that was a couple of years later to star Basil Rathbone is not clear, though he had taken the precaution of buying screen rights to several of the Wodehouse tales. Only this one was made by him, however, and David's loan-out from Goldwyn was as usual for just one picture; moreover, the title made it appear that if this was to be a Wodehouse screen series about anybody, it was to be about the butler rather than the master.

Still, Niven as Bertie was an intelligent and attractive idea. Though by no means the first or last of the screen

Woosters, he seemed at last to have a role which would clarify and consolidate casting directors' ideas of what he could actually do on film. The upper-class twit was a role well within David's grasp and Army memory, and it at long last gave him a professional foothold within the colony of expatriate actors. This colony was now happily divided into *Upstairs, Downstairs*-type groupings harking back to the *Cavalcade* filming in 1931 which had represented one of its first great American gatherings. 'Upstairs' were still to be found the old paternal aristocrats, men like George Arliss and C. Aubrey Smith, along with the occasional old-buffer uncle like Nigel Bruce and one or two more poetic loners such as Leslie Howard and Ronald Colman. These were now being joined by younger bloods like Niven and John Loder, renegade types but still on the right side of the green baize door that separated them from the servant classes led by Arthur Treacher, the immaculate *Jeeves* of Niven's latest film.

Bertie Wooster gave David a kind of idiotic credibility. The character was already rather more familiar than the actor, but at least the casting meant that David could now be classed an official member of the colony, no longer a tennis-playing extra who might embarrassingly be about to ask Colman for a kindly mention next time he was in the studios. Niven was now a fully-fledged, though still very junior, member of the Hollywood British, and if ever a man and a role were born for each other then surely they were Niven and Wooster, as Frank Nugent of the *New York Times* observed: 'Mr Wodehouse must have been one of the fates in attendance at the births of Mr Treacher and Mr Niven, marking them down there and then to play the characters he had been writing about these many years.'

The screenplay credits had the grace to note that *Thank You, Jeeves* was by Joseph Hoffman and Stephen Cross 'after' P. G. Wodehouse; most critics said a long way after, for 'Plum' himself had recently retreated from what even he considered the unfathomable lunacy of life in Hollywood, where only a couple of years earlier he had been paid $104,000 for writing a film called *Rosalie* which nobody much wanted to make.

The one person who emerged with real credit from this film was, of course, Jeeves himself. It led to years of tray-carrying screen employment for Arthur Treacher, who was soon able to hire his very own butler and set new standards for gentlemen's gentlemen on camera. When, a couple of years later, Mary Pickford had cause to sack her American houseman for incompetence, he was heard to scream at her from the doorstep, 'Madam, you don't require an ordinary mortal like me: the butler you are looking for is Arthur Treacher.'

Socially, however, David was still far from accustomed to Hollywood ways. It had only been this past Christmas that he had decided to push the boat out and present Norma Shearer, one of his most faithful hostesses, with half a dozen lace handkerchiefs. Her gift to him turned out to be a Studebaker.

Chapter Eight

1936–1937

'Bring on the empty horses.'

Just as they had in India a century or so earlier, the upper-class British in California were divided into at least two teams, the respectables and the renegades. Since he had played Wooster (and in Hollywood at that time you were what you played) David clearly belonged to the respectables, but he tended to side with renegades like Sir Guy Standing and John Loder, the disreputable mirror images of C. Aubrey Smith and Ronald Colman. Standing was, at the age of sixty-five, reliably reported to be living with the then nineteen-year-old Betty Grable, while Loder went even further towards offending local susceptibilities by starting an affair with Marion Davies until it was explained to him that the last man to try that, the director Tom Ince, had mysteriously disappeared overboard from the yacht owned by Miss Davies's lover, William Randolph Hearst.

Niven's Stowe and Sandhurst background was perfectly in keeping with those of C. Aubrey Smith (Charterhouse and Cambridge), Basil Rathbone (Repton) and Clive Brook (Dulwich) but, like Loder and George Sanders, Niven was temperamentally much more of a rebel, and one of the things he was beginning to rebel against was Goldwyn's continued refusal to treat him as anything more than a taxi, useful for short hirings to other destinations.

It wasn't just the meanness of Goldwyn's $100 a week that irked Niven. As Ronald Colman had once told him, 'Before God we are worth $35 a week; before our agents we are worth whatever they can get for us.' What worried David was Goldwyn's continued refusal to cast him in a decent role at his own studios, and even the latter agreed that the time had come to put up or shut up. It was now the middle of 1936, and David had been in Hollywood for almost two years. He had appeared in speaking roles in seven films, of which the last had offered him co-star status on an admittedly minimal budget, and yet he had managed to make almost no discernible professional impression on anyone. Even *Thank You, Jeeves* was only being shown in New York at the bottom half of a double bill featuring as its main attraction a new Goldwyn drama starring Niven's perpetual and more successful rival Joel McCrea.

Goldwyn recognized that David would either have to be tried and tested in a major film or quietly 'let go' and allowed to drift back to New York or London in whatever professional capacity he chose. So far as David was concerned, there was still no other choice. As he told Roxburgh in one of his many letters back to Stowe, he was finding an actor's life more fun, more interesting and far more lucrative than that of a soldier and had every intention of persevering with it even if the films themselves were proving to be pretty dull.

That, however, was about to change, thanks not so much to Goldwyn as to the director William Wyler, who was later to drag David kicking and screaming up *Wuthering Heights*. At this time Wyler was working for the Goldwyn Studios on a major film version of the Sinclair Lewis novel *Dodsworth*, which had already proved a considerable if wordy success on stage in New York. Goldwyn had acquired it for Hollywood under the mistaken impression that it was a saga of America's new automobile industry; on closer inspection it proved to be nothing of the kind, but a long and rambling account of the deterioration of the marriage of a retired car executive. However it was conveniently written in a large number of round-the-world scenes rather better suited to screen than stage, and even on stage it had survived two Broadway years, so Goldwyn's screen rights investment of $165,000 was no longer looking too disastrous for him.

Goldwyn was so keen to cash in on the Broadway success of *Dodsworth* that he brought in Walter Huston, who had played the title role there for two seasons, and cast opposite him another very stagey character, Ruth Chatterton. The rest of the casting was left to Wyler, who had just been working with Merle Oberon on *These Three*, the first screen version of Lillian Hellman's famous tale of two lesbian schoolmistresses. As soon as Merle knew that Wyler was going on to *Dodsworth*, she began talking to him about the possibility of David playing the small but showy part of Major Lockert, the suave English officer who has a brief shipboard romance with Mrs Dodsworth early in the picture.

Oberon's feeling about Wyler was that he was the most difficult, tempestuous and demanding of directors but that he was also one of the very few who could actually teach Niven the art of screen acting, and that was a view shared by the best. Two years later Laurence Olivier was to acknowledge that Wyler was the man who taught him, for the first time, how to perform in front of a camera, and it was Wyler whom Olivier always hoped would direct his Shakespeare films.

An irascible, intriguing and unusually intelligent movie-man with a love for turning apparently intractable novels into films, Wyler was one of the best arguments for Hollywood nepotism, having first arrived there at the suggestion of his cousin Carl Laemmle, the head of Universal, who not only had a very large 'faemmle' but was kind enough to employ most of them whenever possible. Wyler had started with him as a publicist and studio messenger, worked his way up through two-reel westerns and was now the most meticulous and erudite director on the Goldwyn roster, not that this was saying a great deal.

He agreed, however, with Oberon and Goldwyn that David would be well cast as Lockert, though it is not easy to assess whether he did so simply to avoid a row with a useful star and a studio boss who now also felt that Niven needed at least one good scene in something, or because he really thought he could make him into a film actor. At all events the film was not a happy one: Huston had played the title role so long on stage that he resented any changes of dialogue or emphasis, while Chatterton who had not played it on stage was understandably eager to get as far away as possible from the original version lest it just look like a photographed stage play. Paul Lukas and the formidable Maria Ouspenskaya led a starry support cast, though most off-screen attention focused on Mary Astor, not so much because of her so-so performance in the film as because of sensational revelations about her private life which were to be unveiled to David's huge and gossipy delight during the shooting.

Miss Astor was now having to play 'the other woman' in the law courts as well as in *Dodsworth*. For the past year she had been carrying on a flamboyant affair with the Broadway playwright George S. Kaufman, one which hit the headlines during the shooting of the film because her husband, a distinguished local doctor, had on discovering the affair sued for divorce and custody of their daughter, winning also a $60,000 property settlement. This decision Miss Astor was now trying to overturn, but the subsequent hearings were to prove the spiciest even in the history of Hollywood divorce cases. It transpired that the actress had kept a diary in which she was inclined to note the number of times that Kaufman managed to make love to her in a single night. There was considerable speculation as to what this total actually was (one magazine quoted twenty, though on what evidence was never clear) but for a week or two the story managed to push Hitler's Berlin Olympics, the Spanish Civil War and the worst corn crop since 1881 to the side of even the *New York Times* front page.

The hearings were nocturnal affairs, since the local Los

Angeles judge had graciously agreed that Miss Astor could go on filming *Dodsworth* by day and testifying to her sex life by night; Kaufman, summoned to give evidence by the prosecution, thought better of it and escaped across the back of the MGM lot dressed in one of their old officers' uniforms from *Mutiny on the Bounty*. By now the proceedings had taken on the air of a full-scale sex farce, and David was doubtless happily reminded of his own days in Malta with Trubshawe and the Husbandometer. Perhaps Californian life was not so very different after all.

For several days the case came near to closing down *Dodsworth*. Several other studio chiefs, still jumpy after the Fatty Arbuckle sex scandal and the murders of Ince and William Desmond Taylor, urged Goldwyn to invoke the ritual morals clause that was now standard in all studio contracts. Goldwyn, however, had a better idea: was not Miss Astor a much-maligned mother fighting for the custody of a child? And if that didn't get cinema audiences weeping, was she not now playing the 'other woman' in what he had privately and rightly always considered to be a remarkably dull film, and might not the current publicity do *Dodsworth* a little good at the box office even six months hence?

On those wise grounds shooting was allowed to continue, and David would arrive each day at the studio eager for fresh revelations. By night he was being heavily coached by Miss Oberon in the art of acting for the camera, and the result of her nocturnal tutoring and Wyler's daily haranguing was that Niven finally turned in his first really adequate screen performance. It was not especially good and neither was the part, but it was recognizably the work of a professional actor, and for that David owed a debt to Wyler which he acknowledged somewhat grudgingly, and a debt to Oberon which he acknowledged not at all.

True, Wyler's on-set teaching methods were not of the most charitable. When David started a scene, he would bury himself behind the *Hollywood Reporter* asking to be informed when Mr Niven had quite finished. At that point he would simply call out, 'Again,' until David, on about the twentieth take, got it right. It took several large men with contracts to persuade Niven to work for Wyler again a couple of years later, when he had clambered up into some kind of negotiating position at last. But by then he was an actor, largely as a result of the head start that Wyler had given him on *Dodsworth*. Professionally he was now among the grown-ups, and not before time.

Privately he was living happily enough with Merle (though 'still playing the field occasionally', says Fairbanks) and enjoying his new-found respectability and status as a member of the Hollywood Cricket Club (C. Aubrey Smith, president). Boris Karloff and P. G. Wodehouse had been the other founding members, and the team also featured Alan Mowbray, Herbert Marshall, Philip Merivale, Reginald Owen, Nigel Bruce and H. B. Warner. 'When the grand old man asked you to play,' said David once, 'you played,' and indeed he once found himself in a game against Pasadena batting at number five in a team which also included two former and one current England captains, all of whom happened to be visiting California at the time.

Confident of Merle's love and of his new-found stature within the Goldwyn studios, David went with her to New York on a publicity trip and then together they drove back across the country in Oberon's new car, taking their time and ignoring increasingly desperate cables from Goldwyn asking David to call in urgently. When, ten days later, they showed up in Hollywood, Goldwyn was about to tear up Niven's contract. It was the first he had heard of the seriousness of the Oberon affair, and while he had been prepared to forgive Mary Astor her liaison with Kaufman because of the publicity it brought to *Dodsworth*, this was very different. Merle Oberon was at that time on semi-permanent loan to him from Korda (whom she was later to marry) and Goldwyn regarded her as one of his studio's most valuable assets while Niven was just another vaguely useful English supporting player. He wanted nobody to tarnish Oberon's still-virginal on-screen image, least of all somebody on his own payroll, so when he heard that director Michael Curtiz at Warner's was planning a long location shoot on *The Charge of the Light Brigade* and would be quite interested in hiring David for Captain Randall, Goldwyn saw a heaven-sent opportunity to split the lovers.

Niven's first uniformed epic was not well received at the time of its first release ('The acting is negligible, the bloodiness is all,' said the critic of the *New Statesman* in London), but it introduced him to Errol Flynn, with whom he was soon to share a beach-house, and it possibly gave him the title for his second volume of memoirs when Michael Curtiz, a Hungarian whose English was always problematic, issued his famous command for a hundred riderless chargers. Intriguingly David doesn't actually tell this story when recounting the filming in his first volume of memoirs, and the command 'Bring on the empty horses' may well have been issued by Curtiz on some altogether different film location – he went on to make a number of other costume cavalry epics as well as such varied classics as *Casablanca, Night and Day* and *Angels With Dirty Faces*. But his English was to remain a problem: 'You men think I know fuck nothing,' he once told Flynn and Niven who were as usual mocking him, 'whereas in fact I know fuck all'; and on another well-documented occasion he issued instructions to one surprised extra to 'go stand about in huddles' while telling another to 'stop standing in bundles'.

Apart from the good old public-school sport of mocking the foreigner, Niven's chief delight on the location shooting of *Light Brigade* was the discovery of Flynn. The film itself bore little thinking about, consisting as it did of a minimal script which, according to the credit, was 'inspired by Alfred Lord Tennyson', presumably in the hope that Mid-western audiences would assume yet another distinguished and aristocratic British writer had been tempted on to the Warner payroll. Yet it was to serve as a useful mounted vehicle for Flynn, whom Curtiz had shot to instant stardom in the previous year as the swashbuckling hero of *Captain Blood*, and there were even those prepared to overlook the fact that the British Army flies its own Union Jack upside down throughout the film, while the entire location of the famous charge has been shifted from the original Crimea to a wholly fictional Indian setting, presumably because that was already familiar to American audiences from the 1935 *Lives of a Bengal Lancer* which David had somehow missed.

Curtiz did not himself direct the charge of the title, leaving that to subordinates who managed to get several horses killed, thereby launching the film's publicity in a less than ideal way. All else went reasonably well, however, and Niven found himself with a showy little part involving a valiant death during the charge. By the time this was in the can, he and Flynn were firm friends and had decided to rent Rosalind Russell's house at 601 North Linden Drive as a bachelor pad. Flynn was at that time separated from Lili Damita, but he was by no means the only other tenant of 601 – Robert Coote stayed there for a while before Miss Damita returned briefly to the Flynn marital nest and Coote and Niven had to move down to the beach, and the address later became a kind of refuge for actors on the run from tricky marriages and/or girl-friends. It was Miss Russell herself, a sharply witty woman, who therefore named it Cirrhosis-by-the-Sea; it was also she who christened a nearby church Our Lady of the Cadillacs in view of its wealthy congregation.

For a while, Niven and Merle Oberon were still to be seen at all the right parties and premieres, often in a foursome with Oberon's great friend Norma Shearer and her husband Irving Thalberg. But with Thalberg's death towards the end of that year and Oberon's increasing determination to marry Niven, David himself drew away from anything so settled or apparently irrevocable. He was still a young twenty-six, and his new-found friendship with Flynn offered a wilder life with its own sexual and alcoholic energy. Much of their time at 601 North Linden was spent covering up for each other when confronted by irate husbands, and with Flynn David was able to find the kind of aged-schoolboy life he'd last enjoyed with Trubshawe on Malta five years earlier.

There was, perhaps, another and less attractive side to the Flynn–Niven alliance. David by his own admission always liked being around big stars, and he had not much cared for Errol before *Captain Blood* made him just that. Flynn was at this time vastly the richer and better-known of the two men, and though you could charitably assume that David found in him the big brother he had lost when Max first went off to the Army, you could not so charitably wonder whether he had just found a less demanding star than Merle to hang around with. Certainly it is true that Flynn features in the Niven autobiographies at far greater length than Niven features in Flynn's, though that may well be because, by the time Errol started writing, his career and his life had fallen into considerable disrepute and Niven was no longer anywhere in sight. It is also true that if David did not behave particularly well towards Errol in his many post-war times of trouble, he did leap almost alone to Flynn's posthumous defence when a 1980 biography solemnly suggested that he had been a Nazi spy.

For now, however, Flynn and Niven were a couple of the likeliest lads around town. Female stars were extra-maritally bedded, films made, bars broken up; it was a case of 'no job too big or small'. 'In like Flynn', David was now able to escape the faintly claustrophobic and musty world of the Hollywood British and revert to the teenage tearaway who had smuggled a prostitute into his public school. Whether smuggling Joan Bennett into Flynn's bedroom under the nose of her understandably aggrieved husband Walter Wanger, or merely claiming to have salvaged Harry Cohn's yacht (a claim which meant that neither Flynn nor Niven worked at Columbia for several years), Niven now began to lead with Errol a life that contrasted sharply with the more conservative and conventional world of Merle Oberon and C. Aubrey Smith's

Hollywood Cricket Club. It is a considerable tribute to his social dexterity that he managed for several months to carry on being simultaneously Bertie Wooster (whom he had just played) and the more caddish Raffles (whom he was about to film).

What separated Flynn from Niven was, in the end, little more than caution and an eye to the main chance, both of which David had tuned to perfection and Errol totally lacked. Niven would buccaneer alongside Flynn so long as Flynn remained a bankable star and therefore morally untouchable, but he would also keep his other contacts in good repair and avoid the legal and professional traps into which Flynn was later to fall with such depressing regularity. 'The more stories David told about a fellow actor or a director, the less you felt he knew them,' says an American actor who saw them both professionally and privately a good deal in the late 1930s, 'and I don't think Flynn really thought of David as a great or loyal friend; he was just somebody to bang about with, while to David, Flynn increasingly became just a source of good stories and occasional women.'

The Charge of the Light Brigade was one of the only two films they ever made together. After it, David went smartly back to Merle (who had now begun giving discreet press interviews about her love for a young but unnamed Englishman) and to another film that she had lined up for him at the Goldwyn studio. This was *Beloved Enemy*, an underrated thriller made in the mould of John Ford's *The Informer* and concerned with the daughter of a British civil servant stationed in Dublin during the 1921 troubles who falls in love with an Irish revolutionary leader. Niven had the small and rather caricatured role of the civil servant's ultra-stiff-upper-lipped military secretary, while the daughter was of course Merle herself and the Irishman was played by Brian Aherne, yet another of the young English actors whose careers seemed to be moving so much faster than David's up the studio ladders of the 1930s.

'David at that time was still going through the female

population of Hollywood like a knife through butter,' remembers Brian, 'and Merle was getting to hear about it, which didn't make the shooting any too easy. His gaiety and apparently inexhaustible fund of amusing stories about his Army days made him welcome everywhere. He was one of the most charming companions of that era, but I doubt if any of us realized that behind the charm lay an extremely canny mind that was even then planning the course that led him on to fame and affluence. Behind all the anecdotes there was something extremely careful and calculating about everything he did. Mind you, we didn't get along too well because I had a thing about Merle too, and one afternoon she was in my house and we had all the blinds down and my houseman came upstairs and said, "There's a Mr Niven at the door." So I hastily went down and said, "Just the man I wanted to see, let's go for a long walk"; but as we set off he kept looking back toward the house thinking it odd that the blinds were all drawn in the middle of the afternoon. I think he suspected Merle was in there, but he never said anything and nor did I. It just wasn't the kind of thing one could talk about, really.' So they kept on walking around the reservoir and by the time they got back to Aherne's house Merle had left; afterwards they carried on making the film and the afternoon was never referred to again.

'Hollywood was always like a big joke to David,' says Aherne, 'but he wanted the last laugh. Oddly enough, some of the best of the Army stories he used to tell in those days never found their way into his own books, like the time in Malta when he was a second lieutenant and one of his duties was to preside over the sergeants' dinners in the mess. One day a Russian ship had come into the harbour there and been unable to pay the dock dues or something, so the Maltese had seized the cargo which was largely composed of caviare, and the mess sergeant managed to buy it up very cheaply. So there were all these jocks eating the caviare, and David walking up and down between the tables making sure everything was all right, until he got to the last table and asked for any complaints and a huge Scot got to his feet and said, "Aye, Sirr, this jam tastes of fish."'

Beloved Enemy was the first of Niven's 1937 films, and though not particularly successful, it did at last bring him to the attention of several English critics. Until now he had been so far down the castlist of major films like *Light Brigade* that he had hardly been noticed at all at home, while the occasional B features like *Jeeves* which gave him better billing had not always made it across the Atlantic at a time of still-strict quota import regulations for cinemas. Even in *Beloved Enemy* he achieved only seventh billing, well below Aherne and Oberon and such lesser-known figures as Karen Morley and Jerome Cowan. It was still a small cast, though, and David's tense, frozen portrayal of the military aide at least ensured a fleeting mention towards the bottom of the film columns that were being eagerly scanned by his sisters in London.

Chapter Nine

1937–1938

'Goodnight, Fritz: I'll talk to Cromwell tomorrow.'

1937 did not look like the most promising of Hollywood years for Niven. It had started with his routine stiff-upper-lip job in *Beloved Enemy* and with the chilly discovery that Merle was also coming to regard their alliance as something rather less than an exclusive or binding contract. Racketing around the beach bars with Flynn was all very well in its way, but unlikely to lead to anything much more than the occasionally embarrassing close encounter with the Beverly Hills traffic police. Moreover, Flynn was about to return to the formidable clutches of his wife Lily Damita, and Niven would be left alone to come to the painful conclusion that he was fast losing his early shine as a cheery young expatriate party guest, one who a year or so ago had been as useful and prestigious at top Hollywood producers' tables as a really classy English butler.

Good-looking young English actors were now fairly pouring off the trains from New York, many of them with already established theatrical careers, and David had begun to look somehow faded after three years out in the California sun. Even he had noticed that his invitations almost always came from the wives of the moguls, denoting in a small community alive to every nuance that his social standing was considerably higher than his professional one, and though this still meant that he could be sure of free

Saturday night meals and even Palm Springs weekends whenever he chose to turn on the charm, it still didn't add up to much of a career. He had made almost a dozen films but no real mark in any of them, and was already finding rather too many familiar faces of those who had arrived with him in 1934 turning up as down-town bartenders or the kind of blazered English tennis pros always beloved of wealthy American matrons.

What he needed, to avoid all of that, was a prestige hit, but it was unlikely to be *We Have Our Moments*, the dire little caper-comedy for which Goldwyn hired him out to Universal. David was wearily cast as a smooth shipboard Englishman, leader of a gang of petty thieves and confidence tricksters but billed well below such minor character comics as Thurston Hall and Mischa Auer in a plot for which not even the local trade papers could find more than tepid enthusiasm. David's main career problem at this time was that he was undefinable. Almost all the English who had made it big in Hollywood thus far had been either romantic heroes like Ronald Colman and Cary Grant, sinister heavies like Boris Karloff and Basil Rathbone, elder statesmen like George Arliss and C. Aubrey Smith, or knockabout comics like Chaplin and Laurel. Niven fitted none of those categories, though at various times he was to try all of them. Like the old 'walking gentlemen' of the Victorian theatre, he was often useful in a film but never vital. Most of his movies benefited from his casually elegant presence but almost all could have been made equally well without him, and that was a problem which, over nearly a hundred films, he was never quite able to solve.

Help was at hand, and it came once again from the community of English gentlemen players which was gathering for one of its masterpieces, Selznick's *The Prisoner of Zenda*, which was to star Ronald Colman in the dual role of the Ruritanian king and his look-alike cousin Rassendyll and to feature such other all-English performances as those of Madeleine Carroll, C. Aubrey Smith and Raymond

Massey who, though Canadian by birth, counted as honorary Englishman. The cast was also to feature Douglas
Fairbanks Jr, another honorary Englishman, and it was
during a gathering at Colman's house one Sunday that the
colony began to realize that here too could be found
useful employment for Niven as the king's aide, Fritz van
Tarlenheim.

First the producer David O. Selznick and the director
John Cromwell had to be convinced. Merle was enlisted
to plead his cause, as was Fairbanks, and Niven was in no
doubt that it was entirely due to their combined urging
that he duly got an invitation from Irene Mayer Selznick
to lunch with her husband David and play a little tennis.
That took up most of the afternoon and was followed by
some sustained drinking since the Selznick brothers, David
and Myron, were renowned for the aridity of their Mar-
tinis. At the end of a long evening, Selznick finally acknowledged that Niven might just be all right, and that
he would duly pass this information on to his director.
'Goodnight Fritz,' he said to Niven, 'I'll talk to Cromwell
tomorrow.' David had at last joined the first team.

This version of *The Prisoner of Zenda* was being made
largely as a result of the fascination with romantic royalty
which had suddenly erupted all over America at the time
of the Edward VIII abdication a few months earlier, and
which Selznick had sharply realized *Zenda* was really also
all about. Here too, in this old Ruritanian warhorse (which
had already been twice filmed as a silent in 1913 and 1927,
and was to turn up in two more sound versions, one a
shot-for-shot replica of the Colman), was the story of a
king in romantic trouble, and as the shooting was now to
coincide with George VI's coronation, an astute Selznick
publicist had all the British members of the cast line up for
a photograph 'sending a loyal message of congratulation to
Their Majesties'.

By that time, however, David was nearly not of their
number. He had decided early in the shooting, out of a
combination of desperation and boredom, to play the vain

Fritz largely for laughs in the hope of breathing life into a dead character. He had forgotten to inform his director of the decision, and after his first major scene he was sent for by the deadpan Cromwell and told that, if this was his larky attitude to the role, his services would no longer be required. Niven went off to drink with Flynn that night in some alarm: the sack from *Zenda* would certainly mean the sack also from Goldwyn, and an ignominious court-martial from the Raj in their finest hour.

Luckily, that night some early rushes were shown to Selznick by Cromwell, and both men suddenly realized to their surprise that what David was doing with the part actually worked on screen. His own recollections of the filming grew somewhat distorted thereafter (he somehow became convinced that the Mary Astor diary scandal happened while she was working with him on this, instead of a year earlier when they were together on *Dodsworth*) but there is a reliable report of one of the film's funnier moments from Raymond Massey, cast as the villainous Black Michael: 'Niven as Fritz had been given a skittish and handsome mare to ride in the coronation scene and I got a big, black stallion. Both of us wore our dress uniforms, "Chum" Niven with an eagle-topped helmet and I with a great hussar busby. We both carried sabres in slings, and in addition I wore the hussar empty jacket over my left shoulder and a long sabretache with four straps hung from my sword belt. To cap it all I had a monocle. In short we were loaded like Christmas trees. In tasselled boots and long, goose-necked spurs we were scarcely able to move. I mounted with some difficulty. My horse must have been 17 hands, and I was carrying a handicap of nearly 50 lb in medals and accoutrements. My wrangler said, rather ominously, "Don't get your mount too close to the mares," but as the cavalcade moved slowly forward at the shout of "Action!" my great beast plunged forward. Snorting with determination he leaped at Chum's mare. I must have nearly broken his jaw with the curb, shouting "Jump, Chum, jump!" He'd already done so, and his mare was almost as quick in her getaway. My horse missed her, but hit the coach full on. Madeleine Carroll received the full shock of his arrival, the huge horse's head thrust through the open window and the bit rattling in her face. As for me, I landed on the roof of her coach, sword between my legs, busby over one eye but the monocle still secure in the other, as embarrassed a horseman as I could be and awaiting a stepladder to make an inglorious descent to mother earth.'

Fairbanks, Massey and Niven formed an unholy trio of musketeers for the rest of the shooting, a lot of which was spent trying not to laugh at the greater lunacies of the plot. But this was still an ambassadorial mission, presided over by Colman who would dole out stiff gins to the troops at the end of each day's shooting. As for Aubrey, he would sit at the side of the set with three-week-old copies of the London *Times*, the only paper he ever believed, bringing him news of the Hitler–Mussolini pact. 'Bloody whipper-snappers' was his only comment on that, though he was fractionally more talkative when one day Ray Massey, having a little problem with the characterization of Black Michael, decided to take his troubles to the master. Smith looked up from his *Times* and told Massey, 'In my years as a stage actor, young man, I have played every single part in *The Prisoner of Zenda* except that of the princess. And you know, old boy, I'll tell you a funny thing. I never discovered how to play Black Michael either.' And with that, he turned off his hearing aid and went back to his copy of *The Times*.

Not all the filming of *Zenda* was as amicable, however. Cromwell soon began sending acid memos to Selznick complaining that Fairbanks and Niven appeared on the set 'overindulged and lazy' while Colman 'never knows his lines: I don't know which of them annoys me most. Also, both Colman and Carroll insist they have a "bad side" to be avoided by the camera, but as it's the same "bad side" shooting them face to face is all but impossible.' In the end, both W. S. 'Woody' Van Dyke and George Cukor were brought in by Selznick to shoot retakes, but the result turned out well enough and C. Aubrey Smith even managed, with David's help, to preserve his tear-jerking last line to Colman: 'Goodbye, Englishman, you are the finest Elphberg of them all.' Not a dry eye in the house.

Zenda marked an immediate change in David's thus far sluggish Hollywood fortunes. Now that he had worked alongside Ronald Colman on a Selznick picture, even if he was billed well below not only the star but also below Massey, Fairbanks, Carroll, Mary Astor and C. Aubrey Smith, he was clearly an actor of some note, no longer to be farmed out by Goldwyn on just any assignment. Henceforth he would have to be farmed out only to the classy ones, and the first of these was to take him back to London after an unbroken absence of almost five years.

Dinner at the Ritz, not to be confused with the vastly superior *Dinner at Eight* made a few years earlier by MGM, was a curious little comedy-melodrama designed to introduce to English-speaking audiences Annabella, the French actress (born Suzanne Charpentier) who had made her name in Abel Gance's epic *Napoleon* and was later, as Mrs Tyrone Power, to give a party which turned into the most tragic night of Niven's life. For the time being, all that really mattered to David about the film was that it gave him the chance to make the ten-day journey home to his sisters and Trubshawe and all the London friends he had left behind at the time of his abrupt resignation from the Army in 1933.

He had of course always kept in touch with home, writing long and rambling letters to Trubshawe and Roxburgh, assuring them that he was earning good money every week from Goldwyn and putting some of it away so as not to end up 'a tumbledown actor'; in one letter he even suggested to Roxburgh that he was planning eventually to come home with his Hollywood earnings and go into British politics, though this seems to have been a remarkably short-lived ambition, as was the desire to 'do something for the

Empire' which David expressed to an interviewer on his first return home.

By this time his name was at last becoming visible in the fan magazines. One Hollywood reporter who interviewed him on the set of *Zenda* solemnly informed her readers that Niven 'had won early fame as an athlete, gaining his place in Army football, polo and boxing teams. He also represented Great Britain in the 1930 eight-metre yacht race, got into the South African Revolution [which one is not specified], shipped on a tramp steamer, joined hunts for buried treasure on the Spanish Main, did bicycle and pony racing, wrote for British magazines and sold advertising in New York.' The combination of an expansively chatting David and a journalist none too keen on double-checking the facts was already proving lethal to any kind of biographic truth, and even English papers were beginning to follow this American lead. Just before David got back to England in 1937 the *Evening Standard* announced: 'Niven arrived in New York with little money and joined the staff of a horse-racing establishment. After that he wielded an axe in a Canadian lumber camp, tired of that and began operating the rollers in a Manhattan steam laundry. Washing of linen palled on him after a while, so he went to Cuba where he secured a commission in the Cuban Rebel Light Infantry. For some weeks David taught the rank and file how to fire their rifles away from rather than at themselves, and how to equip their camps with sanitary contrivances, but when hostilities began he found his soldiers deserting him on the battlefield, leaving him to face his enemy alone. That was when he left Cuba for Hollywood.'

Family and friends, at least, had learned to discount most press interviews on principle, and Trubshawe was of course at the docks in Southampton to greet his friend and learn the truth of his last few years. Married now, and a Norfolk squire, Michael had arranged a village fete 'to be opened by the well-known film star D. Niven'. In fact at this time David was not particularly well known, certainly not to Norfolk villagers. *Zenda* had yet to be released in Britain, and if local filmgoers did know him at all it would probably have been from his appearance in *The Charge of the Light Brigade*. Nonetheless, the posters were a wonderfully confident welcome-home present from his still-devoted friend. Trubshawe recalled: 'David, at the time of that first return from Hollywood, certainly hadn't yet hit the jackpot, but he wasn't exactly an unknown quantity either. We persuaded him to turn out for the village cricket team, and he seemed still the same splendid chum I had last seen in the Army. There was none of the cynicism or the bitterness that was to overtake him after the war. He wasn't at all spoilt by the beginnings of his success; he was tickled pink by it and only terrified that it was all too good to be true and might disappear overnight. There was no real sense of seriousness, nor of exile. The world was his oyster and he'd just started to prise it open and gobble. The ebullience, the enthusiasm, the initial euphoria of fame was still carrying him along.'

On this occasion the visit home was to be a flying one, for Goldwyn had a film waiting for David back in Hollywood that was vastly more attractive than *Dinner at the Ritz*, so he was only allowed a minimal six weeks at Denham to give his performance as 'Paul de Brack, a debonair man-about-town' in a so-so tale of high-society blackmail, before heading rapidly back to California and a director who had once told him he had no future in films whatsoever.

That director was Ernst Lubitsch, and since their early meeting in New York he had had time to rethink his announcement to Elsa Maxwell that Niven would never make an actor. The great stylist was now starting work on a Billy Wilder script called *Bluebeard's Eighth Wife*, a comedy about a multi-millionaire industrialist with seven broken marriages behind him falling in love rather more successfully on the French Riviera. There was, of course, still no question of David playing the lead, a role that went to Gary Cooper, but Lubitsch did have another one to offer: that of a young Frenchman who tries to divert the eighth wife before she gets into Bluebeard's den, and this was why Goldwyn had recalled Niven with such speed from London. The wife was to be played by Claudette Colbert.

'David sometimes used to say that he had been an extra on my 1934 *Cleopatra*,' she says, 'but I certainly don't recall meeting him then. Mind you, there were about a thousand on that Cecil B. de Mille epic, so I suppose he could have been one of them. But by the time we got to *Bluebeard* three years later I certainly knew who he was, and I think in the very early days I had done a screen test with him when they were trying him out for something at Paramount where I then had a contract. At the time of *Bluebeard* he was fast becoming a star, and Goldwyn was already getting irritable with him. "The trouble with that young man," he once said to me, "is that his body has gone to his head."

'I never saw much sign of that. On *Bluebeard* he was divine, very funny and behaved extremely well, even in the scene where I had to knock him out. Actors usually learn how to duck, and I just assumed that David had, so I landed him one straight on the chin, but he never really complained, just picked himself up and went on telling the stories which even by then I'd begun to know pretty well from all our Sunday afternoon tennis parties. He was always much more outgoing than Gary Cooper, and terribly uncomplicated: what you saw was what there was.'

Although Colbert and Niven got along well enough, *Bluebeard* was not the easiest or happiest of films to make. Cooper resented having to take second billing to the star of *It Happened One Night*, and wasn't really then at home with light comedy in the way that Colbert and Niven already were. Indeed, Cooper took the generous view that Niven should have been playing the lead, and he and Merle Oberon took David with them on to the film they were about to start shooting a few weeks later, *The Cowboy and the Lady*, only David's scenes all got cut from the final edit. Still, he and Cooper were to appear again two years later in *The Real Glory* as a likeable team, and though their *Bluebeard* got off to a disappointingly slow critical and box-office reception, it has latterly been restored to the shelf marked 'minor Lubitsch classics', not least for the scene where David surfaces beside Colbert on a life raft. 'Mr Lubitsch', noted *Variety*, by way of explaining the film's original failure to grab the then all-important family audience, 'works for the carriage trade: he does not address his art primarily to those in kiddycars.' Already there was the feeling that the potent combination of Lubitsch and Wilder was somehow too adult for Hollywood tastes. Certainly Colbert as the evocatively evasive virgin and Coop as the frustrated male set up a very sexy chemistry indeed, but this was essentially the reworking of an old 1920s stage comedy which Ina Claire had done on Broadway and Gloria Swanson had once filmed as a silent. Lubitsch and Wilder rebuilt it into something rather closer to *Design For Living*, though its staginess was underlined by a famous background shot in which Sacha Guitry can clearly be seen emerging from a Vienna hotel.

What really mattered about the film from David's point of view was that he was in his first upmarket comedy, and in the hands of masters. It was Lubitsch who taught him that 'nobody can play comedy until they have a circus going on inside them', and Wilder who gave him his first really worthwhile screen dialogue. The best advice he got came from Charlie Chaplin, when at a dinner party one night the film was given a sneak preview. Courageously, Niven asked him for a verdict on his performance. 'Don't be like the majority of actors,' replied Chaplin, 'standing around on screen just waiting your turn to speak. Instead, learn how to listen.'

David had a great deal else to learn, mainly about rebuilding his own Hollywood image. Up to this time he had been generally known either as the handsome young English actor whom Merle brought along to dinner parties, or as one of the infinitely rowdier Flynn cohorts, forever crashing polo ponies into Darryl Zanuck or getting into trouble by pretending to salvage Harry Cohn's yacht. The trouble was that neither image was doing him much professional good. Sooner or later he had to get known in his own right as the actor David Niven, or preferably the film star David Niven, and he was astute enough to realize that it had better be sooner.

By now it was the beginning of 1938. David had *Zenda* and *Bluebeard* on release testifying to his new-found status as a potential leading man, and he began looking for star or at least co-star billing, a promotion in which he was much helped by the earliest of his Hollywood landladies, Loretta Young. Miss Young, who had always taken a warm sisterly interest in his career, was making a series of romantic dramas at Twentieth Century-Fox and suggested that David should join her in a couple of them. In fact they went on to make four films together over the next ten years, failing in every one of them to become the kind of William Powell–Myrna Loy romantic duo that had clearly been intended, but nevertheless enjoying themselves very much along the way.

Their first venture for Fox was also Niven's only film for John Ford, like himself an elaborate practical joker on the set but one of the few directors for whom David seemed to retain a grudging regard: 'They all had their own little idiosyncrasies. Lubitsch had his cigar and his step ladder. Michael Curtiz strode about wearing breeches and riding boots and brandishing a fly whisk. William Wyler liked to make anything up to forty takes of a scene, and then would only print the first. Otto Preminger seemed to enjoy working in an atmosphere of tension, and would generate it by screaming at people. Henry Hathaway objected to chairs on the set for actors because he said he had to stand all day and so should they. Woody Van Dyke chain-sipped gin out of paper cups. And John Ford? He sat beneath the camera chewing a grubby white handkerchief.'

The picture was *Four Men and a Prayer*: the men were brothers (Niven, George Sanders, Richard Greene and

William Henry) and their prayer was that they might
manage to get their Indian Army officer father (C. Aubrey
Smith – who else?) reinstated after a court-martial had
found him guilty of causing the death of his troops. Loretta
Young was an American girl in love with Richard Greene,
and the casting also included such other stalwarts of the
Hollywood Raj as Reginald Denny and Barry Fitzgerald.

Ford fans were not impressed with this uncharacteristic
little programme filler and the great man himself made it
clear that he was only in it for the money: 'I just didn't
like the story or anything else about it,' said Ford later,
'so it simply became a job of work. I kidded around a lot
with all those Englishmen.'

Niven himself appears rather less debonair than usual
here, and for a very good reason. After *Zenda* and *Bluebeard* seemed to be getting his career off the ground at
last, he was less than delighted to be taking inferior billing
not only to Loretta Young and George Sanders but also
to Richard Greene, an English actor four years his junior
who, on the basis of some London stage work, had suddenly been flown out to Hollywood on a starring contract
and rather better money.

As Greene said: 'That was my first film. I was twenty-
four and I do recall David being rather less than delighted
to see me, which was understandable, I suppose, considering that he'd been out there for four years working his way
up through the ranks. But I always felt he was watching
me rather too closely, and I remember an ambitious,
calculating and very sober man who for some reason
wanted to appear to be a cavalier drinker. Behind all that
bonhomie and the endless anecdotes and good cheer, there
seemed to be a sort of nervousness, as though he was
trying to estimate the opposition you might represent to
his career. There was always a sting in that tail, and one
never really found out what was going on behind the grin.
I never really knew who David was or what he wanted,
except perhaps for me not to be there playing a slightly
better part, in that I was the one who got Loretta Young.'

As soon as that film was safely in the can, however, it was David and Loretta who moved on to *Three Blind Mice*, an undistinguished romantic Fox comedy chiefly notable for what might charitably be called the eccentricity of its director, one William A. Seiter, whose habit it was to walk around the set with a goosing stick – a long cane fitted with a clenched plaster fist at one end from which protruded an extended second finger for the purpose of surprising female cast members from the back.

Seiter's film was very nearly as unfunny as his on-set behaviour, concerning as it did Loretta Young and two poultry-farming sisters suddenly inheriting $5,000 and deciding to use the money to entrap a wealthy suitor; but David got co-star billing for which he had to thank not only Loretta but also the film's other leading player and another long-standing champion of his Hollywood fortunes, Joel McCrea. Recalls McCrea: 'There was no question of an affair with Loretta, and at the time of *Three Blind Mice* David was still quite involved with Merle, but there were great jokes about the early days in Loretta's mother's house. David was always very careful at this time not to get too involved with any big star who might conceivably one day want to marry him. I don't think he had any intention of ending up as a Mr Oberon or even a Mr Young: he wanted his own kind of fame. He had great confidence in himself, and he was still doing the kind of vaudeville routines around the set that were always his trademark.' He had stopped doing his imaginary skating by the time he filmed *Three Blind Mice*, and instead was doing one about an absent-minded Indian chief who kept putting his hand up to the back of his head to shield where he thought his eyes were. David, Cesar Romero and Tyrone Power were regarded as the three best escorts in town. If ever a big female star needed an escort for a premiere or a party they would invite David because he looked good and could dance a bit and tell jokes. 'I remember once,' said McCrea, 'we were both invited up to the Hearst ranch to meet Churchill when he was out there on a visit long before he became prime minister, and after dinner David turned to me and said, "Just tell me one thing. How can a man who drinks that much brandy be quite so clever?" He was very impressed by that.'

By this time, the early spring of 1938, David had become a star of minor pictures as well as of the California social circuit. What he now had to find was a film worth starring in, and two of those came along before the year was out.

Chapter Ten

1938–1939

'Mr Wyler, I've done this scene thirty times now;
what do you really want me to be in it?'
'Better.'

If there was a single film in which David grew up on screen, that film was Edmund Goulding's *The Dawn Patrol*. Made in 1938 immediately after the appalling *Three Blind Mice*, it reunited Niven with Flynn for the second and last time and, more importantly, brought him under the charge of the director who had, along with Loretta Young and Joel McCrea, been one of that small but persistently loyal band of his earliest Hollywood enthusiasts. *The Dawn Patrol* had already been made once in 1930 with young Doug Fairbanks in the Niven role of the hard-drinking First World War airman who goes into battle against the Germans armed with crates of champagne, but who later has to see his own brother shot down and his great friend and hero taking his own place on a suicide mission.

Lieutenant Scott was, in short, a very good part, and it seemed to trigger in David some old English military memories. Though he had not yet served in a war, he had known men like Scott, men who, unlike his own father, had somehow managed to survive the 1914–18 armageddon, and he knew something of their tight-lipped bravado, that curious mix of schoolboy humour and immense courage. Whereas there was always something phoney and

suspect about Flynn's screen heroics, David's had a useful
air of underlying and understated reality. If only they had
made *Journey's End* a little later than 1930, he would have
been marvellous casting first for Raleigh and later for
Stanhope.

As it was, *The Dawn Patrol* was the next best thing. A
remarkably similar story, only set among the airmen of the
Royal Flying Corps instead of in the trenches beneath
them, it allowed David for once to stop trying to be an
actor and get back to what he was best at being, a damn
decent English officer and gentleman. With a strong Raj
line-up (Flynn may have been a Tasmanian colonial, but
the director was English as were Basil Rathbone, Donald
Crisp and Melville Cooper who played the other officers),
the film was among David's few real screen triumphs.

Eight years earlier, the first version of *The Dawn Patrol*
had made Fairbanks into a star. This one, thanks to Goulding, was to make Niven into an actor. Its castlist also
included another young English actor, later to become a
distinguished television producer in Britain and one who
took a distinctly less than favourable view of Niven as a
man – Peter Willes. He says of David, 'He was an extremely mean and deeply heartless figure. I think perhaps
his real tragedy was having less heart than anyone I ever
knew. I suppose in a way I knew him too well, but I was
always surprised all through his life by the contrast between
the genial public image and the darker private reality. I'd
been to school with him at Stowe, but when I first got out
to Hollywood it was as though I didn't exist, and even on
the set of *Dawn Patrol* he wouldn't speak to me until one
night I'd been out drinking with Flynn, a much easier man,
and that somehow made me socially acceptable. The only
advice he ever gave me was not to sleep with leading ladies
until after the retakes, though if anyone ever profited from
sleeping with most of his leading ladies then it was surely
David. He had a ruthless instinct for survival and self-
preservation, and the people he liked best were almost
always the ones who could do him a bit of good. There

was an odd sort of insecurity always hanging over him, and he often seemed frightened of wasting his charm on the wrong people – as though it was all he had, and it might one day run out.'

If you look carefully at David's performance in *Dawn Patrol* you can actually see him growing in confidence and stature from scene to scene (Goulding shot largely in sequence). It is as though he gradually realized that he was at last on home territory, where he could handle all the behaviour and emotion required of him without giving the usual self-deprecatory shrug to the camera which was supposed to denote his own awareness of his inability to be much of an actor.

It was here too that Niven began to distance himself from Flynn. Like a younger brother, he began to emerge from Errol's sphere of influence, aware already that the other man's sexual reputation was getting beyond a joke, and that he himself had now graduated into altogether more eminent company with a new-found air of distinction, which would evaporate as rapidly as it had arrived if he continued to get publicly caught up in Flynn's alcoholic and promiscuous escapades. A new Niven was emerging from *The Dawn Patrol*, one who had earned his Hollywood wings at last, and among the first to notice that here suddenly was an actor instead of a performer was the film critic of the *New Statesman* in London: '*The Dawn Patrol* seems to me to contain scarcely a false note; the references to the futility of war are plausibly and naturally introduced, and the film allows no women to add a note of false romanticism; among the men, David Niven emerges as a deeply sensitive, natural actor as well as a potential star of great magnitude. The film allows no prospect of release to palliate the horrors, and its last scene shows Niven, dazed by the loss of his brother and his greatest friend, welcoming a fresh wagon-load of eager youngsters with his same old routine of cheerful informality . . . his is one of those characters without whom a picture of war conditions would be incomplete: the soul of all good nature and good fellowship, he has the gift of making ghastly situations not only tolerable but at moments almost preferable to the shabby humdrum of ordinary life.' Not a bad description of the man, as well as the performance.

Someone else who had noticed Niven in that last re-markable scene of controlled good cheer was his old spar-ring partner from *Dodsworth*, the director William Wyler who was now back at the Goldwyn Studios setting up what was to be Sam's prestige production of the year if not the decade – the first filming of *Wuthering Heights*. Few productions of such subsequent success can have started more unpromisingly. The original casting idea for Heathcliff had inevitably been Ronald Colman, Goldwyn's regular first thought for anything vaguely to do with cos-tumes or literature or England. When he proved unavail-able, Wyler was told to consider Douglas Fairbanks Jr or possibly Robert Newton, but the director had other ideas. It had already been decided that Cathy would be played by Merle Oberon, still on intermittent loan to Goldwyn from Korda, and during those negotiations Alex had sent out to Hollywood the print of an undistinguished romantic comedy he had made in the previous year with Oberon called *The Divorce of Lady X* in which her co-star (though billed well below the title) had been Laurence Olivier. Wyler decided that they worked well together and flew to London to try to persuade the actor to give Hollywood another try, his only previous professional visits having been fairly disastrous – a couple of uninspired RKO dramas in the very early Thirties and then ignominious dismissal by Garbo after only two days on *Queen Christina* (1933), on which he was replaced by John Gilbert.

Olivier took an understandably dim view of Hollywood, and moreover had just started a passionate extra-marital affair with Vivien Leigh; he would thus only be interested in *Wuthering Heights* if she could be cast opposite him: Wyler refused, but added that she could have the second lead of Isabella and that 'she'd never get a better start in pictures', a prophecy that seemed to make perfect sense a full three months before the final casting of *Gone With The Wind*. In the event Vivien turned down Isabella (the role went instead to Geraldine Fitzgerald), but Olivier's great friend and Old Vic colleague Ralph Richardson convinced him that he should not turn down Heathcliff. In the memorably brisk words of Sir Ralph, 'Yes. Bit of fame. Good.'

Olivier was bitterly unhappy at being parted from his beloved Vivien, and found Merle Oberon distinctly 'lacking in passion'; for her part, she had decided she was going to marry Korda and was missing him since he too was back in England. She was also annoyed that the affair with David seemed to be over, and that Olivier appeared to be interested only in Leigh. Goldwyn meanwhile was furious with Wyler for hiring 'that damn ugly English actor' instead of a more glamorous Heathcliff.

Then there was David. Now that he had professionally come of age with the semi-heroic role in *The Dawn Patrol*, he had no particular desire to return to the milksop support role of Edgar, as he saw it more of an actor's nightmare than a reasonable offer. Nor did he much want to work with Merle now that their affair had cooled, and least of all did he want to work again with Wyler who had made his life such hell on *Dodsworth*. He therefore went to see Goldwyn and told him he would rather go on suspension for three months than take any part in *Wuthering Heights*. There was little enough Goldwyn could do about that, but Wyler did not give in so easily. Having gone after Olivier and got him for Heathcliff, he was now equally sure that David was the perfect casting for Edgar, so sure in fact that he twice took Niven out to dinner and promised faithfully that he would never once raise his voice to him on the set.

Deciding either to believe this unlikely promise or, more possibly, that he was in no financial condition to stay on unpaid suspension for long, David caved in and signed for the role, only to have his first day on the set deafened by Wyler's increasingly hysterical attempts to get him to give a reasonable performance. In fact he succeeded to such an extent that the *New York Times* noted 'Niven's Linton, so namby-pamby in the novel, is here a dignified and poignant characterization of a young man whose tragedy was not in being weak himself but in being weaker than the abnormal pair whose destinies involved their own destruction'.

Goldwyn himself took a thoroughly dim view of the proceedings, threatening to close down the picture altogether after he'd seen Olivier's earliest takes. 'He's a mess: dirty, unkempt, stagey, hammy and awful,' he grumbled. Wyler, seeing something more, fought to keep him and, in the process, turned Olivier for the first time into a film star. The rest of the *Wuthering Heights* casting was another of the great Hollywood British gatherings: it included not only Niven but also Flora Robson and Donald Crisp plus Leo G. Carroll and Miles Mander and Cecil Kellaway, three London actors who were to be dried by years of Californian sun until they appeared almost like parchment figures in a vast range of other Hollywood work.

Some critics still didn't care for any of it, however; Graham Greene, writing in the *Spectator*, thought 'how much better they would have made *Wuthering Heights* in France. There they know how to shoot sexual passion: but in this Californian-constructed Yorkshire, among all the sensitive, neurotic English voices, sex is cellophaned. There is no egotism, no obsession. This Heathcliff would never have married for revenge (Olivier's nervous, breaking voice belongs to balconies and Verona and romantic love) and one cannot imagine the ghost of this Cathy weeping with balked passion: Miss Oberon cannot help making her a very normal girl.'

By many other critics, though, and most audiences around the world, *Wuthering Heights* was reckoned a considerable success, despite the fact that Goldwyn had ordered Wyler to shoot an alternative ending because 'nobody will want to look at a goddamn corpse at the fade'. Wyler refused, so Goldwyn had an assistant make the shot of Olivier's stunt double and a girl seen in double-exposure walking on some clouds – no worse a mistake, perhaps, than the Yorkshire heather being allowed to grow about 3 feet higher on screen than nature ever intended.

Billed on its New York posters as 'the strangest love story ever told', *Wuthering Heights* won Olivier an Oscar nomination, though in the event he lost out to another English actor, Robert Donat, who was honoured for his performance as Mr Chips. The film also led to what was perhaps the greatest single gift the Hollywood British ever made to the colony that supported them, for it was during the shooting that Vivien Leigh arrived to join Olivier and was taken on to the burning Atlanta set of *Gone With The Wind* for that brilliantly staged 'accidental' encounter with David O. Selznick, one in fact engineered by his brother Myron, who just happened to be both Larry's and Vivien's agent.

Another indirect result of the film was the start of a long friendship between Olivier and Niven. Almost half a century after the shooting Olivier had these memories of David at that time: 'He was a great joy to be with on that film, because we both started it with a deep hatred of Willie Wyler, who could be very cruel and sarcastic and knew that we were too well-mannered and well-trained and English to answer him back as he deserved. In fact, later we grew to like Wyler very much, but it took that picture to break the ice because he really wasn't very charming. David was always a lightweight, but I think that was probably why we got on so well, because I was no threat to him and he was no threat to me. He couldn't have done a stage classic to save his life, but he had enormous charm and he was very sincere and very good as Edgar, which is a terrible part really.'

In recognition of Niven's new-found status, he was given equal billing with Olivier and Oberon, if not on the screen then certainly on the film's early posters, and although it hadn't been an especially enjoyable picture to make, it was undoubtedly a good one to be seen in. It also saw the start of one of David's more elaborate running gags. From now on, whenever possible, the name 'Trubshawe' would be added to one of his lines in each film, usually referring to an off-screen character or animal and designed to give Michael himself a good laugh when the picture got to his local cinema in Norfolk. In *Wuthering Heights*, the name was given to one of Linton's snarling dogs during the attack on Heathcliff, but Wyler managed to get it deleted from the final cut.

Niven was now on a winning streak, and the four other films that he made in the first nine months of 1939 did nothing to change his luck. First came *Bachelor Mother*, a Garson Kanin comedy for which Niven was loaned out to RKO to do his usual jovial playboy routine in a silly but surprisingly successful little plot about Ginger Rogers being left with an unwanted baby in a department store owned by Niven's family. Kanin's brisk, angular direction ('He's too caustic,' someone once told Goldwyn; 'Never mind the cost, hire him,' replied the mogul) and the un-usual teaming of Niven and Rogers at a moment when both had sharpened their comic timing turned what might have been just another low-budget romp into a sleeper hit that surprised even its own makers and one that was much loved by Niven's now fast-growing band of English admirers when it was released just before the outbreak of war.

If *Bachelor Mother* was *Bringing Up Baby* without the wit – or, indeed, the leopard – Niven's next 1939 film was another doomed attempt to get the screen partnership with Loretta Young off the ground. *Eternally Yours* was a loan-out to Walter Wanger, who cast Niven somewhat eccentrically as the Great Arturo, a hypnotist-conjuror-stuntman falling in love with the lovely Loretta. Despite a strong support cast of funny ladies (Zasu Pitts, Eve Arden and Billie Burke), C. Aubrey Smith as a bishop and Broderick Crawford as Niven's rival for Miss Young, the whole conjuring trick signally failed to come off, leaving Niven to return to what was now an increasingly tetchy alliance with the Goldwyn Studios.

The problem there was essentially that Goldwyn still couldn't quite work out what he had in Niven. A useful supporting man had suddenly become a sort of star, usually in other people's pictures, and Niven understandably began to feel that he should be getting some of the loving parental care and attention to his career that Goldwyn had always lavished on Ronald Colman. Yet Niven still wasn't really the next Colman, despite certain determined gossip-column attempts to talk that idea into reality. He lacked Colman's poetic grandeur as an actor; he also lacked the charisma that gave the mere mention of Colman's name the power to attract writers, directors and audiences to virtually any classic novel that he chose to film. Thus Goldwyn was now torn between grudging admiration for what Niven had achieved and a secret, almost resentful disappointment at the realization that David was never quite going to reach superstardom of the Colman variety.

At this point Niven behaved towards Goldwyn much as he had in the sixth form at Stowe towards Roxburgh: another surrogate father had to be challenged and tested for loyalty, and if there were no Hollywood exams in which to cheat, Niven would find some other way. Urged on by such cronies as Garson Kanin (who had pointed out to him that on *Bachelor Mother* his salary, by the time Goldwyn had taken his studio cut, was less than half the camera-man's) and his agent Leland Hayward, Niven began to challenge the terms of his contract and by extension Goldwyn's whole attitude to his career. Goldwyn's wrath at what he saw as blatant disloyalty was swift and sure. He not only put Niven on suspension but also barred Hayward from the lot for a cooling-off period while everyone tried to think about what Niven was supposed to be doing next. He was now on the verge of his thirties, and clearly his days of playing weakling younger brothers, charming alcoholic wastrels, or cads who lost the girl in the last reel to butch leading men like Gary Cooper or Joel McCrea were over. Nor could he go on being the gallant young officer to Errol Flynn's war heroes, while his own romantic

partnership with Loretta Young had signally failed to catch
audience imaginations. Moreover, with the recent arrival
of Laurence Olivier and Vivien Leigh from London, new
acting standards were being expected of the Hollywood
English, standards which Niven with his lack of any formal
stage training could never hope to reach.

Despite all of that, he was still much in demand. Even
during his Goldwyn suspension he managed to do a lot
of radio work, playing opposite the likes of Constance
Bennett and Hedy Lamarr in cut-down broadcasts of
current movie hits for the Lux Radio Theater or the Shell
Hour. Sometimes they'd even attempt the classics, with
David and Miss Bennett once doing a memorably catastrophic version of Pirandello's love scenes, under-
rehearsed and curtailed to the point of utter
incomprehensibility. Sponsors of these shows would often
pay their artists in kind rather than cash, and as Goldwyn
still insisted on half of all David's earnings it was with
mischievous delight that Niven once sent over to the studio
a Kraft hamper, earned on the Bing Crosby radio show,
in which all the dairy products had been neatly divided in
half with a knife.

David's older and wiser Hollywood friends, among them
the Colmans and the Astaires, pointed out that this could
not go on forever, and a truce was arranged whereby he
would return to the studio fold on a seven-year contract
rising to $1,000 a week, one which would start moreover
with two extremely prestigious Goldwyn pictures: first *The
Real Glory* with Gary Cooper, and then a remake of
Raffles, the vehicle with which Sam had made Colman a
star a decade before.

Things could not have looked much better for Niven,
but there was just one snag: it was the beginning of the
summer of 1939.

Chapter Eleven

1939

'Raffles Goes to War'

Just before the outbreak of war, King George VI and
Queen Elizabeth paid a state visit to President Roosevelt,
and the Hollywood British gathered themselves together
for one massive if eccentric showing of the flag. In a live
radio broadcast back to Washington from Los Angeles,
Niven introduced Cedric Hardwicke, Nigel Bruce and C.
Aubrey Smith singing *Three Little Fishes*. Basil Rathbone
and Vivien Leigh read love poems by the Brownings, Greer
Garson and Leslie Howard did extracts from *Goodbye
Mr Chips*, Merle Oberon paid 'loyal respects to Their
Majesties in these difficult times', Brian Aherne read
Rupert Brooke, and Dennis King sang *Annie Laurie*.
Some years after this momentous contribution to the royal
visit, one which is now happily preserved on disc as a
collector's piece of considerable, not to say hilarious,
period fascination, David happened to run into Queen
Elizabeth, by then the Queen Mother, at a dinner party
in London and asked what she and the late King had made
of the proceedings. 'Wasn't it awful?' replied Her Majesty,
and before he could take that as a verdict she went on,
'President Roosevelt's radio battery ran out just before
you all came on.'

As soon as the prodigal son had made up his differences
with Goldwyn, shooting started on *The Real Glory*. By

now the studio publicity machine, which only a few weeks earlier had on Goldwyn's instructions been putting out press releases of the 'Niven Hated By Fellow Workers' variety in order to bring the rebel to heel, had gone into swift reverse and local fan magazines were flooded with material on the golden boy who had just signed a new seven-year contract. There were even, said the studio, to be no more loan-outs: from now on Niven was to be an exclusively Goldwyn player.

The first film under this new and unusually loving relationship was a Gary Cooper drama, light years removed from the romantic-comic *Bluebeard* which he and Niven had shot a few months earlier. *The Real Glory* was an unashamed propaganda piece for the American military, though Goldwyn himself always considered it a western since it largely concerned men running around with guns. True to his new promise, he gave Niven not only the second lead (the wonderfully aptly named Lieutenant McCool) but also a lingering death scene and before that the undivided attentions of Andrea Leeds. The film itself ran into a good deal of critical disapproval abroad, since it consisted mainly of large numbers of well-armed American soldiers shooting the hell out of guerrillas in the Philippines. 'In times like these,' wrote one London critic, 'we question the wisdom of rattling the bones in the closet of Yankee Imperialism. To show Filipinos as bloodthirsty savages is fair neither to them nor to history.'

Blithely untroubled by such political considerations, Niven and Cooper turned in performances of considerable bang-bang authority in a film that even Graham Greene thought was 'exactly what cinema should be: a simple story of adventure, and sudden death, and will they arrive in time? Every value which exists in a *Boy's Own* story has been put cunningly into this film – self-sacrifice, misunderstanding, heroism, and if it were not for the intrusion of a couple of females about a third of the way through, it could hardly be improved. The star is Gary Cooper, with David Niven and others sparkling in the background.'

Now Niven was to be allowed to sparkle in the lonely
foreground. From *The Real Glory* he went straight into
Raffles, playing the cricketing burglar who had always been
the hero of E. W. Hornung's English country house-party
stories of snobbery with violence. David was, of course,
by no means the first actor to clamber over those particular
walls for the loot: quite apart from the other sound version
with Colman in 1930, both John Barrymore (in 1917) and
House Peters (in 1925) had made *Raffles* films and the
subject continued to be of lasting fascination, at least to
the British – Graham Greene did a stage adaptation for
the Royal Shakespeare Company in the 1970s, and a
revival of the original play was to be seen with Simon
Cadell as recently as the autumn of 1984.

Goldwyn felt that even by 1939 the story was getting a
little jaded, and accordingly he brought in a number of
distinguished writers to touch up Sidney Howard's 1930
script for Niven. Only John van Druten gets a screen credit
alongside Howard, but undoubtedly the most celebrated
of the writers to have had a hand in this new version was
Scott Fitzgerald, who spent a couple of weeks working on
it in the early summer.

'You always know where you stand with Sam Goldwyn,'
said Fitzgerald later, when recounting a predictably unhappy experience on the film, 'you stand nowhere.' He
had been brought in to add a little polish to a property
that was already shiny but with age rather than class, and
his contributions can chiefly be found in two sequences.
In the first of these, Niven as Raffles is lamenting the
pawning of his automobile, something that the author of
Tender is the Night had just had to do in Los Angeles to
pay off a few of his many drinking debts. In the second of
these, Raffles is gazing into the face of his beloved Gwen
(Olivia de Havilland, hot from *Gone With The Wind*) when
he asks her to part her lips.

'You know,' says Raffles in this rare exchange of Fitzgerald dialogue, 'you have a magnificent . . .'

'What?' asks Gwen eagerly.

'Dentist,' replies Raffles.

Apart from car trouble, Fitzgerald was also having teeth trouble that summer, and he believed in using whatever material came to hand.

Unfortunately he then got caught up in the middle of a major row between Goldwyn and his director Sam Wood over the changes that had been demanded in the script by a still sensitive Hays Office. Not only could Raffles not be seen to escape scot-free in the traditional ending, but he would also have to stop saying 'Good Lord', while a scene showing prostitutes on Bond Street would have to be reshot with them all dressed as shopgirls. Things had been a lot easier in 1930 when Colman had made the earlier version, and sadly enough this, the last film that David was to make for almost three years, emerged as a stale and, though profitable, rather weary affair in which all concerned (writers, actors and even two directors since Willie Wyler was brought in to reshoot some later scenes) seemed painfully aware that they were simply producing a replica of a Colman original without the man himself.

David had more to worry about than his inability to breathe new life into the gentleman cracksman. Away from the Goldwyn Studios his private life had moved into a period of relative tranquillity (apart from a brief renewal of an old London friendship with Jacqueline Dyer) with neither Flynn nor Merle to give it alcoholic or sexual character; in rather more mature mood, he was seeing a great deal of Doug and Mary Lee Fairbanks, and also of Olivier and Vivien Leigh, who were still in California – he having started work on *Rebecca* while she finished *Gone With The Wind* and both were waiting for their respective divorces.

One weekend during the shooting of *Raffles* and *Rebecca*, as Douglas Fairbanks recalls, 'We were all spending the day on a chartered yacht off Catalina, anchored in the harbour of the yacht club there . . . Larry and Vivien weren't yet married, so they had her mother along as a chaperone, and there was Niven and Bob Coote

and my wife and me. We had the radio on, with reports
from London coming through that war had just been
declared against Germany. We listened grimly, each concerned with special thoughts about what to do. The silence
was finally broken not by the usually ebullient Niven, who
had gone very quiet, but by Larry of all people. Without
our noticing it, he had unobtrusively proceeded to get as
smashed as a hoot-owl. Then, very solemnly and carefully,
he had climbed into a dinghy and rowed away. On reaching
the stern of a fairly large anchored yacht, young Laurence
stood up, just steadily enough not to fall into the water
and, like some Cassandra in swimming shorts, he bellowed
to all within earshot: "This is the end. You're all washed
up. Finished. Enjoy your last moments. You're done
for . . . Relics, that's what you are now, relics!" And
before the bemused American layabouts could reply, our
Larry boy was again rowing resolutely off towards the next
yacht that had caught his bleary eye, and again repeating
his prophecy of doom. An hour later, an official protest
was delivered by the club secretary, not to us but to
the owner of a small sailing yacht nearby, demanding an
immediate apology for having insulted other club members. That other owner was a man who still bore a passing
resemblance to both Larry and Niven – Ronnie Colman.'

  David now knew, probably more clearly than at any
other time in his life, what he had to do: he had to get
home and fight. No matter what it said in the small print
of his Goldwyn contract, no matter that the rest of the
Hollywood British were in a state of deep uncertainty,
David almost alone among those of them under forty (and
therefore of fighting age) had actually served for very
nearly five years as a professional soldier. Admittedly he
had resigned his commission and had no formal links with
the Army, but for so long, both on screen and off, he had
behaved like an officer and sometimes even a gentleman
that there was simply no alternative, whatever the effect
might be on a screen career that had belatedly started to
flourish.

Others in Hollywood were not so sure. 'That autumn morning,' recalled Joan Fontaine, whose sister Olivia de Havilland was still on *Raffles* with David, 'when Britain first declared war, calls to the British consul in California were placed from every bedside phone before the morning tea . . . Should every male and female born under the British flag take the next plane home? Were we all needed, expected, commanded?'

An understandably bemused British consul (the California posting never having rated very highly on the priorities of the Foreign Office) said he would be contacting London for further instructions; in the meantime there were films to be made and nobody, least of all the British consul, could see much point at the beginning of the 'phoney war' in a mass exodus from Hollywood of mainly septuagenarian and often First-War-wounded veteran character actors to defend their homeland from the Hun.

Even David in his eagerness to serve the flag realized that *Raffles* could not be abandoned in mid-shoot, and the few weeks he had left on the film came in fact as a welcome breathing space in which to consider precisely what his plan should be. He was, after all, only just at the start of a legally enforceable contract with Goldwyn, and America was still more than two years away from the war. Suppose it was to be a short-lived conflict, and suppose he was to survive it, then he would need some sort of post-war employment. All he really knew about was Hollywood, and a unilaterally broken contract there with Goldwyn would not exactly set him up for the future.

A number of actors of his generation were in almost the same boat, but David's professional military service, his suddenly high profile and the fact that most of his best roles had been uniformed made him the focus of immediate gossip-column attention, and he at once made it clear that he would be going home to fight 'as soon as possible'. In the meantime, on the artificial cricket pitch at the Goldwyn Studios where *Raffles* was being shot, Scott Fitzgerald later recalled an encounter in which David spoke 'nostalgically'

of the Army and England, while Fitzgerald told him he
was going to be the kind of war hero that he, Fitzgerald,
had always wanted to be in the First World War. All that
David was to recall of that same encounter was a drunken
Fitzgerald 'pouring out woe, charm, sadness for lost youth,
boasts, family disasters, nostalgia, fear, hopes, pure bab-
bling and a lot of coughing'.

After Olivier had sobered up from his yacht harbour
declaration of the Second World War, he was the first to
notice a distinct chill in the usually balmy Californian air
that September of 1939: 'It was a painful situation, and
wretchedly embarrassing with the Americans who were,
for once, our now not very enthusiastic hosts. Many of
these seemed far from certain whose side they were on.
There was an enthusiastically pro-German feeling in those
areas of the United States containing extensive proportions
of German immigrants. Milwaukee, for instance, was
largely German-speaking.'

That German-speaking populace was far too important
in terms of box-office revenue for the moguls to allow
audiences there to be decimated by films taking a definably
Allied propaganda line. In Hollywood itself large numbers
of German immigrants were still employed as directors
and designers, and a few like Von Stroheim were regularly
to be seen on camera. With Pearl Harbor still a peaceful
Hawaiian dockyard, and an American policy of non-
intervention in 'the European war' all but declared despite
Roosevelt's constant urging of support for the British,
confusion among the Hollywood Raj now rose to almost
epidemic proportions.

While Olivier and Niven announced that they would be
leaving the moment they could disengage themselves from
Rebecca and *Raffles*, for others the state of affairs was
considerably more complex. Those above the age of immediate call-up, those long settled in America with wives
and children and sometimes even grandchildren, those on
apparently iron-clad studio contracts all urgently wanted
some kind of official advice which would override local

considerations. They were, after all, in an extremely exposed, albeit still physically very comfortable, position. Many were actors with a public as well as a private commitment to Britain. They were actors who for years had been making very good money playing stalwarts of the empire, sons of Victoria, colonels of the Raj. All still had relatives in Britain, as well as audiences there and in America who had come to trust them as quintessentially British. They could not afford to be caught shirking their duty.

The trouble was that nobody, least of all the British government, seemed willing to define precisely what that duty was; indeed, there was now understandable alarm in Whitehall at the sudden realization that if, as Olivier noted, 'every Englishman living abroad were to come gallantly dashing home, the public services would have to face an additional population of anything up to half a million extra mouths to feed and extra hands to find employment for'. Not surprisingly, therefore, a 'stay put' directive was almost immediately issued from the British embassy in Washington, though if that had only been as well publicized in Britain as it was in America a lot of the ensuing unpleasantness might have been avoided.

Led by Cedric Hardwicke (then in his late forties) and Cary Grant (then only thirty-five, but already an American citizen), a number of the Hollywood British flew to Washington to find out precisely what they were supposed to be doing during the 'phoney war' of 1939/40. Lord Lothian, the ambassador of the day, told them briskly that they were actors on legitimate business in California, doing good for their country by portraying 'the best of England' to world audiences. In other words, they were all to shut up and stay put.

Certain other problems then arose, as the British press immediately began to castigate the Hollywood British for having 'gone with the wind up' and being deserters in their country's hour of need. Lothian's cabled reply was strong, but unfortunately it remained for years buried in a pile of Foreign Office briefings. It read, in part: 'The maintenance of a powerful nucleus of older actors in Hollywood is of great importance to our own interests, partly because they are continually championing the British cause in a very volatile community which would otherwise be left to the mercies of German propagandists, and because the continuing production of films with a strong British tone is one of the best and subtlest forms of British propaganda.'

To a BBC radio broadcast repeating these London press allegations of actors' desertion, Lothian further replied: 'The only effect of broadcasts like these is quite unjustifiably to discredit British patriotism and British-produced films; neither do Americans like having British dirty linen washed for their benefit in public.' That, however, was still not enough to deter a number of the British at home from settling some old scores. Michael Balcon was to make Alfred Hitchcock, who had left his studios for those of David O. Selznick only a few months earlier, a constant target for public charges of failure to do his patriotic duty in his country's hour of need: 'I had a plump young technician in my studios whom I promoted from department to department. Today he is one of our most famous directors and he is in Hollywood, while we who are left behind short-handed are trying to harness films to our great national effort.'

As hired actors, most of the Hollywood British in 1939 had no control whatsoever over the kind of pictures the American studios were then making, and their chances of being able to slip in the odd patriotic epic were remote. America had acquired, through the films that David and many others had been making during the 1930s, an image of England that was fixed in some other century altogether. No films had been made in Hollywood featuring the Britain of the 1930s. *Cavalcade* stopped in 1929 and *Rebecca*, though nominally modern-dress, was in fact set in a totally timeless Californian Cornwall. Men like Chamberlain and Baldwin and events such as Munich remained almost totally unknown to Hollywood. Most movie-going Americans thus pictured Hitler invading an England ruled by old Queen Victoria, whose gallant sons were still away defending corners of the empire from heathen blacks. The one element of near-truth that had filtered through to California about Britain in the Thirties was the wonderfully filmic fairy-tale story of a humble Baltimore girl stealing from his throne a British king whom many Americans thought was Victoria's eldest son. It was as if, in reverse, all British knowledge of 1930s American life had been derived from a close study of *Gone With The Wind*.

Rallying round the flag in 1939 was thus no easy matter, though David was still determined to be seen doing it as soon as possible. When he first approached Goldwyn, on the Monday morning after that weekend afloat with Fairbanks and the Oliviers, his employer announced that he had immediate plans for at least three more *Raffles* pictures, followed by a new series about a Scotland Yard detective, all of which would take Niven well into 1944 under the terms of their newly signed contract. David went away to think about that for a while, before wiring his family in London for help. Wiring them for help was not always a great idea: when he'd been trying to get back into California from Mexico a few years earlier he had needed some documentation, and had therefore wired Grizel in Chelsea, 'Send birth certificate'. After about three days he got a cable back from her. It read simply, 'Whose birth certificate?'

This time he thought he'd try a wire to his brother Max instead. Although David had resigned his commission in the Highland Light Infantry five years earlier, that was a technicality with which he had never really bothered Goldwyn. If a cable could be sent by Max posing as Niven's old commanding officer and demanding his immediate return to uniform, Goldwyn could surely not object? Max was duly found and told what to do, and while David was waiting for this plan to take its course, he set about capitalizing on his new-found fame. Articles headlined RAFFLES GOES TO WAR began appearing in local fan magazines already forecasting his imminent departure, and

David himself began writing for them about his early life, either recounting or more often inventing anecdotes which he had sadly and uncharacteristically forgotten by the time of *The Moon's A Balloon* thirty years later. In one August 1939 article bylined 'Just A Diplomat', he wrote:

The world, it seems to me, is in dire need of diplomats. At the moment I am occupied with other matters, or else I'd turn my hand to that most fascinating of all professions. That I am an actor instead of some fortunate nation's emissary is due to chance. But one of these days, because of that same law of chance, I shall no longer be an actor and then I shall go about settling such simple matters as the partition of Czecho-Slovakia. How long this present job of mine will last I do not know. It won't last forever, that's certain. It never does. One day you're up and the next day your little world is down about your ears. One day you have a leading part in a picture like Goldwyn's *The Real Glory* and the next you can't get extra work. That's why I have my eye on this diplomacy business. After all, why shouldn't I? All my training has been in that direction. As I look back at my life, I realize more and more that I should have gone into the diplomatic service rather than the Army or the cinema. A man with my particular talent for smoothing things over owes it to his country to put that talent at his country's disposal. In time I shall.

I think that an incident which occurred on the Isle of Wight in the early 1930s illustrates better than anything else my fitness for diplomatic work. At that time I quite fancied myself as a sailor, and rightly so. Hadn't I been a member of the eight-metre team that won for Great Britain the Cumberland Cup? Anyway, I had gone down to do a bit of sailing at the club. A stiff wind was blowing, and I saw at once that I would need another man for the small boat. So I cast around for a shipmate. A friend pointed to a little man sitting in the club. 'Why not take him?' he said. 'That little squirt?' I said. 'What does he know about sailing?' 'That,' said my friend, 'is Admiral Jellicoe.'

Another time I was courting the very lovely daughter of one of England's great industrial magnates. He was a self-made man and had a low opinion of me. He felt that I was not the sort of chap who would make a suitable son-in-law, so I set out to impress him. 'You know, Sir,' I said one day, 'what I really need is toughening up. This army business isn't the sort of thing for me. I should be in the Northwest Mounted Police. That's what I should be in, by Jove, and I shall be.' 'So you shall,' said the man whose daughter I coveted. 'I'll fix it at once.' And he did. It took me a week to keep from being shipped off to the Canadian wilds, and after that he would have none of me.

Then there was the incident in Washington when I first arrived in America. I had gone down there to visit a friend in the British embassy, and he took me to a very swell social affair. 'Look, Davy,' he cautioned, 'watch yourself. These are the most important people in the country, and we must not offend them.' I assured him that he need not worry, and for a while I got along beautifully. Then I met a lovely girl and we danced together and she seemed quite taken with me, so I decided to impress her with my wit. Not far away was a very odd-looking fellow and I nodded toward him. 'Funny looking bloke,' I said. 'That's my brother,' she said. 'I mean the other one,' I said. 'That's my father,' she said. I was now covered with confusion, but making one last desperate effort to redeem myself. 'Thank Heaven your grandfather isn't living,' I said. 'Oh, but he is,' she said. 'He's right over there.' I left the party at once.

Most movie stars' articles of the time were of course ghostwritten by hacks in their studio publicity department. It seems unlikely, however, that Goldwyn had on his staff a publicist sufficiently talented to recreate that breezy, sub-Wodehouse prose style of David's. Niven himself was already, before the war, a comic writer.

In due course the cable he had ordered arrived from Max. Signed simply 'Adjutant', it read, 'Report regimental depot immediately.' In the interests, presumably, of telegraphic economy Max had not bothered to visualize where the depot might be, or what regiment might be involved. Mr Goldwyn, unversed in the technicalities of the British Army, was nevertheless suitably impressed by the suggestion of a rival and presumably pre-dated contract for Niven's services.

Chapter Twelve

1939–1940

'The star who came home to join the Royal Air Force, and failed.'

So it was that David, with a little inventive help from his brother Max, now became the first Hollywood film star to be 'called up' into the Second World War, and if that call-up was on inspection to prove totally mythical, Niven could at least reflect that it was no more unreal than the Hollywood he was now trying so hard and fast to leave. Goldwyn's avuncular pride in his brave young war hero rapidly overcame his commercial fury at having to shelve what might have proved a lucrative new *Raffles* series. He agreed to keep David on a low retainer during his enforced absence from the studios (something that Niven, in his post-war raging against his employer, usually forgot to credit), and announced that he would 'tell that bum Hitler to shoot around you'.

Young Doug Fairbanks then gave Niven a lavish and much-photographed farewell party at which the entire Hollywood English community turned out to wish him well. There was also a bagpiper to signal his presumed return to the Highland Light Infantry. As Fairbanks recalls: 'In fact, it was a Canadian Piper because the Black Watch happened to be in town at the time and that was the nearest I could manage; there was a feeling that night of general admiration for David as the one who'd managed to get off to England first, and Goldwyn made sure of a lot of publicity for him, since it also reflected well on the studio that was letting him go.'

Next morning David flew to New York, the first time he had crossed the continent by air, and began to have severe second thoughts – not about fighting for his country, exactly, but about fighting for it from England. His ties there were distinctly shaky. Since his mother's death almost a decade earlier, his only and final contact with his hated stepfather had been an icy lunch at which the sole topic of conversation had been who should pay for the upkeep of her grave. He still felt naturally more attached to his sisters and brother (who had gone back into the Army as soon as war had been declared), but apart from Trubshawe he had no other real friends at home and not the remotest idea what he would do when he got there, especially as the message from Washington had deeply discouraged the idea of a return to any sort of uniform.

Once back in New York among such old Broadway cronies as John McClain, however, a better war campaign began to develop. Instead of travelling on to London across an already perilous Atlantic he would go north to Canada, a considerably cheaper and easier journey, and there join the Canadian Army. Unfortunately, that idea had already occurred to just about every English actor on Broadway (and there were almost as many there as in Hollywood) with the result that the Canadian Army now regarded itself as overbooked. After a short visit to Washington, where Lothian again urged him unsuccessfully back to California, David then boarded the Italian liner *Rex* which was bound for Europe.

His destination was Naples, from where trains could still be taken to Rome and then London. David spent a few days in Roman bars with some Italian skiers he had met in Sun Valley and who were now on a similar army-joining mission, though in their case the army would of course be Mussolini's. He then travelled on to Paris, where he found Noël Coward already installed in a flat near the Ritz and working to set up a British bureau of propaganda in liaison with the French Commissariat d'Information which was then run by another distinguished dramatist, Jean Giraudoux. This proved to be a somewhat hopeless assignment, but it did lead to at least one brief and remarkable encounter. David arrived at Noël's flat one night to find him in conversation with a distinguished RAF group captain. 'Ah, Niven,' said the man as he entered the room. 'You won't know me, but I'm Pope. Remember? The man you played in *Dawn Patrol*.'

Niven told Pope that, on reflection, he would rather join the RAF than go back to the Army he had resigned from so abruptly in 1934. Pope thought he was probably already too old at twenty-nine for training as a fighter pilot, but that there might be some other RAF position for him on reaching London.

There, living in his brother's small Mayfair flat, David found Grizel already driving for the Chelsea Fire Service and the barrage balloons already up over the City. It was then that he made his first real mistake.

The Goldwyn office in London had been alerted to expect his arrival, and to make the best possible publicity out of it. *Bachelor Mother* was on release all over the country by now, and with *Raffles* on the way the London publicists had already ensured that his name on all the posters was crossed with a sticker reading THE STAR WHO CAME HOME TO FIGHT.

Not surprisingly, the campaign immediately backfired. David agreed to give a press conference to establish his arrival in London and hence his availability to the RAF. Fleet Street journalists decided, for once in their lives, not to side with Niven. Early in the phoney war his homecoming reeked of a Goldwyn publicity stunt, and they gave it cynical attention under such headlines as RELAX, THE DAWN PATROL IS HERE which did remarkably little to further his application to the RAF. Nobody, as Niven ruefully told an old school friend at this time, seemed to want a Hollywood star in uniform unless he stayed safely on film.

'But the curious thing is,' he added, 'that I actually hate myself on film. For the last year I've been terribly lucky and had some marvellous parts. Not counting Sundays I've only had four days off in fourteen months and have finally emerged as a star, God knows how. And now nobody wants me.'

The RAF didn't even seem to believe that he was only twenty-nine. At any rate, they went so far as to send a telegram to the headmaster at Stowe reading, 'Grateful if you would wire us David Niven's age.' And when they got that, they decided they still didn't want him in any capacity. Actors, said one recruiting officer, were usually trouble and tended to alcoholism under pressure.

The Navy took a similarly dim view of his usefulness, and David was determined not to go crawling back to his old regiment, where they would doubtless still recall some of his and Trubshawe's less than finest hours. By now it was almost Christmas, and Niven was getting more than a little desperate, as Michael recalled: 'He had come all the way home from Hollywood because he simply had no alternative. As an Englishman and an ex-regular officer it was the only thing he could do, and it was therefore very depressing for him when every door slammed in his face and no branch of the armed services seemed to want him at any price. One weekend he came down to us and I suggested that he should overcome his pride and write to our old commanding officer and ask to be taken back into the Highland Light Infantry, but he was still utterly determined never to do that. "Old chum," he said, "everybody has to change their butcher now and then." But luckily Celia, my wife, knew somebody in the Rifle Brigade, and he was the one who finally opened the door after all those RAF buggers had turned him down for the tenth time.'

David had some other important friends now rooting for his return to active service, not least Lord Beaverbrook's son Max Aitken and most of the members of Boodle's, the club where David spent a good deal of time on his return lamenting his failure to enlist. It was there, one afternoon in late 1939 when his face was on posters all over London as the star of *Bachelor Mother*, that he was addressed by one of the club's more elderly members who thought he looked vaguely familiar and that they must have met before. Unlikely, said David, as he had been abroad for the last six years. 'Doing what?' asked the old member. 'Pictures,' replied David. 'Really?' said the other. 'Water colours or oils?'

It is almost possible to sense the sigh of relief that runs behind this report from the London *Times* of 10 March 1940:

> Mr David Niven, the film actor, has at last succeeded in joining the army as a subaltern in the Rifle Brigade. He returned to England last October hoping to join the RAF but was over the age limit; in January his name was accepted by the Officers Emergency Reserve, and a commission in the Rifle Brigade now follows. Formerly Mr Niven was a Lieutenant in the Highland Light Infantry.

Even now he wasn't altogether in the clear. A medical revealed that he was missing about 2 inches of his jugular vein as the result of a childhood operation, but urged on by a stiff letter to the authorities from Mrs Trubshawe's friend he was accepted, and noted in a letter back to California his delight at finding some old friends from Sandhurst and Stowe in the brigade. If one were going to get bumped off, thought David, it would be a lot more pleasant to have one's chums around immediately prior to the bumping.

Though he was already missing the bright lights and indeed the climate of California, Niven had not been exactly idle while waiting around for a uniform. *Time* magazine of 15 January 1940 reported that he had got himself engaged to 'war nurse Ursula Kenyon-Slaney, a granddaughter of the Duke of Abercorn', but that engagement, if it happened at all, appears to have been so short-lived that David later had no recollection of it whatsoever.

Interest in his affairs, both romantic and military, was still considerably higher in the American press than it was at home, and David made the most of this. If and when the war was to end, he knew that his life and career would still lie on the other side of the Atlantic and that contact there had to be maintained with a notoriously forgetful and fickle film-going audience. When therefore he wrote back to Los Angeles, it was usually to Nigel and Bunny Bruce and their schoolgirl daughter Pauline, to whom David had always been devoted. These letters were then to be handed around the acting colony in Beverly Hills, while a strongly edited and somewhat less scabrous account of his romantic and other activities would also be regularly sent by David to the likes of Hedda Hopper and Louella Parsons for fan-magazine consumption. Thus could the Niven profile be kept in high definition for the duration.

Other American publications were also interested in David's wartime progress. Early in 1940 one New York paper commissioned from the London film critic C. A. Lejeune a piece entitled 'A David Goes To Battle' which noted in part:

No event has fired the imagination of British filmgoers more strongly in recent weeks than the homecoming of David Niven who flew in from France, chin-deep in mailbags at the bottom of a bomber, on the last lap of his ten-thousand-mile journey to join the fighting forces. Arriving without gas mask, identity book or ration book he did not officially exist. 'I remembered', he said, 'the sort of thing we used to say at Sandhurst about ham actors who played in war pictures, and I wondered what people at home would think of me.' Mr Niven's one great fear is that his own people will see his return as an actor's stunt. Mingled with public interest in his return is however a very real regret for its occasion. The British

film fan does not want David Niven in the army, the
navy or the air force. We want him in his proper place,
right up there on the screen, helping us to forget this
war a little. In the last two years, and especially since
Dawn Patrol, Mr Niven's trim little star has been climb-
ing irresistibly toward the top place in popular favour.
He is to us today what Ronald Colman was yesterday –
higher than the Gables or the Taylors or the Powers,
comparable perhaps only with Spencer Tracy and
Deanna Durbin whom all the English love. This taste
is not confined to a class or sex. Schoolboys and Mayfair
matrons share it. There isn't one of us who wouldn't
gladly pack him back to Hollywood tomorrow. We like
him for being at such pains to come home and fight with
us, but we have a feeling that his conscience may have
done him wrong.

Though she had put it as kindly as she could, Caroline
Lejeune's message to David was much the same as the one
he had been getting from the RAF: he would be a lot more
useful to the British war effort on the screen than off it.
But David wasn't really concerned only with England or
the English or what they wanted of him; subconsciously I
think he already knew that if he were going to survive in
a post-war Hollywood as the kind of screen character he
had established in the pre-war years, that image required
him now to be seen in the real uniform of his country.
Cary Grant might have elected to stay in California, but
Cary Grant was nearly forty where David was not yet
even thirty; moreover Grant's image as the suave lover of
Katharine Hepburn in *Holiday* and *The Philadelphia Story*
was wildly different from David's as the officer and gentleman of *The Dawn Patrol* and *The Real Glory*.

Niven's early months in the Rifle Brigade were a time of
irritating inactivity. He was assigned to the 2nd Battalion, a
motor-training unit on Salisbury Plain, and early in June
was told to stand by for a posting to the 1st Battalion which
was already fighting in Calais. Then came Dunkirk, and

with it the total decimation of that battalion, all of whom were either captured or killed while David carried on drilling his way around Salisbury Plain in much the same kind of deadening routine from which he had fled in 1933.

Being now something of a celebrity, albeit one still denied any real part in the war action, he was invited at weekends to a series of country house-parties where he managed to renew old social acquaintances and mix with politicians, including Winston Churchill to whom, like almost all actors, Niven took an instant shine. His frustration, however, at being on such inactive service, and his irritation with most of the old-guard English county squires who were his hosts at these weekends, was remarkable; it never surfaced in the rather glossy pages of his own war memoirs in *The Moon's A Balloon*, but can be found in some detail in his last novel, *Go Slowly, Come Back Quickly*, where the hero (the RAF pilot officer that David had so wanted to be) goes racketing around the English shires in a state of sustained if impotent rage at the way the old landowning classes appear to be avoiding most of the dangers and the deprivations of the war.

At one of their weekend meetings, Churchill had the grace to acknowledge David as the first of the few who had come home from Hollywood for the war, while adding pointedly that 'it would of course have been despicable if you hadn't '. As David now saw it there was not a lot of point in his having given up a career, travelled 10,000 miles (at his own expense, as he used frequently to point out when his Scots family blood was near-boiling) and fought his way into the Rifle Brigade after considerable humiliation at the hands of recruiting officers in other regiments, if now he was merely to be kept on Salisbury Plain far from any sight or sound of the action that the journalist and self-publicist in him wanted so badly to report back to California. Nor did the occasional letter from his newly married brother, already fighting in the desert, do anything but add to David's frustration at being so far from any real front. It was never like this in films.

Some time towards the late summer of 1940 he found an escape from Salisbury Plain. Volunteers from the Rifle Brigade were wanted to join a new and top-secret force training in Scotland. They were to be the first commandos, and Niven proved acceptable to them. Things began to look up at last, and not only on the military front. On a brief London leave that summer he met (precisely where depends on which of his memoirs you select, though the most likely location seems to have been the Café de Paris) a member of the Women's Auxiliary Air Force by the name of Primula Rollo. She was twenty-two, the only daughter of Lady Kathleen and Flight Lieutenant William Rollo, MC, and by the time they met again (at a cello concert in the National Gallery) David had decided that he was going to marry her, preferably within the next ten days. In this he seems to have met with remarkably little opposition, either from Primmie or her separated but enthusiastic parents. To marry your only daughter to a man who was both a film star and a commando must in 1940 have seemed as close to the social ideal as could then reasonably be hoped, and besides they were patently very much in love if somewhat vague about each other's backgrounds, characters and interests.

With a war on, there wasn't a lot of time for personal case histories of that kind, and the frenzy of the period seems to have suited David who was to make a point even in the relatively calmer time of his second marriage of allowing only another ten days to elapse between first meeting and altar. There was, in his view, no doubt at all that Primmie was 'the one' and an announcement in *The Times* duly noted on 16 September that 'a marriage has been arranged and will take place shortly'. In fact it was within the week, at the parish church of Huish on the Wiltshire Downs, with the Battle of Britain then at its height in the skies above them. The best man was of course Michael Trubshawe, now of the Royal Sussex Regiment, who said of Primmie: 'She was an absolute darling, the perfect English rose. She was kind, she was fun, and she was to be the most wonderful mother for the short time she was allowed. She was one of those lucky people who can take fire without the aid of any alcohol: her adrenalin was flowing all the time just naturally. David always used to say he was the luckiest man in the world, but it was only when he met Primmie that I began to believe him. She was a radiant girl, and at once she gave David something he had never really had before: a sense of purpose and continuity, as well as a sense of what his life was supposed to be about. More than anything, he suddenly now wanted to be a husband and a father and that was all to do with Primmie. Living as he had for so long in California and before that in New York and Malta, I don't think he'd ever really met anyone like her. She wasn't at all like an actress, she was just the best sort of English girl of that period and one of the last of them; after the war women somehow stopped being like that. Primmie was England in the 1930s: country cottages and small children and all that gentle, lost world of the upper classes at home.'

David and Primula Niven were to have two sons and nearly six years together, five of them wartime ones; yet those who knew David best have always reckoned that they were far and away the happiest of his life. Though he was to grow increasingly bitter about the war and what he came to see as its utter futility and waste, domestically and privately he now knew as he entered his thirties exactly where he was. For the first time in his life he was at home.

That home was first of all a cottage on Dorney Reach from where Primmie would cycle each morning into Slough to work at the Hurrican fighter factory; David was now a major commanding 'A' Squadron of Phantom, the special regiment that had been formed out of those volunteer commandos. As their historian Philip Warner has noted:

> Phantom was – and still is – one of the least known of the wartime special regiments. It began in 1939 with the mission of finding out exactly where all the Allied forward positions were – a task which required linguistic

ability, unlimited tact and radio expertise. After Dunkirk its squadrons at first kept an eye on all invasion points, then sent a unit to Greece and more to the Middle East. Soon it proved an indispensable direct communication link between the forward patrols and command headquarters . . . Phantom took the fog out of war by informing the British, the Canadians and the Americans exactly what their forward troops were doing and what was the enemy's reaction. Phantom was at Dieppe with the Commandos, in France with the SAS, at Arnhem with the Airborne and in Germany until the surrender . . . It was a private army, a great success story and a happy unit.

Those who served with David in Phantom at some stage of the war included the actor Hugh Williams, the journalist Peregrine Worsthorne, the police chief Robert Mark, the MPs Christopher Mayhew and Hugh Fraser, and Lord Hailsham, who as Quintin Hogg shared a Whitehall office with Niven early in the proceedings. At last, as Trubshawe recalled, Niven felt that his journey home had been worthwhile: 'After the rejection by the RAF and the discovery that all the things he'd asked to have shipped home from Hollywood had been on a cargo boat which got sunk by a torpedo, David deserved a little good luck and his rapid discovery of Primmie and Phantom certainly changed his life in 1940 for the better. He even volunteered for parachute training, and I remember distinctly having to leave the bedroom window of the cottage at Dorney with him, umbrellas held aloft as part of that training. David was a very good officer, you know. His men respected him because he would always do anything and everything that they were expected to do themselves, from cleaning out latrines to correcting a number one stoppage on one of the guns.'

It was all coming together in public as well as in private. Blissfully happy in his marriage, he was also finding in Phantom that his original Army training a decade earlier, together with the years he had since spent as an actor, were a good and unique preparation for 'A' Squadron. The Hollywood fame, if rightly handled, could be used to break down the usual barriers between officer and men, and David was shameless at using his old showbusiness contacts to provide special film shows and celebrity concerts for the troops. Unlike most actors who were now suddenly finding themselves in uniform, David still knew his way around the Army well enough, knew exactly how to behave and where the boundaries were and which of them were best not crossed. Now that there was a war on, all his old feelings about the pointlessness of Army life disappeared. Phantom was everything he had always looked for and never found on Malta, in what already seemed another life.

There is some indication of David's new-found marital and military contentment in a letter he wrote from Brooks's club in St James's to his old studio boss Sam Goldwyn on 30 October 1940, a little over a month after his marriage – a letter which by some extraordinary coincidence then happened to find its way from Goldwyn's desk to just about every gossip column in Los Angeles:

My dear Sam:
Well! I am now married and extremely happy about it. The only snag to the whole thing was that I didn't have the lovely moment I had been looking forward to so much – seeing you when I walked into your office and broke the news. I have been doing a special job for the army lately, and have been working in the War Office these last two months. London has been a little noisy lately, as you may have gathered from the newspapers. But everything is still running well, and people have readjusted themselves marvellously to our new way of living. You really ought to write a scene into one of your pictures between two women on the corner of Bond Street at night – both now wearing steel helmets. There are so many great stories being written every day here

and I am so happy that, even if I missed Dunkirk, at least I have not missed a day of the victory of London.

We will never leave this city, Sam, until pestilence sets in which is impossible even if they could bomb us 100 times as badly, and we'd only leave it then to make room for the fumigators. I miss Hollywood dreadfully. I never realized how much I enjoyed my life and my work out there until I came home. But real pride is one of the greatest sensations on earth. I love Americans. They were simply swell to me for eight years, and the best I could wish them would be that they could experience the same sensation of PRIDE that I have today. But I hope the States will avoid active complications in this chaos, because it's no fun and anyway they don't desire to be mixed up in them. On the other hand, I hope you won't all go and think it's a pushover for us just because the police and fire-women and taxi drivers here are so great.

                    Yours ever, and with great affection, David.

Chapter Thirteen

1941–1942

'Going to war was the only unselfish thing I have ever done for humanity. I hated it. Detested it. Loathed it. If you push me, I will admit that I am pleased about having passed the test of not behaving badly. But believe me, that's all I really did. I was inclined to lie down and wait until it was all over – but there were people watching, and that made me behave a little less like a coward. I did my best, but it was never better than what I was told to do.'

For the whole of 1941, and well into the spring of 1942, there were really only two things in David's life: Primmie and Phantom. Daily he would leave her going to work at the Slough factory and head up to London where, behind desks in the same Whitehall room, he and Quintin Hogg began sorting out the secret liaison work which was their main concern. David's war was not, as he himself was always the first to note, an especially flamboyant or heroic affair; but by the time it ended he had risen from major to lieutenant-colonel with the additional honour of the American Legion of Merit, one of only twenty-five British soldiers to be so awarded. Precisely what he did to earn that is still buried in the classified files of the Phantom unit, but as their historian Philip Warner has noted, 'Niven is so well known that it is difficult to realize he was also a dedicated and very professional soldier . . . in Phantom

he commanded a colourful group of men including stock-
brokers, burglars and poachers. According to them he was
even more colourful.'

He was also determined not to disappear from the public
eye or ear altogether and used at this time to take part in
a number of radio shows for the BBC. As a regular member
of the British panel of two in *Transatlantic Quiz* which was
heard throughout Great Britain and North America all
through the war, he acted as an admirable foil to his
co-panellist, Denis Brogan, professor of political science
and American history at Cambridge, whose encyclopaedic
powers of recall were said to have been unrivalled since
Trevelyan and whose scholarly optional extras, astounding
in their detail, were often in danger of trailing away from
the microphone as he casually removed a stone from his
shoe. Listeners later recalled how David sparkled, often
anticipating the professor's reply, always giving it that
witty and memorable turn that, combined with his own
panoramic knowledge of British life, made the programme
compulsive listening and helped to ensure that the odds
were tipped marginally in favour of Great Britain despite
the gallant efforts of the United States side, co-ordinated
and championed by Alastair Cooke. David also took part
in other morale-boosting wartime radio programmes such
as *Answering You* (with Leslie Howard), in which questions from Canadian and United States listeners were
answered by British speakers. Both on and off screen, the
British gentleman of Hollywood was faithful to his origins.

Of course, David still had his more traditional ways of
keeping in touch with the great American public during
this period of their non-involvement. Another of his letters
back to the Nigel Bruce family in Hollywood made its
usual way into the film magazines of 1941, only now
his forced cheeriness was giving way to something more
reflective of the war at its darkest time for Britain:

There still seems to be an abundance of food here, and
everybody is perfectly calm just waiting for the balloon

to go up . . . Thank God we have now got a real government and in Churchill a real leader at last, but there is going to be a little scalp-hunting when the smoke has cleared off the battlefields. I am unimportant, but besides cousins and relations I have now lost practically all my old friends and all in the last few weeks . . . they need never have been sacrificed if the people then at the top had been doing their jobs as well as they said they were doing them. I want to stick a knife into them just as much as I want to fix Hitler. I promise not to come back to you a bitter and disillusioned man when this is all over. I've seen a lot of things since I last saw you, and I have never been so impressed by anything as I have been by the British character. If we ever went under, at least a standard would have been set that the rest of the world would have a hell of a job to copy. I have a feeling now that something will end this war quite suddenly . . . it might even be God pulling a few strings. He certainly pulled one at Dunkirk, and I feel He will come through in an even bigger way next time. Will you please thank Ed Sullivan for that marvellous article making me out to be a hero. I hope he never sees my face when I'm being bombed.

There were still people, even in England, who could never forget that Niven was an actor as well as a soldier, and one of them was his new radio-panel partner, Leslie Howard. The two men had never worked together before, though they had of course at least been acquaintances through most of the late 1930s in Hollywood, where both had lived with Merle Oberon. Leslie Howard had, like Niven, come home from Hollywood (and in his case *Gone With The Wind*) as soon as war had been declared, but at forty-six and not in the best of health he was deemed unfit for military service, and instead dedicated himself to producing and directing as well as starring in films that would promote aspects of the British cause. By this time he had already made *Pimpernel Smith* and *49th Parallel*, and was starting to think about a life of Reginald Joseph Mitchell, the designer of the Spitfire that had done so much to win the Battle of Britain.

With the sole exception of Ronald Colman (who went to his grave more than a decade later totally convinced that a knighthood had been denied him because of his decision to wait out the war in California, a theory called into some question by the knighting of C. Aubrey Smith in 1944), Leslie Howard was beyond doubt the ideal of the screen Englishman. Even if he was Hungarian in origin, he had, as C.A. Lejeune once noted, 'a passion for England and the English that was almost Shakespearian', and in the early isolationist months before Pearl Harbor it was Howard who had broadcast back to the USA from London most often, trading his celebrity value there for the chance to urge America into the war.

As his most intelligent observer, Jeffrey Richards, has noted, Howard spoke then and in his last films 'of the quiet spirit of an England roused to action by a monstrous evil'; his classic screen image was of the aesthete deeply angered when Nazi submariners destroyed his books and pictures (the role he played in *49th Parallel*), and suitably enough it was Howard who had spoken, anonymously, the epilogue to Coward's *In Which We Serve*. He was the Scarlet Pimpernel who became Pimpernel Smith, getting first the aristocrats out from under the guillotine and then the Jews out from under Hitler, and it was Howard who came to personify a particularly anglicized blend of nation, empire and mysticism in his first broadcasts back to the USA from a Britain at war: 'I can't explain the mystery of the call that comes to people from the land of their birth – I don't have to explain it to you, anyway. The call of Britain seems particularly potent, doesn't it? Look at the way they've come hurrying from the four corners of the earth, especially as that call comes at what must be the most critical moment of our whole long history. Most of you, I'm sure, will know what I mean when I speak of the curious elation which comes from sharing in a high and mysterious destiny.

The destiny of Britain we cannot know for certain, but we can guess at it, and pray for it, and work towards it as we find ourselves singled out of all the nations of the world for the rare honour of fighting alone against the huge and ruthless forces of tyranny.'

The chances are that Howard in the end gave his life to those forces, for his plane was shot down over the Bay of Biscay by two German fighters in June 1943, when he was returning from a lecture tour of Spain and Portugal with a man who looked very like (and may conceivably have been taken by the Germans for) Winston Churchill. By then Howard had made his greatest contribution to the war effort. In stark contrast to the 'colourful rubbish' which was his own definition of his Hollywood work, this was to be a sober black-and-white study of the birth of the Spitfire, and for it Howard made it very clear that he wanted David Niven.

Niven was in many respects the other side of the Howard coin – the man of action as against the philosopher, the jovial extrovert as against the thoughtful introvert – and it was astute of Howard to realize that they would make a rare screen team, very much the same kind of team which was to work so well a decade later in another hugely successful war film, *The Dam Busters*, in which Richard Todd was to be the dashing airman and Michael Redgrave the thoughtful scholar who provided the machinery for action.

Though Howard could see the propaganda value of *The First of the Few*, with himself cast as the philosophic inventor and Niven as the pilot who has to get the Spitfires off the drawing board and into the skies in time for the Battle of Britain, David himself was a lot less enthusiastic about the idea of going back to the cameras, as Trubshawe recalled: 'He felt that he had come back to fight not to film, and that if he was going to make films now he might just as well have stayed in Hollywood. Also I think he felt that all the publicity about him joining the Army might backfire if he was seen to leave it again after less than three years. So in the end his adjutant said, "Well, if you won't volunteer for this, we shall have to make it a direct order. Is that understood?" And it was.'

So Niven, under military orders, took a month's 'special duty' leave and (keeping a radio transmitter in his dressing room so that he'd never be totally out of touch with Phantom) played the test pilot who, at the height of the Battle of Britain, takes a little time out to tell some young pilots the story of the man who invented their planes. *The First of the Few* was an intelligent, semi-documentary attempt to tell the story of the birth of a plane. It had a wonderfully rousing score by William Walton, and Howard's production included one or two marvellously cynical touches such as the glimpse of a 'Trust Baldwin' poster. For the first time Niven was working on home territory with an all-English cast of mainly theatre-trained professionals, and his initial nervousness and diffidence, not only at getting back to the camera after a long absence, but also at acting for the first time as a professional in Britain, are evident. Yet by the end of the film, when he has to play a remarkably haunting scene where Howard is dying in the garden while his planes soar overhead, there is a confidence about Niven's performance and a subtlety which was never visible in his earlier Hollywood work. *The First of the Few* is the film in which Niven comes home as an actor, and it marked the start of a trio of war films which contain almost all of the really good work he ever did on screen.

The distributors were nonetheless extremely nervous about its chances, as it was opening at a moment in the autumn of 1942 when war films were suddenly dying at the box office, presumably because people did not wish to pay good money to look at what they already knew far too well. Cinema managers were urged in their trade papers:

Explain to your audience that *The First of the Few* is *not* a war film. Tell them that it is a human story of a great man who helped to put Britain in the forefront of world aviation . . . be careful not to give the public the idea that this film is merely a repetition of previous flying pictures. Go all out to tell them that flying is merely incidental to the plot, and that it is the great human story and the brilliant acting that make up the entertainment total.

Nobody seems to have thought it worth mentioning that this was also David's first native picture, and the early reviews were respectful rather than hugely enthusiastic. Dilys Powell thought it 'a story well told, with a careful balancing of professional and domestic incident' and that David gave 'a performance of instinctive gaiety and confidence – one of his best to date'. In America, where it opened as *Spitfire* in the very week that Howard was himself shot down, *Time* magazine alone noted the way that he and Niven 'suggest the subtle interdependencies which may develop between a man of vision and a man of action' and the fact that the film contained Howard's own best epitaph: 'We've all got to pack it in some time. It doesn't matter when. It's what we do before that is important.'

But with *The First of the Few* safely in the can, Niven hurried back to his Phantom duties, limiting his public appearances to the occasional mock-solemn letter to the editor of *The Times*. On 27 June 1942 he wrote:

Sir,
During last night's air raid warning, all taxis were ordered to stop and pull into the side of the street. Their occupants were then told to go into the shelters. This seems to me very reasonable, but the taxis kept all their lights on for the duration of the warning, and traffic lights continued to work busily. This seemed to me rather peculiar.

I am, Sir, David Niven.

Later in the year *The Times* carried an even more important communication from Niven, one also conveyed to his
old headmaster at Stowe in a telegram dated 10.30am on
15 December: SON BORN 9.30 THIS MORNING STOP PLEASE
PUT HIM DOWN FOR GRAFTON HOUSE STOP BOTH SON AND WIFE
DOING WELL AND FATHER DOING EVEN BETTER STOP KINDEST
REGARDS NIVEN.

The birth of David junior, and David's increasingly
responsible liaison work at the War Office for Phantom,
meant that he and Primmie were not exactly unoccupied
during the winter of 1942–3. Nevertheless, there was now
an odd distinction between his working and his private
life. Where the former was purely military and largely
concerned (to his increasing frustration) with pushing
papers round a desk, the latter was becoming ever more
theatrical. Noël Coward had come back into his life as a
godfather to young David, and while Noël was filming *In
Which We Serve* and Olivier was planning *Henry V* they,
and such other actor–officers as John Mills and Rex Harrison, would gather at the Niven cottage, ideally placed as
it was about half-way between London and most of the
studios. John Mills recalls:

I'd just been released from the army,' and we were all
living around Denham making war films of one kind or
another. David was still in uniform, very reticent about
his Phantom work, but still inclined suddenly to appear
on the doorstep at eight in the morning in full dress
uniform and wearing a gas mask. He and I were great
jokers, but you never really knew what David was thinking. He didn't fit easily: he wasn't stage-trained, or
England-based, or interested in the theatre like the rest
of us. He was already a Hollywood creature, but happy
in his new life with Primmie.

She was a glorious creature, rather aristocratic, but
evidently terribly proud of him, very much in love and
always happy to let him be the star turn, which is why I
think that first Niven marriage was so much easier than

the second. Primmie wanted no part of David's limelight; he was the limelight one in that marriage, and every time he told a story she'd laugh uproariously, even though she must have already heard it a dozen times.

I never worked with Niv, and I only really knew him well in those war years, but I always thought he was an amazing character. He had managed to create himself out of nothing. In the short yardage he performed in, he was totally expert. He was always the first to admit he could never cope with costumes or character roles or false noses, but on the screen he did have something remarkable. He knew his own territory, and he stayed within it. If he suffered from anything, it was, I suppose, a lack of background – you never really knew where he had come from, as an actor or as a man. That perhaps was why, before and after the war, California suited him so well. Unlike England, it's a rootless place.

In long conversations with the Millses and the Oliviers, David's determination to give up all acting for the duration (a determination which had already been severely dented on official instructions for *The First of the Few*) now became more and more shaky. If men like Olivier, Coward and Ralph Richardson were going back to the greasepaint and the arc lights occasionally, perhaps he could too.

Early in 1943 his commanding officer seems to have arrived independently at the same conclusion. Niven was sent for on 13 January by the adjutant-general, who took the view that what Coward had done for the Navy with *In Which We Serve*, a massively successful propaganda film based on the sinking of the *Kelly* and the maritime heroism of Lord Mountbatten, should now be done for the Army by Niven. Quite how was never specified, but the next day David found himself seconded to the Army's director of public relations and negotiating with Carol Reed and various commercial film companies on possible future projects.

After months of complex negotiations about whether

this was to be a Ministry of Information documentary or
a commercial feature film, a form of compromise was
reached whereby it was agreed that the ministry would put
together a script, key personnel and Army facilities, and
then make these available to an experienced commercial
producer, in this case Filippo Del Giudice of the Two
Cities company with which Coward had made his now-
triumphant *In Which We Serve*. That, too, had gone
through considerable and prolonged teething troubles with
a ministry which at first considered it 'unpatriotic' to show
a British destroyer being sunk by enemy action, but now
that it had become such an unexpected critical, box-office
and propaganda success, Brendan Bracken's Information
Office was determined on an Army equivalent.

Niven's first instinct was, logically enough, to turn back
to Coward, but Noël was canny enough to know that
lightning seldom strikes the same idea twice, and that
he totally lacked in the Army the long-standing service
connexions which had made it so easy and natural for him
to work with his beloved Navy. Niven therefore now had
another problem, quite apart from finding a script and a
director: he had been told by Del Giudice that if his film
was to have a chance of breaking into the all-important
American market, it would need a major British star. At
that time, said Del Giudice, there were precisely four and
a half major British stars: Vivien Leigh, Robert Donat,
Laurence Olivier, Leslie Howard and the half – David
himself.

Given the total unavailability of the other four, it was
therefore rapidly agreed that David would be taking part
once his role as a kind of glorified production manager
could be handed on; it was further agreed that Carol Reed
should direct, and that a script should be sought from
Eric Ambler. But what should it be about? After further
discussions with the War Office on one side and Del
Giudice on the other, David set out his own ideas in a
memorandum:

(1) The film must have one object only, and that is to make everyone who sees it say either, 'There, that's what our Bert is doing: isn't it wonderful?' or 'See, we old-timers started something in the last lot' or, in the case of an American audience, 'The British Army is OK.'

(2) In order to accomplish the above, the film must be on a really important scale and must certainly not be just a small propaganda short.

(3) The movie-going public, which in this country, the Dominions and the US numbers nearly 200 million, after three years of war can smell pure propaganda a mile off.

(4) Therefore the film must be of first-class entertainment value, with the benefit to Army prestige coming as a natural result of the story.

The film was to be called *The Way Ahead*.

Chapter Fourteen

1943–1945

*'My fast-becoming-forgotten movie face was oc-
casionally pressed into service as I appeared in
fog-filled cinemas all over Glasgow, haranguing
paying customers whom I could hardly see about
the need for more volunteers in the Women's
Army.'*

War Office records show that Niven spent a little more
than a year in 1943–4 first setting up, then developing and
finally starring in *The Way Ahead*. It was the only one of
his ninety-plus films of which he could genuinely be said
to be the creator as well as the leading actor, and it was
received at any rate in England with considerable critical
and box-office acclaim. Yet in the 500 pages of his collected
memoirs it rates rather less than four lines – whether
because of the film's subsequent commercial failure in
America or because he just thought it was not the kind of
thing he should have been doing in the middle of a war is
not clear.

Around him on *The Way Ahead* Niven gathered, de-
fended, encouraged and in some cases spotted some very
considerable talents. This was, for instance, to be the first
film featuring Peter Ustinov as a writer/actor (he appeared
fleetingly as an enraged North African café proprietor)
and the first to suggest, in its famous closing shot of the
patrol advancing uncertainly into a smokescreen, that if

any of them did make it back from this war they were going to have some tough questions to ask of those who had sent them into it.

The film has its roots in an earlier short made by Carol Reed in the previous year and also co-written by Ustinov and Ambler, whom he now brought forward with Eric Linklater to write the greater Niven project. *The New Lot* had been a forty-minute Army indoctrination short, made under the supervision of Army psychiatrists, which looked at the ways in which humour could bridge the gap between Army and civilian life. The seven recruits, used in that film as a cross-section of British humanity pressed reluctantly into service in their country's hour of need, were now to be used as the platoon of Lieutenant Perry, the character to be played by Niven himself.

Even this idea was not without its problems. David was still technically under contract to Goldwyn, and now that the film had left the safe confines of an Army training documentary to become a major feature, Goldwyn would have to be first consulted and then bought off his Niven exclusive with the promise of the American distribution rights – though in the event the British production company then bought these back for $100,000. The British were, for once, able to drive a hard transatlantic bargain, since they claimed that if Goldwyn proved obstructive they would simply tighten their military grasp on Niven and order him to star in the film regardless of any non-military pre-war Hollywood contract stipulations.

For Peter Ustinov, this was, as he recalls, a time of considerable hilarity: 'I was in the Army as a private with the Royal Sussex Regiment when I had a play produced in 1942 which got one rave review in the *Observer*, so the Army suddenly realized they had a writer in their ranks whose services on a typewriter could be had for nothing. That was when Carol Reed and Eric Ambler and I did the short film about recruits and, because it was a success, at least with the soldiers who saw it, we were told to start thinking of an extension to it.' Ambler was a major, David

a colonel and Carol Reed a captain, though when anyone
saluted him he always used to remove his military cap and
say good morning very politely. 'My status was still rather
obscure,' continues Ustinov. 'I was stationed at Wembley
Park, and although I had a sleeping-out pass I used to have
to go on parade there every morning, march to the Express
Dairies place, have my breakfast, wash up my utensils and
then take the underground right across London to the War
Office and eventually to the Ritz where Niven and Ambler
and I were given an office.'

In order to keep in daily contact with Niven it was
decided by the Army that Ustinov should be officially
considered his batman. 'David at that time was very chipper indeed, very bright: it was all violins. Those cello notes
only came in later, after the death of Primmie. She was
charming, rather like a minor member of the royal family.
She had that same kind of constantly interested expression;
you felt that she could make herself frightfully keen on
knowing how much underwear was being produced by a
certain factory during her visit and then move on to something else entirely, only taking the same sort of interest.
She had that kind of English rose-lavender look, rather
small eyes and very big cheeks.

'I think they kept us working in the Ritz because we
were judged too eccentric to contaminate the War Office
with our creative presence; we had one of the bedrooms
there, and I used to sit at the desk with the typewriter and
David would sit by the door and occasionally he'd shout,
"Cave!" so then I'd seize his belt and pretend to be
polishing while a visiting general would look in and say,
"Everything all right?" and we'd say, "Yes, Sir," and he'd
say, "Aha, very good, carry on," and then I'd go back to
the script. It wasn't an ideal way of working, but David
was a character so full of gaiety that I look back on it
all now almost with nostalgia. He once wrote on my
sleeping-out pass, "This man may go anywhere and do
anything in the course of his duties, according to his own
best judgement."

'The great thing about David is that he was ostensibly a product, and a very typical one, of the officer class that he was so vitriolically funny about. He was one of them, but what set him apart was that he could see how comic they all were and they couldn't. He needed friendship a great deal of the time, and he depended on a kind of loyalty. He was vulnerable and tender and very affectionate, and those again were not qualities which often went with the kind of chap he seemed to be. Like my own father, he was really much more intelligent and profound than he ever let on to being: he would pretend that the superficial cheeriness was all, whereas in fact it wasn't even the beginning.'

The importance of *The Way Ahead* is that it raised, in many cases for the first time, questions of class and economics in warfare. The Labour victory of 1945 might not have come as such a nasty shock to the officer class in Britain if they had looked more closely at what Ustinov and Ambler were saying in that film about the new social order that was to emerge from the war, and David's value was that he provided an acceptable front behind which many 'subversive' things could be said. As the film's only star he maintained a stiff-upper-lipped Hollywood officer dignity, but further down the castlist a group of superb character actors (Stanley Holloway, James Donald, John Laurie, Hugh Burden, Jimmy Hanley, Leo Genn) could express what Dilys Powell called 'the exasperation, boredom, disappointment, suspicion, irony and readiness to get on with the job that characterizes many recruits to the British army'.

The Way Ahead did badly in America, where it opened in 1945 to audiences already weary of war films and uninterested in the local British social issues it raised, and by early in 1946 it had still not recouped more than about two-thirds of the £250,000 it had cost to make, even with considerable below-the-line Army subsidies of men and machinery. Yet it remains, in my view, the most important film that David ever made, and it was certainly the one to which he committed more time, more energy and more of himself than any other in his near-fifty-year career in the cinema.

Then it was back to Phantom and the life of a regular soldier, one that David was coming to regard with increasing frustration and depression since he was being kept so totally deskbound. During the shooting of *The Way Ahead* the actress Dinah Sheridan, then married to Jimmy Hanley, remembers, 'Late at night, after the filming, when David would come home and tell all those young English actors marvellous stories about Flynn and Fairbanks and Hollywood before the war, you could sense that in some ways his heart was still there.'

There was yet more nostalgia for the USA in a meeting late in 1944 with the bandleader Glen Miller. Niven was introduced to him by Cecil Madden at a time when both men were organizing entertainments for the Allied Expeditionary Forces. As Madden recalls, 'Niven was there representing the British Army. Absolutely charming – wore a brand new uniform, turned up at all our meetings ahead of time, immaculately dressed. He'd chat with everybody, get his name on the books as Present, then vanish. He would say before the Chairman sat down at the planning sessions, "Well, gentlemen, I don't think I shall be able to contribute this morning, so I bid you goodbye," and off he'd go. But he did once come with me to meet Miller, when we were planning a concert for the troops. At that meeting, however, Miller was mainly interested in showing David and me plans for the "dream house" he said he was going to build somewhere in England after the war. "But you know," Miller said to us, "sometimes I have a funny kind of feeling that I'll never get to see that house." A few weeks later he was reported missing in a plane over the Channel.'

Partly as a result of the long months David had spent working on *The Way Ahead*, his own view of the war was no longer nearly as clear-cut as it had been when he first dashed home to be a part of it. The *Boy's Own* paper heroics had been replaced by a weary cynicism about futile loss of life, and the tone of his letters to the Nigel Bruce family in California had by 1944 changed considerably – this one was dated early November:

I have made a definite decision as far as what happens after the war. Once this thing is over and I have been demobilized, I hope I shall never have to mention it again. I have slogged along for five years with millions of my countrymen and I am just as happy as they are that the end is in sight. But during these years I have seen too much misery, horror and suffering ever to want to brag about being even a small part of it all. And more important, with the one blessed exception of my elder brother, who is still with the Eighth Army in Italy (and has been all the way from El Alamein) all my closest friends and most of my male relatives have been killed in this war.

So, witness this: if I ever get back to Hollywood, you will never hear me giving interviews along the lines of 'returning warrior'; and above all you will never hear me get into arguments as to who or what won the war and when. As far as I am concerned it will have been five of the best years of my life not, pray God, wasted. Though that we shall see later, when the politicians get on with their job of winning the peace. I am proud to have been fit enough in body and mind to have had those years to give for our cause. It must be awful for young and healthy men to have stayed away from all this. They will have lost something, however thick-skinned they may seem to be. They may have made themselves famous and wealthy during the last few years, but their insides will still be rotten at the end of it. We pity them. I met one the other day in London, an English actor who took out American citizenship papers in 1940 to avoid the war over here. He was now in the uniform of one of Uncle Sam's GIs. I laughed a lot. This may look rather bitter on reading it but don't worry, it won't be mentioned by me again. I just want to forget it all, except the funny bits which were legion and which I shall never forget. See you soon, I hope . . .

At last, almost five years after he had first come home to fight, he was to see some active service. Following a long period of training for the final assault on Europe, training which for David's 'A' Squadron seems to have consisted largely of eccentric attempts to survive on the middle of Dartmoor with only wild pony dung for sustenance, he was sent in 1944 on to the Normandy beaches to act as a liaison officer (newly promoted lieutenant-colonel) between the British and American Armies during the landings.

Niven's devotion to the Americans and their film community in particular now paid off in trumps. Clark Gable, James Stewart, Douglas Fairbanks Jr, John Huston, John Ford, Willie Wyler, Garson Kanin and the critic John McClain were all over in Europe on one wartime mission or another, and David's ability not only to recognize them in uniform, but also to trade on the friendships he had built up a decade earlier in California, was to prove invaluable in his new contact work with the invading Armies.

It was while David was, to his great relief and pride, in the thick of the fighting that was to lead through France to the spring 1945 crossing of the Rhine that he one day received a rare letter from home. Hoping that it might be from Primmie back in Dorney with news of how she and young David were getting along without him, he tore it open eagerly. 'Dear Sir,' it read, 'This is to inform you that we, the Music Corporation of America, have now absorbed the Leland Hayward Agency of which you were a client. We therefore shall be handling your business from now on.' As Niven later noted, the message came as a considerable relief: 'I was greatly cheered by it. The thought of death no longer chilled my heart. I was in safe hands. MCA had never lost a client, and they weren't about to start now.'

Sure enough he got home safely – 'It's all right for you,' he told his men after one attack, 'but I shall have to do all this again later with Errol Flynn' – and went back to some increasingly secret service liaison work. Years later, when he was filming for television the story of William Stephenson, the man called Intrepid whose spy network had at various wartime moments also involved Alexander Korda, Noël Coward, Leslie Howard and Ian Fleming in an all-star cast of transatlantic couriers and liaison men, he began to recall some of the more eccentric moments such as the day when he was told to report to MI5, given the address but then told to memorize and destroy it before murmuring it only to a cab driver. 'Ah yes,' said the cabbie, 'that'll be MI5 you're wanting, Mr Niven; all the stars go there in the end.'

On another occasion he was sent for by MI5 and asked if by any chance he could impersonate General Montgomery. 'I said all they had to do was cut several inches off my legs, which they didn't seem to find at all funny or helpful. Oddly enough, I did know Montgomery slightly. He used to have this huge blackboard inside his HQ with the words "Are you 100% fit? Are you 100% efficient? Do you have 100% binge?" and none of us ever dared ask him what was meant by "binge".

'Another time I was told that in view of *The Way Ahead* I had been promoted to Deputy Director of Army Kinematography, and asked if I had any other ideas for films, so I suggested a morale booster for the troops called *Great Moments in British Sport* but they didn't seem desperately keen on that. Then, thank God, they found a man to impersonate Monty so as to fool the Germans into thinking that the invasion of Europe would come not from England but instead from North Africa. He was a man called Clifton James. He later made a film about the incident and became quite a star, but even at the time it happened I managed to do him a bit of good. Being an actor myself and knowing those ropes, I made sure that for the time he was playing General Montgomery he got the full Equity acting rate for the job instead of his usual Pay Corps salary.'

Soon David himself would have to start wondering about Equity rates, but with the war now almost at an end he went back to France one more time, finding himself again with his old Phantom battalion behind the American lines. On one occasion he actually managed to capture a fleeing German general, though only momentarily: a kind of war-weariness combined with a sudden realization of the utter futility of reprisals now made him simply send the man on towards the next Allied patrol. 'Years later,' Niven once told Charles Champlin, 'I used to wonder if it had been Martin Bormann.'

David was in any case far more worried about his own chances of survival than those of captured Nazi generals. As the Ustinov–Ambler script for *The Way Ahead* had pointed out, the important thing now was not surviving the war but surviving the peace, and Niven had very little idea of how he was going to achieve that in what had become a very different actors' world.

All David knew for sure, as the VE celebrations rang out over London in May 1945, was that, 10,000 miles away, buried somewhere in the pre-war files of the Goldwyn Studios, was a long-term contract with his name at the top of it. That contract was now six years and a world war out of date, however. David's last two films, the only ones he had made since *Raffles* in 1939, had been wartime English critical successes but neither of them had made very much impact on America, and meanwhile his position as the star of *Bachelor Mother* had been invaded from two sides. On the one hand there were the men who had somehow managed to avoid the fray and improve their studio status at a time of very little masculine competition in California, while even more frighteningly on the other was a whole new generation of actors, one that had suddenly grown up in the war and which bore almost no relation whatsoever to the 1930s concept of a British officer and gentleman that had been Niven's main cinematic stock in trade.

Moreover, he no longer had only himself to consider. Now there were Primmie, young David and another baby on the way – the beginnings of a family which would somehow have to be transported back to California and paid for out there. Niven would have to start thinking like a settled husband and father instead of the carefree roving bachelor who had left Hollywood in 1939.

There was yet another change wrought by the war. David had now begun, in *The First of the Few* and *The Way Ahead*, to live and work among stage-trained actors instead of the usual Hollywood film stars, while his continuing friendships with Noël Coward and the Oliviers meant that he was constantly coming up against acting talents that he regarded, in fact rightly, as vastly superior to his own. None of that made for a sudden post-war burst of confidence in his own professional future, though he was (as he later told Charles Castle) relieved to note that even Coward had his moments of professional crisis: 'After a wartime trip to the Middle East, Noël had written this terrible book called *Middle East Diary*, and in it he described going into an American hospital which he said was full of "snivelling little boys from Brooklyn". Well, this caused an understandable stir in the United States and the *Stars and Stripes*, which was the American Forces newspaper, carried a review of the book under the headline: "Kick this bum out of the country." Now, on the day that "Kick this bum out of the country" was being read by all the troops in Paris, it so happened that Noël was to open in cabaret there at the Marigny Theatre with Maurice Chevalier, whom the American soldiers were sure was a collaborator, and with Marlene Dietrich whom they were convinced was a German spy. I was on leave from my unit and had decided to go to this opening night. I went to see Noël before the performance and I said, "You know, there are about 5,000 people out there and I am afraid they are all going to kill you. What are you going to do about it?" So Noël said, "First I shall calm them, and then I shall sing them some of my very excellent songs." "Well," I

said, "I'll stand by the exit door because . . . you know
. . . just in case . . ." So I went and stood at the back by
the exit, and Noël came on to a deathly hush which he was
not used to. A deathly hush. And then he looked at them
and said, "Ladies and Gentlemen and all you dear, dear
snivelling little boys from Brooklyn," and they fell down
and absolutely loved it.'

Back in England, David took Primmie and young David
on a brief Cornish holiday to celebrate his sudden freedom
from the Army, and then wrote to Goldwyn with the news
that he was once again available for filming. He was
understandably nervous of the reaction ('six months is too
long for an actor to be out of the business – six years is
almost certain disaster') and when it came, there was a
certain ambivalence about it. Goldwyn was, so the cable
said, delighted that Niven had survived the war safely, and
he would of course be taken back on long-term contract
at a suitably raised figure to allow for the change in world
economics since 1939. There was, however, just one little
snag: Goldwyn didn't actually have anything for him in
Hollywood just at present, so in the meantime he would
be loaned out in England to Michael Powell and Emeric
Pressburger who were just setting up a curious fantasy
called *A Matter of Life and Death*.

If David was disappointed that Goldwyn was not summoning him back instantly to Hollywood like a long-lost
son, he was astute enough not to show it. This was, after
all, not exactly one of the humiliating loan-outs to which
he had been subjected at the very start of his Goldwyn
contract a decade earlier. Powell and Pressburger were
then a much admired team of film producers with *One of
Our Aircraft is Missing, The Life and Death of Colonel
Blimp* and *I Know Where I'm Going* already to their joint
credit as writer–directors, and a film in England would
mean that there would be plenty of time to pack up the
house and prepare Primmie and young David for the
culture shock of the new world. Moreover their second
child, like their first, could now be born in England.

Chapter Fifteen

1945–1946

*'I knew. I knew as soon as I saw them come out of
the elevator. I knew by the way they walked. I knew
by the way they stood murmuring together without
looking at me as I waited across the hall.'*

A Matter of Life and Death (an all too horrendously apt
title for what was to be the immediate post-war pattern of
David's private life) was filmed through the summer and
early autumn of 1945. Niven was cast once again as an
airman, but this time a squadron leader shot down after a
bombing raid and then forced to plead for his life in
front of a heavenly tribunal and a strongly anti-British
prosecuting counsel played by Raymond Massey, his old
adversary from *The Prisoner of Zenda*.

What was to become the first production ever screened
at a Royal Command Film Performance had in fact started
out, rather like *The Way Ahead*, on instructions from the
Ministry of Information who told Powell and Pressburger
that, with the war nearly over, they should perhaps turn
their attention to the vexed question of deteriorating
Anglo-American relations. Their reply was a film which
took on a great deal more than that: it became a story of
the battle of two worlds, one existing only in the dying
airman's fevered imagination, for control of his wounded
body, and it was far and away the toughest role that Niven
had ever been asked to play. For the *News Chronicle*,

Richard Winnington took a thoroughly dim view of the ethereal proceedings here:

> The film has technical originality, and a firmer narrative grasp than anything we have seen before from Powell and Pressburger. But it is even farther away from the essential realism and true business of the British movie than their recent films. Niven plays a pilot who after a poetic conversation with a WAC (the American actress Kim Hunter) on the radio from his burning plane then throws himself parachuteless into the sea. Surviving and suffering from serious concussion, he has hallucinations. These involve a claim from the Other World that he has been allowed to live only through the error of a celestial clerk, and must quickly vacate the nice technicoloured normal world of bombers and WACs for a monochrome heaven. But he has met his WAC and loves her; so he makes an appeal, in an hallucinatory period, to the High Court of the Other World. Love, you will be astonished to find, can bridge these two worlds and win. But was it really necessary to base the prosecution on a facetious cosmic clash between Britain and America in which Britain is presented as the nation everybody hates? I suppose, for American box-office purposes, that does help.

But not a lot: in the year of *The Lost Weekend* and *Brief Encounter* and the 'new realism' throwing its light on to cinema screens from Italy to the United States (where *A Matter of Life and Death* was more romantically known as *Stairway to Heaven*, thereby making it sound like a Ginger Rogers musical and causing even more audience bewilderment), a Technicolor phantasmagoria about the afterlife was bound to seem more than a little anachronistic. A film which started by quoting Andrew Marvell and Walter Raleigh and then went on to invoke the collected works of Plato, George Washington, Benjamin Franklin, Dryden, Pope, Coleridge, Shelley, Keats, Milton and Donne was not quite the usual cinema fare. Though it reflected (as did Coward's contemporary *Blithe Spirit*) an understandable wartime fascination with what happened to your body and spirit after you were killed, it badly lacked either the humour or the coherent philosophy that might have made the theme acceptable at a time when people were still going to the movies in search of a little light relief from post-war rationing gloom, or at the very least an escape into such readily definable and even curable problems as those outlined by *The Lost Weekend* and *Brief Encounter*.

Therefore, when Powell's and Pressburger's 'stratospheric joke' was courageously chosen for the first Royal Command Performance, all hell broke loose. A leader in the *Daily Graphic* thundered:

> There will be widespread indignation at the choice for the first Royal Performance last night of a picture which might have been made specifically to appeal to Isolationist and anti-British sentiment in the United States . . . Ancient charges against British imperialism, which for the most part never had any real substance, are paraded here and no defence is offered . . . It is a pity that the film should cross the Atlantic carrying the cachet which comes from its Royal showing.

It is unlikely that many cinemagoers in, say, Minneapolis, would have rushed to see the film simply because it had been royally and formally witnessed in London by King George VI and Queen Elizabeth, and in fact American critics were generally unimpressed and unmoved by the old arguments about British imperialism, which now had no more than historic interest. *Stairway to Heaven* was not really the popular success that David might have hoped for his return to commercial film-making, though news on the domestic front more than compensated for that minor professional set-back. On 6 November 1945 *The Times* announced the birth of a second son to Primula (née Rollo) and David Niven: he was to be christened James, and was also put down for Stowe within hours of his birth.

No sooner had the boys been christened (with David Jr being given a silver cocktail shaker by his godfather Noël Coward, 'because, my Godson dear, I rather/Think you'll grow up like your father/My gift is this, and with it given/ A toast, fine health, to Master Niven') than Goldwyn decided the time had come for David's triumphal-warrior return to his studios in Hollywood. He still had no real idea what he would do with David once he got there; what he knew was that the publicity that could accrue to his studios from a rightly handled hero's return would rapidly disappear if David were left drifting around England making films for other people.

Getting back to Hollywood was not easy, with every plane and ship still jammed with returning GIs, and it soon became clear that David would have to travel alone, leaving Primmie to bring the boys on after him when their passages could be arranged more easily in the new year. So in December 1945, almost thirteen years to the day since he had first arrived in New York as the guest of Barbara Hutton, David made a carefully studio-managed return to the city. His press conference after an over-crowded and generally very rough crossing on the *Queen Mary* was a model of understated elegance, and bore no trace of the long and bitter row he had just had with tax officials in Britain. They had taken the view that, since he had returned voluntarily to the Army in 1939, and at his own expense, he had thereby confirmed his intention to remain a British resident. In this case he could be back-taxed to 1934, as one of His Majesty's citizens who had never really given any formal notice of a decision to live abroad.

A tax bill of just under £6,000, even if the Inland Revenue were prepared to give him three years in which to pay, was not exactly the reward that David had been hoping for on demobilization, and it had given him a lot to think about on the voyage over the Atlantic. Even on his new Goldwyn contract, he only stood to make the kind

of money that could pay for his new family and his new
tax bill if he stayed in constant and starry work, but
precisely where was that kind of work now to come from?
What work would there be in California for a nearly
thirty-six-year-old, still non-trained actor who had made
his name in a different pre-war world as Raffles?

It was while he was seriously pondering these problems
that he was greeted in New York by several Goldwyn
publicists and a fair number of reporters eager to find out
how he had fared 'over there'. Under the headline 'Soldier
of Good Fortune' the *New Yorker* noted that 'Mr Niven,
tall, thin and handsome in brown tweed, was dispatching
glass after glass of orange juice. "I never thought I'd live
to see the day when I preferred this stuff to whisky," he
said, "but an orange is now as hard to come by in England
as the Kohinoor diamond." We suggested that he tell us
something about the raids he'd been on. "I'd rather not,
if you don't mind," he said. "I'm not being coy but I did
very, very little. I was simply a one-pip subaltern during the
phoney war, and then I got into Phantom Reconnaissance
which was set up as a counter-invasion system . . . we
were supposed to be the beginnings of an underground
movement if the Germans landed, which, thank God, they
didn't."'

To another reporter Niven confided his problem with
American restaurants. 'Years of potatoes, bread and por-
ridge with an occasional egg thrown in have dulled the
edge of my appetite. I see all these good things here and
I want to feast myself and I start out but shortly I'm full
up. I'd like to be allowed to come back and finish the steak
later in the week. I'm still staggered by the way New York
looks compared to London – it's so clean and whole and
painted. I can't tell you what it means to me to see a city
without the scars of battle on it. I went out to the Colony
for lunch today and spent half an hour just reading the
menu. Last night when I got in somebody here offered me
a glass of milk and without thinking I said, "Are you sure
you can spare it?"'

In response to other questions, David managed to sound simultaneously depressed and reassuring about the state of England at the end of 1945: 'We all built up a terrific illusion of Paradise, of what we'd find when we got home at the end of the war. But the returning soldier is now pretty disillusioned. There's little thanks except on the first day: after that comes a lot of standing at the back of fish queues. I think an actor should act and not give off with speeches about politics or things that he can't possibly be up to top form on. But I will say that Mr Bevin is the idol of Britain at present and with good cause, though don't imagine that Winston is done for. He'll be heard from many a time again. The English love him, but they were fed up with some of his advisers and that was why there was a Labour election victory. Don't think for a minute, however, that the English are going to do anything radical. They never have, and they never will.'

Thus reassured that the Commies were not at the doors of Downing Street, New Yorkers went on to present David with the American Legion of Merit, a rare military honour, before seeing him off on the Chicago train at the start of his cross-country trek back to Goldwyn in Hollywood.

There, too, the flags were out. Niven happened to reach Los Angeles on the same day as another returning gentleman–actor who had distinguished himself in the European war, Douglas Fairbanks Jr, and at a huge celebratory lunch on the Goldwyn lot the surviving veterans of the Hollywood British, men like Nigel Bruce and Herbert Marshall, were lined up to greet the homecoming heroes. Not surprisingly David was asked to recount his war stories, and not surprisingly he stuck to his earlier promise of silence to the Bruces: 'I will, however, tell you just one thing about the war, my first story and my last. I was asked by some American friends to search out the grave of their son near Bastogne. I found it where they told me I would, but it was among 27,000 others, and I told myself that here, Niven, were 27,000 reasons why you should keep your mouth shut after the war.'

Sam Goldwyn was not about to let the afternoon drift away into such unaccustomed reticence. After allowing that he had been 'fooled' by Max Niven's telegram recalling David to the Army, Goldwyn added, 'But you know, folks, when David got up there in that plane to fly back to England he was crying. Crying. That was how much he loved Hollywood and hated to leave us.' Having thus set the right sentimental scene, he went on to offer Niven just about the best advice he was ever to come up with for the man he was now unashamedly calling his 'son': 'You know, I wish that David would now promise me one thing. I wish he would promise to write a book.' In five years' time Niven was to do just that, though only in the hope of making up the income which had been somewhat abruptly cut off from the Goldwyn Studios.

For the time being, however, all was sweetness and light. Young Doug's stepmother, Sylvia Ashley, made the Fairbanks' beach-house available to David while he was hunting for somewhere for his family to live, and in the meantime Niven himself was to be reunited with his pre-war co-star and landlady, Loretta Young, for a light marital comedy of near-divorce called *The Perfect Marriage*.

True, this was to be another loan-out (Goldwyn to Hal Wallis Productions), but David's employer made it clear that very soon there would be something big for him at the home base, and in the meantime, with the tax bill and the family's travelling expenses to pay, not to mention the cost of the Pink House he was now trying to buy for them up in Pacific Palisades, Niven was eager for any kind of work, however undistinguished. *The Perfect Marriage* certainly was that. Though Loretta Young and David were always the greatest of private friends and allies, on screen their partnership was as leaden now as it had been seven years earlier in *Eternally Yours*. 'They made a good team and looked good together,' recalled their producer Hal Wallis, but David's main interest during the shooting was naturally enough getting Primmie and his boys settled into the house they were renting in Beverly Hills, as Mrs Eddie

Albert (whose husband was the other star of that film) recalls: 'As soon as David opened the door there you knew it was already his family home, even if he had just moved into it a day or two earlier, and when Primmie came into the room the sunlight just used to hit him. He was wonderfully happy with her, and it was amazing how they put their mark on that house right away. It had to do with books and flowers, but Primmie at once managed to make it stop looking like just another rented Hollywood house: it became an English home away from home, and for those very few months that they were together there, I think David had the happiest time of his life. He had that very strong capacity just to live in the moment for the moment, which I think came probably from his experiences in the war, and the way he now introduced Primmie to us and talked softly to her, leading her gently into a world that must have seemed strange enough to this country girl who had hardly ever been out of England and certainly never to America, that was all just wonderful to see. They were a champagne couple; just being with them, and sensing their happiness in each other, made you feel better.'

David's evident and utter delight at being back in his beloved Hollywood as a family man in that spring of 1946 was tempered by the increasing realization that he had come home to a very different film industry from the one he had left in 1939. With Leslie Howard killed, Ronald Colman turning now to radio for *Halls of Ivy*, and the other First World War veterans of that British colony already well into their seventies, the Hollywood England in which David had been trained and earned his spurs during the late 1930s had gone forever, a change lamented by this leader which appeared in *The Times* during 1945:

What a loss it is never again to see that enchanted or at any rate transmogrified land, wrapped almost all the year round in a dense fog – that will indeed be a deprivation. It was a land which we had all learned to love, for not only had glimpses of it redeemed many a bad film from dullness but it had a quaint, dreamlike charm all its own. Its House of Commons (in which Sir Aubrey Smith almost always sat, often as a Duke), though generally rather smaller than our own, was infinitely more animated as well as being rather better lit; it is indeed scarcely possible to recall a session which was not rendered historic by the denouement of some major international crisis. Its policemen, barely discernible as they patrolled the fog-bound streets, resembled our own; but their helmets were slightly different, they never took their thumbs out of their belts, and the only traffic they were called on to regulate was the occasional hansom cab. Its aristocracy were, though not particularly powerful, numerous, and though stupid, generally condescending; they often had beautiful American daughters. They lived in castles of the very largest size, and were much addicted to sport, particularly foxhunting. This was normally carried on at the height of summer (fog being perhaps less prevalent at that season) and though much of the densely wooded and often semi-precipitous country appeared unfavourable to the sport as we know it, the rather small packs never had a blank day. The lower orders, a cheerful lot, wore gaiters in the country but in London, being mostly costers, dressed in a manner which befitted this calling. The army, except of course in wartime, consisted almost entirely of senior officers, most of them in the Secret Service. There were two universities, one at Oxford the other at Cambridge. Cricket and football were not much played and – possibly as a consequence – there was a great deal of crime. But it was a wonderful place, and the only general criticism which can be levelled at the inhabitants is that when, as frequently happened, they met an American they betrayed an almost complete lack of understanding of the American Way of Life.

As the GIs on war service in London discovered to their amazement, the real England had changed too. Just as the

war altered British social life by introducing vast numbers
of women to the concept of work outside the home, so it
was also to make it impossible for the Hollywood dream
of this country to go on turning up on reels of cinema
celluloid. So what should the British in California do now?
The demand for films about the empire had declined
almost as rapidly as the empire itself, and newer forms of
Hollywood movie (the big-band musical, for instance, or
the Bogart–Ladd police thriller) seemed to have precious
little need of the British. Even the great *Casablanca* had,
from the old guard, used only Claude Rains and then as
a French police chief while the newcomer Sydney
Greenstreet, great though he was in every possible sense,
was not exactly the kind of Hollywood Englishman likely
to endear himself to Rathbone or C. Aubrey Smith. The
thought of his vast, evil bulk on a cricket pitch was curiously
implausible.

The only wartime British immigrants to Hollywood had
either been women or children like Roddy McDowall and
Elizabeth Taylor, and the ones who began to appear there
after the war belonged to a more racy breed, one that the
Americans, long used to the suavities of Colman, Howard
and Niven, simply did not begin to understand. These men
were savage and rowdy, given to physical violence and
often drunk. Some were dirty in their personal habits.
Most were graduates of the J. Arthur Rank Organization.
James Mason, to quote an example, was quickly described
by one columnist as 'the rudest man in Hollywood'; his
irascibility reached a peak when he smacked William Sa-
royan across the face for chattering during a movie. One
well-known actor fought out his best love and hate scenes
in public with his ex-wives, while another lashed out at
several of those who came within hitting distance. Of yet
another famous star, Sheilah Graham once wrote that he
was the pin-up boy of the publicity girls at MGM,

'but only because they have pinned up his picture with a
knife through the heart. Robert Newton drifted through

several alcoholic years in post-war Hollywood, while Rex Harrison fought such a bitter feud with California journalists in general and Louella Parsons in particular that he left, raging, and did not return for years.

These new arrivals drove Thunderbirds instead of Bentleys. They read Los Angeles papers instead of the London *Times*, and they wore Wilshire Boulevard sports shirts instead of old school ties. They did not seem to like Hollywood very much, but they clearly liked it a damned sight better than they liked England. They were Englishmen all, but no longer willing or able to create, in Hollywood, a little corner that was forever England. The roots sunk by these post-war Britons were to be shallow, and at the first wind of trouble they blew away. When the movie industry in Hollywood began to slump, they quit. They sold or sublet their houses. Those who still had friends said goodbye and moved to Rome or Switzerland. Some quietly let their American citizenship lapse and resumed British nationality. Through the early 1950s they were, however, still in demand to man the now CinemaScopic ramparts of the Khyber Pass or to eat grapes while ordering the Christians to the lions; to play light comedians, silly asses, pirates, brave but slow-witted Army officers who infuriate the American heroes. Any parts that suggested decadence or decay. Only the English could do these things.

This, then, was the new movie order to which David had returned, and if it seemed to him both inimical and confusing after the sun-dappled cricketing days of the 1930s, at least he had Primmie to guide him over the generation gap.

One weekend in mid-May, when David had just finished *The Perfect Marriage* and was about to start costume and make-up tests for another loan-out, this one to Universal, he and Primmie took the boys up to Clark Gable's retreat near Monterey, from where Primmie wrote to her father in England that she had never been so happy in her life.

On the Sunday, they returned to their rented home to find an invitation from Tyrone Power and his wife Annabella (with whom David had made *Dinner at the Ritz* just before the war) to a party a few streets away. John McClain was in from New York and Niven was keen to see his old journalist friend; Richard Greene was also there, and Lilli Palmer and Rex Harrison and Gene Tierney. The actor Cesar Romero was among the guests too, and almost forty years later he described the occasion to me.

'I had known David from way back, the mid-1930s in New York, when I was playing on Broadway and he was a liquor salesman for Jack and Charlie at the 21 Club. Then a couple of years later I was out in California and I had a date with Sally Blane, who was Loretta Young's beautiful sister, and I went to pick her up at her house and who should come in but young Niven who was then living with them. So we kept in touch over the years, and then when we all came back from the war he and Primmie and the boys were living right near me and we used to go over to Ty Power's house in the evening and play charades. And this particular night I said, "Let's do something different, let's play sardines," which is the game like hide-and-seek where you turn all the lights out and one person goes off to hide and whoever finds them hides with them, so eventually you're all clustered into a closet or under the bed or something and one person is left wandering around the house looking for all the others. So they agreed and we put out the lights and somebody went and hid and we all started looking. And then in the dark I heard this door open and a crash and I knew exactly what had happened. Somebody had opened this door in the hall thinking it was a closet, whereas in fact it opened on to a flight of stone stairs leading down into the basement. So I felt my way over and turned on the lights, and it was Primmie. I guess nobody had told her that in America we have doors opening from the hall on to downward stairs like that: it's not something you see that often in England.

'We ran down to her, and Oleg Cassini and I picked

Above: David aged two (Alec Mellor)
Above right: Joyce, Grizel and David with their father (Miss Grizel Niven)
Below left: David with his father in 1915 (Miss Grizel Niven)
Below right: His mother with his brother Max (Miss Grizel Niven)

Above left: Alec Mellor, David and John Cockburn, 1929 (Alec Mellor)
Above right: In Trubshawe's room in barracks, Malta 1930 (Estate of Michael Trubshawe)
Below left: Recovering from a route march, Malta 1931 (Estate of Michael Trubshawe)
Below right: The 'raspberry pickers' of the HLI (Estate of Michael Trubshawe)

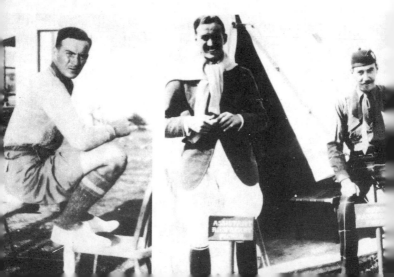

At the start of his affair with Merle Oberon (National Film Archive)
With Merle Oberon in Hollywood, 1935 (National Film Archive)

A scene from
Wuthering Heights
(National Film
Archive)

Solo stardom in
Raffles, 1939
(National Film
Archive)

David in uniform photographed by Anthony Beauchamp (Miss Grizel Niven)

Above left: Primmie and David at the Stork Club (Private Collection)
Above right: Wedding photograph of Primmie and David, 1940 (Photo Source)
Below: Primmie visiting David in Porthcawl (Estate of Michael Trubshawe)

The christening of James Niven, 1945 (Photo Source)
With Cary Grant in the *The Bishop's Wife* (Andrew Sinclair)

Above left: At Primmie's memorial service, 1946 (Photo Source)
Above right: With the boys in the Pink House (Graham Payn)
Below: The wedding of Hjordis and David, 1948 (Photo Source)

Above left: With the boys beside the pool in Hollywood
(Keystone)
Above right: Outside the boys' playhouse (Private Collection)
Below: Showing Hjordis his oil-painting technique (Private
Collection)

At the theatre with Kay Kendall, Vivien Leigh and Gladys
Cooper (BBC Hulton Picture Library)
With Hjordis, Marlene Dietrich and Noël Coward (Popperfoto)

Greeting Lauren Bacall and Humphrey Bogart (Private Collection)

In Hollywood with Douglas Fairbanks Jr (Private Collection)

Separate Tables with Deborah Kerr (Private Collection)
A scene from *Separate Tables*, 1958 (National Film Archive)

In *The Guns of Navarone* (National Film Archive)
With Charlton Heston in *55 Days at Peking* (National Film Archive)

Fred Astaire with David (Jerry Watson/Camera Press)
With Peter Ustinov on the set of *Lady L* (Rex Features)

Above left: Celebrating his paperback bestsellers (Rex Features)
Above right: Princess Grace presenting David with an award
(BBC Hulton Picture Library)
Below: With Bette Davis and Peter Ustinov in *Death on the Nile*
(National Film Archive)

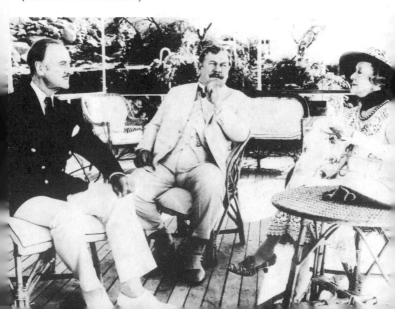

David Niven (General Foods/Maxwell House)
Hjordis and Prince Rainier after the funeral (Rex Features)

Primmie up and carried her upstairs, while David went to call a doctor and an ambulance.'

Lilli Palmer takes up the story: 'By this time she was lying on the carpet upstairs, her head in my lap. The others stood in an anxious circle around her, but there were no abrasions, nothing . . . Annabella brought a bowl of ice water for compresses. Slowly Primmie opened her eyes, tried to look around, but didn't move . . . it was a while before she spoke: "Lil, I feel so . . . strange . . . even when I had babies I never felt so . . ." She closed her eyes again. Tyrone opened the door and asked in a whisper if she had come to. We applied more compresses. She opened her eyes again and looked at me questioningly. "David's gone to get the doctor, Primmie. Just in case, you know." She nodded and tried to smile. "We'll never be invited again," she said, hardly audible, and closed her eyes again.'

'David came back with the doctor,' continues Cesar Romero, 'and the two men went with her in the ambulance to the hospital. After about an hour, David came back to the party and said, "She's going to be all right. She has a bad headache and concussion, that's all." The next day he was filming, but he kept calling the hospital from the set and after work he went straight back down there. Late that night I had a call from Ty Power, and he said, "I've got terrible news for you," and I knew immediately. And I said, "Primmie died," and he said, "Yes." They had taken her into surgery the next day, and she never came out again.

Primmie died of a fractured skull and brain lacerations on 21 May 1946 at St John's Hospital in Santa Monica. She was just twenty-eight (though David was later convinced she had died at twenty-five) and had been in California for a little less than seven weeks. They had been married almost six years, and she left David two small sons, one of them not quite seven months old. The inquest recorded a death by misadventure.

Chapter Sixteen

1946–1947

'Rita is a darling and probably the only really sweet girl out here, but neither of us want to marry and she will never become Primmie II; I doubt that anyone could.'

An entry in Noël Coward's diary for 27 June 1946 reads: 'Profoundly moving letter from David Niven. He is homesick for England and heart-broken over Prim, but is obviously behaving beautifully.' The bachelor of the late Hollywood Thirties had become the widower of the late Hollywood Forties, and the change in David was as sudden as it was irrevocable.

'Something went out of David the night that Primmie died,' says Doug Fairbanks, 'and it never returned. The champagne-fizz of his character just wasn't there any more. He had the actor Robert Coote, always known as "Coote old man", staying with him for a while to help with all the letters and the funeral arrangements and finding a nanny for the boys. Then he came to stay with us for a while and it was terrible to see the change in him. The last time we'd really been together was in the war, when we both had a London leave together and we decided to go on the town pretending to be Australian soldiers in search of a good night out around Soho. Then we'd both gone back to California and I'd bought the old Elissa Landi house up on Amalfi Drive and David was buying the Pink House next door. But they still hadn't moved in when Primmie died, and he couldn't bear to go there alone with the boys so he used to come to us and we'd all help with the letters. At night he couldn't bear to have any of the doors in our house closed, because of what had happened. It was just an awful time.'

Some days, when David could bear it, he and Lilli Palmer used to go over to the Pink House and carry on decorating the boys' bedrooms and nursery for which Primmie had picked all the colours; once there, Lilli recalled, 'David would sit on the terrace steps, looking over towards the ocean. I knew exactly what he was thinking. Dozens of times during the war Primmie had been in mortal danger and come through without a scratch. And at her first Hollywood party . . .'

Once he'd got the boys and their nanny settled in the house, David threw himself back into work, doing in the first few months all the rubbish that Goldwyn hired him out for, apparently hardly bothering to read the scripts, just knowing that if he could stay at the studios from dawn to dusk then there'd be less time to think, to remember, to wonder how he was going to bring up the boys. Gradually, his thinking cleared. The first plan would be to get Primmie's ashes back to England, back to the little church at Huish where they had been married in 1940. There would be no question of staying there, however. David had seen enough of post-war California to know that it was an easier, sunnier and richer place to bring up two small sons. Besides, his career had always been there, even though that career was now going through a very undistinguished time, and there was no sign that any film studio in England was particularly eager for his services or could even begin to match his Goldwyn money. Unlike Olivier or Harrison, Niven still had no professional life on Broadway or in the West End. He was a creature purely of celluloid, and California was still where most of that got wound on to the movie reels.

Accordingly, he put his head down and ploughed on

through *The Perfect Marriage* to *Magnificent Doll* which
reunited him with Ginger Rogers for the first time since
Bachelor Mother. Where that had been a frisky light comedy, however, this was a leaden historical romance which
cast him as Aaron Burr looking, in the opinion of the
Sunday Times, 'traitorous in a gentlemanly sort of way'.
Even the normally enthusiastic trade paper *Kinematograph
Weekly* regretted that 'popular appeal here is likely to be
jeopardized by long and platitudinous speeches on freedom and democracy'.

Away from the studios, and the desperate loneliness of
the Pink House, David now had found something else in
his life: he'd become a journalist. Years of giving interviews
to the dreaded Louella Parsons and Hedda Hopper had
made him realize that his ability to tell good Hollywood
stories could be traded for hard cash. In the summer of
1946 he therefore signed an agreement with the London
Daily Express to write a series of monthly reports from
Hollywood. These would be unique in that they would be
written entirely by him rather than some studio publicist,
and they would take the form of 'open letters' to his
old English friend Trubshawe. There was, of course, an
immediate outcry from the Los Angeles branch of the
Foreign Press Association, a group of men well able to
recognize whole loaves of bread now being taken out of
their mouths by an English actor. But these columns were
in fact the start of what was to be a second and, in the
end, rather more successful career for David as a chronicler
of Hollywood social and professional life; in them undoubtedly lie the hesitant beginnings of *The Moon's A
Balloon* and *Bring on the Empty Horses*, which is why one
of the three columns he wrote in this 'Dear Trubshawe'
series is quoted here. It is dated 17 September 1946, just
four months after Primmie's fall:

When you ask me to write giving you all the news, views
and wisdom of Hollywood, I don't think you realize
exactly what you are doing to me. To start with, every

studio, a large percentage of the directors and most of the stars here employ highly-paid lawyers to lurk behind them twenty-four hours a day, thumbing expectantly through the libel laws of the United States and just waiting for somebody like me to open his mouth too wide. Much as I would enjoy dipping my fingers into the paper bag of my local knowledge and distributing the crumbs of my information to the pigeons who are your inquisitive friends, I shall have to be very, very careful how I set about this. I have no wish to end my screen career making background shots for other people's prison pictures. I have always made it a golden rule never to knock other actors, for the obvious reason that I am not nearly a good enough one myself to withstand the recoil. Conversely, I am ashamed to admit that words of praise, where other actors are concerned, usually flow from me like glue. I am, therefore, somewhat surprised to find myself gibbering and twittering with excitement over the performances of Ingrid Bergman and Cary Grant in *Notorious*. This Hitchcock picture is really good, and the love scenes are the best, the most beautifully played and the best-directed that I have ever seen on the screen.

Of the other artists about whom you seemed in your letter to be particularly anxious to hear news, Rex Harrison has scored a great personal success in *Anna and the King of Siam*. Beautiful Vivien Leigh is, of course, one of the top box-office attractions over here, so *Caesar and Cleopatra* is doing tremendous business. *Henry V* is a smash hit. So, between them, Mr and Mrs Olivier must be putting up a world's record for family popularity. The recipe for this is as follows: take Mr Olivier's fantastic success with the Old Vic company in New York, mix with that the beauty and bravery of his *Henry*, showing all over the United States, now add Mrs Olivier's triumph every time she appears on the American screen, stir slowly and season with their own personal charm and power to make everybody who comes into contact with them love them. Pour liberally, never allowing to cool, and you have the perfect mixture for promoting admiration in American hearts for British art and artists.

Ann Todd arrived last week and I happened to be in New York at the time. We had supper together the first night she was there, and she was as full of enthusiasm as a child. She had spent the day window shopping, stepping inside, being appalled at the prices, and stepping outside again. Then in the evening she and Nigel Tangye, her husband, went to see the great Broadway musical hit *Carousel*. After that Nigel delivered her to a grateful Niven and went off to attend to some business meetings on her behalf. She ordered a fruit salad and got it – American style. That means the same as an ordinary salad, complete with lettuce and tomatoes and so forth, but sitting on top is some fruit. It shook her considerably, but she was undaunted and soon climbed outside it. She is going to make a picture for Hitchcock with Gregory Peck – as nice a set-up as an actress could want, and one she richly deserves after *Seventh Veil*.

Robert Donat is a great favourite over here, but all complain that they don't see enough of his pictures. The same complaint could safely be made in England. Margaret Lockwood arrived here, and at the request of local cameramen struck the traditional pose of all visiting actresses – that of balancing precariously on the ship's rail displaying shapely legs and waving to some object far above the ship. I often wonder what it is they all wave at; I suppose it's somebody in a skyscraper nearby, or perhaps just a passing seagull. She is going to make a picture at Universal. That's a very pleasant place to work, and incidentally the whole studio fell in love with Patricia Roc when she was making a picture there a short time ago.

Danny Kaye is probably the most sensational comedian to appear over here for the last ten years. Before the war he was entertaining at the Dorchester in London

where he tells me ruefully that he didn't think he went
down very well. Perhaps he wasn't so good then – he's
terrific now. You will be glad to know that British
pictures are enjoying a tremendous upswing in popularity over here. Wherever I go – and I don't mean only
in Hollywood but all over this enormous country – I
always hear the same thing: 'How wonderful British
pictures are these days.' Nobody in the world is more
violently anxious than I am that British pictures should
soar up to the heights of world popularity and stay there,
but on the other hand the fact remains that – with regard
to personnel at any rate – the British film industry was
pampered during the war years, whereas the Hollywood
industry was hampered. This probably sounds peculiar
to you, and I can almost hear you ordering another
furious half-pint to steady yourself, but it happens to be
true. You see there were no 'reserved occupations' in the
American film industry. Actors, producers, directors,
cameramen and technicians were just called up for service and that was that. In England, however, producers,
directors, cameramen and key technicians were all 'reserved' and so of course were actors – provided they
remained actively employed at their job of acting. Some
of the finest Hollywood directors were away for years in
the army, and the local scene will soon be brightened
considerably when the productions of Frank Capra,
William Wyler, John Ford, George Stevens, John
Huston and Garson Kanin appear once more on the
screen. Among the actors, old favourites (but by no
means old men) have now been demobilized and have
finished top-class productions so you will soon again be
seeing Jimmy Stewart, Robert Taylor, Tyrone Power,
Henry Fonda, Melvyn Douglas and many others. All of
this adds up to a healthy competition, and without that
we would all be sunk. Just imagine if Mr Austin and Mr
Morris and Mr Rolls and Mr Royce had not looked out
of the window one day and said, 'We can all do as well
as Mr Ford.' Goodbye for now. I will write again soon.

Quite apart from establishing his career as a post-war journalist, and therefore paving the way to *The Moon's A Balloon*, this column seems to me remarkable for a number of Niven features: discreet logrolling for friends like the Oliviers and indeed Ann Todd (with never a mention of their pre-war alliance), coupled with a sharp final warning that the honeymoon period of British movies in America was coming to an end as the native product sharpened up again in 1946. There is no mention of the fact that both Ann Todd and Vivien Leigh were already in marital trouble, and above all not a word – in a gossip column – about the fact that its author was currently at the heart of two of Hollywood's then-favourite topics of cocktail party conversation: Primmie's tragic death and the start of his own short affair with Rita Hayworth a few months later. Clearly David was going to be a discreet and flattering columnist, but there was a limit to the length of time even he could stay on that particular tightrope without falling into any of the legal or social hazards he had outlined in his first few lines. His second column was a lengthy and not entirely gripping account of a dinner party given by Douglas Fairbanks, and by the time of the third column in November the *Express* was already billing it as 'the last of the series'. This one was again full of local gossip about the upcoming Oscars and Rex Harrison's future film plans, though Niven also managed to break the story of Fred Astaire's 'retirement' to open a chain of dancing schools, and the column ended with a paragraph perfectly in keeping with the patriotism of both David and Lord Beaverbrook. Under the heading 'Forever England', Niven wrote:

Cat's Eyes Cunningham suddenly appeared at my Holly-wood home last Sunday. It was good to see him again and to hear his inspiring views on the future of jet propulsion and Britain's part in its development. He has now become chief test pilot for de Havillands, taking over the job from Geoffrey de Havilland who was killed

so tragically on his last test flight. Cat's Eyes is surely
one of our greatest war heroes, and one we will never
forget.

But by now David had realized that he could not go on
being simultaneously an actor and a columnist without
getting into a lot of trouble, as well as a certain amount of
confusion – in one of these columns he had even announced
that Rex Harrison was to play the Scarlet Pimpernel and
added what superb casting this would be, unaware that
two years later he'd have to take on the appalling script
himself after Rex had declined it. Moreover Trubshawe,
now himself an actor in London, was wearying of being
used by Niven as a kind of transatlantic stooge, and even
David was noticing a certain wariness among his Californian friends as they passed on to him the gossip that he
had always found one of the most enjoyable aspects of the
studio life. Clearly he would have to stop trying to work
both sides of the street, and by Christmas the *Daily Express*
was looking for a new Hollywood columnist, much to the
satisfaction of the Los Angeles branch of the Foreign Press
Association.

In later years several actors went into print either denying or adjusting stories that David told about them (Fred
Astaire once spent several pages of an autobiography
correcting a laborious and fairly pointless Niven anecdote
about the painting of Los Angeles mail-boxes), and even
now it was obvious that he would have to tread more
warily if he were to keep his own private life out of the
ever-watchful gaze of Hedda and Louella, let alone his
new-found colleagues among the London press in Hollywood. For, as he was to tell Tom Hutchinson thirty years
later, 'Primmie's death affected me sexually. I was in-
satiable. No woman was safe. It was no disrespect or lack
of love for Primmie – it's just that I was trying to get
something out of my system that was better out than in. I
believe I was very ill in a sexual kind of way.'

He was quick to reassure nervous friends in England

that the Hayworth affair would pass very quickly, as indeed it did, and without ever hitting the headlines despite the fact that both travelled to Europe on film-promotion trips early in 1947 and spent some time together in the South of France. But there was still no real or prolonged escape from the grief of Primmie's death, nor from the knowledge that his own career was now deeply in trouble. Goldwyn had been sympathetic, even fatherly, about his bereavement, but still seemed to have nothing of his own to offer, and instead hired out David yet again, this time to MGM where he was to play the doctor who falls in love with dying concert pianist Barbara Stanwyck in a sanitarium weepie by Erich Maria Remarque called *The Other Love*.

By the time that maudlin mediocrity was in the can it was 1947 and David had sufficiently recovered to start taking stock of his life. With two small boys to feed, clothe and educate (eventually, he still hoped, at Stowe) he was in no position to go into total conflict with Goldwyn. On the other hand it was clear that his employer had no particular use for him except as a profitable hiring vehicle, and every time he got hired out to another studio more than half his contract fee found its way back to Sam Goldwyn, causing David increasing, and understandable, fury and frustration. Moreover, these loan-outs, terrible as they had all proved to be, were fast eroding Niven's professional status. It was a vicious circle, as Goldwyn's biographer Scott Berg told me.

'Niven had come back from the war a hero, and you can be sure that Goldwyn won for his studio every possible line of publicity out of that; but after it began to fade away he found he was left with this ageing Raffles, not an especially accomplished or versatile actor, and not the faintest idea of how to use him. Goldwyn had groomed Niven for a pre-war kind of Colman stardom that just didn't exist any more, and you have to remember that Sam's one big hit around this time was *The Best Years of Our Lives*, his biggest success and the winner of more Oscars than any film had ever won. And that introduced an altogether different kind of screen realism which had nothing at all to do with Niven; the kind of actors that Goldwyn was taking on now were people like Farley Granger, a whole different generation. Sam always regarded David as his wayward son, and he was very concerned that he should get through the war safely. But in the early contract days he would only ever get asked up to the Goldwyn house if he was escorting Merle Oberon there, and then in the late Forties, when Mrs Goldwyn realized that David wasn't doing Sam that much good, he just got kind of dropped from their social circuit.'

Before that, however, Goldwyn did have one last try at establishing Niven as a post-war star. His next production was to be a screen adaptation of Robert Nathan's novel *The Bishop's Wife*, and though the stars were to be Cary Grant and Loretta Young, Niven was offered third billing as the bishop himself whose elaborate plans for a new cathedral threaten to ruin his marriage until all is made well by the arrival of Cary Grant as an angel from heaven. This was at best a whimsical idea for a film, and not much helped by Goldwyn's decision after two weeks of shooting to close down the picture altogether at a cost of nearly $1 million and then re-start it with a new director. Gladys Cooper, who was also somewhere down that castlist, could, when asked later, recall almost nothing about the filming except 'a very faint feeling of tension between David and Cary on the set whenever the subject of the war came up, which was not often'.

Even long before the war which Niven and not Grant had gone home to fight, it was Cary who was always the bigger star, and nothing was now going to change that. Indeed, the original plan had been for Grant to play the bishop and Niven the rather flashier role of the good angel, at least until Grant read the script and announced that the casting would in fact be somewhat altered in return for his agreement to take part. With two directors the film began in more than a little confusion; when William Seiter was replaced at considerable expense of money and time by

Henry Koster, Goldwyn told the latter that he was going to have the inestimable pleasure of working with the great Laurette Taylor.

'Wonderful,' said Koster, 'but, er, there is just one little problem. Miss Taylor has been dead for several months.'

'Nonsense!' said Goldwyn, pointing proudly out of his window to the parking lot where Loretta Young was just getting into her car, 'I was talking to her only a few moments ago.'

With that initial confusion sorted out, filming went ahead rather more easily under Koster, though in the very last stages of editing Goldwyn still had to call in Billy Wilder and Charles Brackett, a couple of the most versatile script-doctors in town, to write three new sequences which would pull the whole thing together into coherent screen shape. So successful were they that the film was then chosen for the second-ever British Royal Command Performance which, in the wake of the previous year's *A Matter of Life and Death*, must have left our royal family (not exactly avid cinema-goers at the time) with the distinct impression that all films starred David Niven.

For Goldwyn, at least, the eventual success of *The Bishop's Wife* (which many critics in England found a welcome Protestant counterblast to the Irish Catholic whimsy of the Bing Crosby musicals of that same period) repaid all the trouble he'd had in making it. He even managed to recoup a little of the $1 million he'd lost on the reshooting, because when it came time to pay Wilder and his partner for their last-minute salvage job, the two writers decided to be magnanimous.

'Sam,' said Wilder, 'about that $25,000 you were going to pay us for those three scenes. We've decided we don't need the money.'

'Funny,' replied Sam, 'I had just come to the same conclusion myself.'

Talking in Hollywood almost forty years later to Cary Grant, I wondered what he remembered of Niven at the time of their only film together. He told me: 'Well, of course I'd known him since way back in the Thirties when he was first out here romancing Merle Oberon and rather trying to model himself on Ronnie Colman. I was about six years older than David, and I'd already been out here for a couple of years when he first arrived, but I don't think we ever thought of ourselves (or were thought of) as rivals because we were such different types on the screen. My great heroes were the light comedians of the 1920s British stage, men like Ronald Squire and A. E. Matthews, whereas I think David was far more impressed by all the movie people like Flynn. But we got on very well. We used to go riding up in the hills and keep bottles of beer hidden along the route. Even then, though, he'd never talk much about himself or his background. He seemed to be terrified of boring or depressing you, felt he always had to be an entertainer. He was more educated, I think more intelligent, than I was but you felt there was always something being held back. I admired him very much for going back and fighting in the war: that was a wonderful thing to have done.

'When he came back he seemed in some ways to have changed, but I think that may have been because of that terrible accident to Primmie. He was still distraught about that when we were making *The Bishop's Wife*, and yet there was also still that urge to entertain, to tell stories, not always true stories maybe but marvellous rearrangements of the truth. He was a funny man and a brave man and a good man, and there were never too many of those around here.'

David's charming and adequate, if somewhat dull, performance in the unexciting role of the bishop did nothing to restore him to his pre-war stardom, and therefore nothing to get him off Goldwyn's transfer list. Indeed the next loan-out planned for him by Goldwyn was to be a great deal further and longer than usual. Alexander Korda, still impressed by David's track record in the wartime English films, had asked for him to be Bonnie Prince Charlie in a major London Films costume epic of the kind that Korda would occasionally make in his increasingly desperate attempts to conquer the American market as he had done once before – all of fifteen years previously – with Laughton's *The Private Life of Henry VIII*.

Goldwyn was once again a little confused by the project, which he constantly referred to in conversation as 'Charlie Bonnie', apparently under the mistaken impression that it was to be the story of a lovable Scots terrier. What he did know, as usual, was the accounting: Korda was willing to pay $150,000 for what was supposed to be a ten-week use of Niven, and of that Sam could keep rather more than two-thirds under the terms of David's studio contract.

This discovery, coupled with the realization that he had no desire to leave two small motherless boys in the middle of California for three months, and perhaps also the discovery that everything about this picture, not least the script, looked nothing less than catastrophic, finally caused David to rebel. He would not, he told Goldwyn, be going to London, nor would he be getting into any kind of kilt. In that case, said Sam, he would go on immediate suspension, which meant no weekly salary and no chance of working anywhere else. Right, said David, suspension it would be. He had conveniently forgotten that Goldwyn knew as well as everyone else around Beverly Hills that Niven could not possibly go on paying his hefty mortgage on the Pink House unless there was money coming in. The £40,000 that Primmie had left him could not last forever: the siege would be a short one.

Chapter Seventeen

1947–1949

'Tomorrow, Trubshawe, I am going to get married again, thereby quite possibly making the greatest mistake of my life.'

In deep tax and mortgage troubles, desperately missing Primmie now that the shock of her death had worn off and he was left with a lot of empty rooms, and on an unpaid suspension from the Goldwyn Studios (where one publicist had already announced that he was 'difficult to work with'), David spent much of the summer of 1947 in retreat, living with the boys and their English nanny up at the Pink House, writing letters home to Trubshawe and Primmie's family filled with nostalgia for the wartime England where he had been so much happier than he was now.

Then, after a few weeks, came the inevitable cave-in. He went to see a somewhat smug Goldwyn and told him that he would, after all, be leaving for London and *Bonnie Prince Charlie*, taking the boys with him and then sending them up north to stay with their delighted Rollo grandfather.

It would be a brave critic who could unhesitatingly pick the very worst of David's ninety-plus movies, because there were now to be so many of them; but certainly *Bonnie Prince Charlie* always came close to the top of his own personal hit-list as 'one of those huge florid extravaganzas that reek of disaster from the start'.

That start had not, in fact, been Korda's idea at all. One

of his studio producers Ted Black had initiated it and then died, though possibly not as a direct consequence. By then too much money had been spent for a cancellation, so Leslie Arliss was brought in to direct and Clemence Dane to write the usual story of the Young Pretender and Flora Macdonald getting him away to Skye after the defeat at Culloden. By the time David arrived on the scene two other directors (Korda himself and Robert Stevenson) were behind the camera, though during the seemingly endless shoot in Scotland they too disappeared to be replaced by the playwright Anthony Kimmins, whose name alone appeared on the final credits.

Years later, Peter Ustinov was to note that when his children were asked what their father did for a living they invariably replied '*Spartacus*', such was the length of time involved in that shooting; but *Bonnie Prince Charlie* was to run it a close second. Indeed, Jack Hawkins, playing the prince's leading general in the film, reckoned that for sheer length of location time it was beaten only by the next Niven–Hawkins costume fiasco, *Elusive Pimpernel*, which started with the birth of one Hawkins son and finished with that of a second.

The kilt calamity did in fact do a bit of good for Hawkins, and for Margaret Leighton who as Flora Macdonald was reckoned to give the only other bearable performance in the picture. It also established a firm friendship between Niven and Hawkins, as his widow Doreen recalls: 'In some ways they were very different, Jack with his Old Vic background and David the Hollywood star, but they got on quite wonderfully from the very first day they met on the set. I think they were united by the sheer awfulness of the film they were making. On that first morning David was kitted out in his blond wig and a kilt with a great tartan sash and a sporran and a claymore and a dirk and his three-cornered hat and he said, "Jack, just tell me one thing, do I look like an utter prick?" and Jack thought about that for a moment and then said, "Yes," and they were friends ever afterwards.'

When the film was finally released to an expectant world almost a year later, critics could hardly contain their glee. Under the heading 'Scots Wahoo', John McCarten in the *New Yorker* wrote of 'a sort of Scottish Western in which Niven as Prince Charlie rallies the hardy Highlanders to his standard in a voice barely large enough to summon a waiter', while others wrote in amazement that £1 million had apparently been wasted on 'two and a half hours of erratic Technicolor'. One of David's best reviews was headed 'Boyish, Clean and Vapid', while the *Manchester Guardian* wondered how it had been possible 'to turn to such dullness the most poignant and romantic episode in the last 250 years of British history'; the *Star* added that David's performance was 'no more animated than the mist-clad Highland peaks', and the *Graphic* concluded, 'Niven seems about as much at home among the Highlanders as a goldfish in a haggis.'

In one horrendous career mistake, one he had easily foreseen but over which he had no real control once Goldwyn had agreed to hire him out to Korda, David had undone all the good of his three wartime British movies. *Bonnie Prince Charlie* was a catastrophic professional homecoming and one from which his career would not recover for at least another five years.

As Judy Campbell, who was with him in that film playing Clementine Walkinshaw, now recalls: 'I really don't think it was David's fault. The original script for the film would have run about eight hours, and Korda's people were forever trying to brighten it up. There was a running battle between the historians who'd been brought in as advisers and the producers who kept demanding more ringlets and cleavage because Margaret Lockwood and *The Wicked Lady* had just been such a success. We kept trying to tell them that was the nineteenth century and we were the eighteenth and people looked and dressed quite differently then, but I don't think they ever really understood. David was in a state of severe depression, and not terribly helpful. It was one thing to have dashed home to fight for your country, quite another to have come home again a few years later to be a disaster in a terrible costume piece and use up all that earlier goodwill. He didn't like period films, hated costumes and had, so he told me, always been unhappy even in *Wuthering Heights*; so you can imagine how he felt about *Bonnie Prince Charlie*. He just couldn't wait for it to finish, which of course it never did. They kept rewriting and reshooting and one actor [Will Fyffe] even died during the film. It was the curse of the Stuarts, another of those desperately unlucky Scots scripts like *Macbeth*.'

Bonnie Prince Charlie did, however, lead David to a couple of remarkable close encounters. The first of these occurred when, during one of the many battle scenes which Korda used as a device to keep his writers a couple of days ahead of his actors, Niven managed to ram his sword about 4 inches into the leg of an extra. There was, understandably, a considerable pause before the man spoke. 'I wonder,' he said politely, 'if you could just slide it out as gently as possible? That's a wooden leg and I don't want a lot of splinters.'

David's other encounter on the set of *Bonnie Prince Charlie* was considerably more romantic, as Doreen Hawkins explains: 'He and Jack came on to the set one afternoon and there was a girl sitting in David's chair. David was not in the best of tempers and about to have her thrown out when Jack went over and had a look at her and then came back and said, "If I were you, old boy, I think I'd want to meet her." That was Hjordis.'

Hjordis Paulina Tersmeden was a twenty-seven-year-old Stockholm model who had just been divorced from her first husband (a Swedish businessman) and was visiting friends in England, one of whom happened to know somebody in the film. 'At that time,' Hjordis told me almost forty years later, 'I had not seen a film of David's because I've always preferred reading to going to movies. But I had seen pictures of him, so when this man in a long blond wig arrived I said, "Oh, I thought you were dark," and that was our first conversation. Then a couple of nights later David ran *A Matter of Life and Death* for me and I suddenly realized what a good actor he was. After that it was all very quick. We began going out every night, and after about ten days we decided to get married. I called up my ex-husband, because we were still good friends, and I said, "I'm getting married again," and he hung up the phone, so I had to call him back because I didn't want him just to read about it in the papers.'

For the second time in less than ten years, David decided on an almost instant marriage. With *Bonnie Prince Charlie* at last in the can, Goldwyn had a picture waiting for him in Hollywood and Niven was eager to get his new wife and the boys back home to the Pink House to start the family life that now seemed to be a real possibility after all.

Trubshawe was duly summoned from the country by telegram to repeat his Best Man performance: 'Only this time I fear I didn't do at all well. There was a party the night before the wedding, given by Audrey Pleydell-Bouverie who was a society friend of David's. That was the first time I was introduced to Hjordis, and for some reason I took it into my head to tell her that if she thought by marrying David she'd have a passport to a Hollywood career, then she was in for a bitter disappointment. Not surprisingly, I suppose, she didn't much care for that, and we didn't speak for fifteen years. But David was now going through an agony of indecision. I was with him late that night when he suddenly decided it had all been too fast and that he was making the most terrible mistake and that it just wasn't going to work out for him, for Hjordis, for the boys, for anyone. It was all going to be a disaster. So I told him that it still wasn't too late, the wedding could still be called off; but he said no, he'd started and he'd go through with it and just see what happened afterwards. As you can imagine, it wasn't the easiest of weddings.'

In all fairness, it was not easy for Hjordis either. Far from acquiring a 'passport to Hollywood', here was a young and childless Swedish model, who had been for a while one of the top cover-girls of her country and was accustomed by her first marriage to a life of considerable Stockholm luxury, suddenly taking on an English actor in career and financial troubles with two small sons she had not yet even met. It is in those circumstances debatable whether becoming Mrs David Niven could have been considered a step up any kind of social, professional or economic ladder. It was not as though she then even spoke very good English or had any great desire to become a stepmother, as she recalls: 'David and I used to joke that he'd only told me about the children on our way to catch the boat back to America, when he said there were a couple of little things he had to pick up on the way; but they had a marvellous nanny and so at first I really didn't see very much of them; I was so besotted by David that I just wanted to be with him. But when we got to Hollywood I found I just didn't understand the mentality out there. At parties I was always introduced as "Mrs David Niven", whereas in Sweden I had always been known by my own name, and then you'd see a face across a crowded room that you thought you knew because you'd seen a photograph somewhere, and you'd go over and say hello and they'd look at you as if you were a beetle that had just crawled out from under their shoe.

'Then, quite soon after we arrived there, *Life* Magazine was doing a feature on "The 10 Most Beautiful Women in Hollywood" and they chose me as one of them; I didn't realize that was supposed to be such a big honour, because I'd often been on the covers of magazines at home in Sweden, but I remember then going to a party at which some actor came up to me and said, "And what did you have to do to get on the cover of *Life*?" It was all rather like that. There were some things about California that I immediately loved – the shopping, the warmth, the freedom to go around barefoot in bathing suits. All that seemed to me marvellous coming from such a cold climate as Sweden. But the social life was something else altogether, and not easy to handle at first.'

If Hjordis was finding Hollywood difficult, David was

by now finding it just about impossible. His old affection
for the Goldwyn who had welcomed him back from the
war like a long-lost son had turned very bitter indeed as a
result of *Bonnie Prince Charlie*. Not only was it a terrible
film, but by insisting that he had to make it, Goldwyn had
shot David straight back into the arms of the British tax
man. Part of the Inland Revenue's post-war agreement
with David about back taxes had been based on the understanding that he was to stay out of England for at least
three years, thereby acquiring non-resident status. *Bonnie
Prince Charlie* had come less than three years after *A
Matter of Life and Death*, so that arrangement had col-
lapsed, leaving Niven with a still larger English tax bill.

In California he was also desperately over-extended on
the mortgage for the Pink House, and painfully aware that
many of his contemporaries and even some of the post-war
newcomers to the studios had managed to cut themselves
free of long-term contracts and were working for vastly
better money on a freelance basis. The late 1940s were not
a good time for Hollywood; the film community there
was torn apart by the first stirrings of the UnAmerican
Activities Committee and, while David was (as a foreigner
bleakly uninterested in politics) able to stay well clear of
that one, he could hardly fail to take account of another
and personally much more damaging change in the climate.
With the one overseas exception of Olivier's *Hamlet*, the
Oscar films of 1948 (the year that David got back to
Hollywood after his 14 January marriage to Hjordis in
London) were *Johnny Belinda*, *The Treasure of Sierra
Madre*, *Key Largo* and *The Snake Pit*: all-American
dramas in which Niven would have been totally uncastable
even had he not been camping around the Highlands in a
blond wig as Bonnie Prince Charlie. The days of the
cricketing English and the Victorian costume caper were
virtually over, and it looked very much as though David's
career was about to end with them. He was not quite
thirty-eight years old.

After a series of further rows and short suspensions from

salary for refusing more loan-outs to other studios, David did get the offer of one more picture at his home base: for it, however, he would have to age thirty years and accept co-star billing not only with Teresa Wright and Evelyn Keyes but also with Goldwyn's new golden boy, Farley Granger. The film was *Enchantment*, and David was to play an old general looking back towards his romantic youth. The role did not exactly fill him with confidence as his old flame Evelyn Keyes recalls: 'David was in all this old make-up, grey hair, grey moustache, wrinkled and a little bit stooped. Farley Granger played my paramour, and one day we were standing around between takes giggling about something when David, who was standing near by, spoke up rather querulously: "You two are ignoring me as if I really were old and couldn't understand your youthful chatter." It was true. I couldn't remember the other David at all. I think he was going through a difficult career time, but he never let that show at all. He was still doing all the jokes and imitations that I'd remembered from way back.'

Farley Granger also recalls a happy time on that film, with no sense that David felt his place had been overtaken at the studio by the younger man, and no realization either that Niven and Goldwyn were at a parting of the ways: 'Though I suppose if I had thought about it, I'd just have thought how lucky David was to be getting out of the kind of studio contract we had all begun to hate for its exclusivity. It would have been like somebody getting out of school early for the day: you envy them rather than pity them.'

That is if they had had somewhere else to go. David did not, but he also knew that he could not stay where he was. If all Goldwyn had to offer was more loan-outs or bumbling generals, clearly he had better celebrate the arrival of his forties by leaving the studio where had spent virtually all of his professional life. Not that it would be easy: Goldwyn still had an iron-clad contract and the role in *Enchantment*, though not exactly glamorous or heroic or even very starry, hardly added up to an insult. Indeed in the view of his co-star, Teresa Wright, it paved the way for the one really great performance he ever gave.

'I believe *Enchantment* was where David first became a character actor,' she says. 'It was the first time he hadn't been able to trade on that youthful charm of his, and in that sense I think it led on to *Separate Tables* ten years later. A lot of people were surprised by the performance he gave in *Enchantment*, including maybe himself. In some ways, you know, he was very self-conscious, all those little gestures like tugging at his ear as he began a story were really to cover up a tremendous shyness, and when he could escape into a whole different generation I think he found a sort of freedom as an actor that he never had when he was playing his own age.'

Something else of tremendous career importance to David happened on *Enchantment*, as Teresa Wright also recalls: 'It was the time when cinemas were forever doing promotions to try to win audiences back from the terrible new threat of television, and David and I, both being Goldwyn contract players still, were sent out across the country with the first release of *Enchantment* to make what they used to call "personal appearances" just before the film started. I used to dread the whole thing, and fervently wished that I could sing and dance or something like that; but David found, when he got up on the stage, that he could just tell these marvellous stories, and he'd move them round a bit so that they referred to whatever town we happened to be in. He'd always done the stories privately, of course, at Hollywood parties, but now for the first time he was doing them in front of paying customers and finding that they worked and that he really was a professional storyteller. I think that was the beginning of a whole new career for him, and one that led straight to the books he then wrote.'

Not that David himself ever cared much for the film, as he later told Hedda Hopper: 'I'd never played a really old man before, and after watching a few I decided that they did everything just a bit slower than I did. So I had about 32lb of lead distributed about my person: my sleeves were so weighted down that I could hardly get a glass up to my lips. Then Sam Goldwyn said I had to bleach my hair to make it look silver on the screen: when I got home that night the dog bit me and the children burst into tears, but what was really embarrassing was that, when it finally washed out, it left my hair looking bright mauve. Then I went for a holiday and the sun turned it magenta, and for about two years I had hair all the colours of the rainbow, mainly in stripes. Then the film finally came out and one critic wrote, "Niven's performance was ruined by a totally appalling wig." I think that was when I really began to lose patience with Goldwyn.'

John Patrick, the screenwriter on *Enchantment*, thought it 'the most lugubrious picture ever spawned by a studio or me', but even he was amused by Niven's apparently endless fund of old Hollywood anecdotes. These did not constitute a living, however, and while David was still considering ways of breaking what now seemed a professionally suicidal Goldwyn contract he found himself being hired out yet again, this time to Warner's for a romantic comedy with Jane Wyman called *A Kiss in the Dark*. Mercifully, all he could later recall about the film was having to play a concert pianist with a real musician's hands stuck through the sleeves of his tail coat. By this time he was not the only one getting more than a little nervous about his future. 'With each of David Niven's current Hollywood pictures,' complained the *News of the World*, 'the same question occurs: what on earth are they doing with that fellow's career?' There was much worse to come. No sooner had Niven clambered off the piano stool and out of the arms of the first Mrs Ronald Reagan, than he was once again sent for by Samuel Goldwyn. It was the middle of 1948. He and Hjordis had settled into the Pink House, the boys were starting nursery school, and David had just about managed to stop waking up in a cold sweat at the memory of *Bonnie Prince Charlie*. There was, therefore, something of a pause when he heard from Goldwyn the news of his next loan-out assignment. It was to be a costume picture. For Alexander Korda. In England.

Yet again he went on suspension for rejecting the script, and yet again he came off it when he realized he couldn't afford to keep his family in the Pink House without his Goldwyn salary. He would do *The Elusive Pimpernel*, the film for which he had so confidently and even optimistically announced Rex Harrison in his *Express* column a couple of years earlier. Now it was to be David who shouldered yet another costumed calamity, 'making his first embarrassed entrance looking,' in the opinion of *The Times*, 'less like Sir Percy Blakeney than the dame in some nightmare pantomime'.

The Elusive Pimpernel had, in fact, started out as a Goldwyn–Korda co-production, and their first idea had been to make it as a musical. Thirty thousand pounds was duly spent finding out that this wouldn't work, but Korda was still convinced, even after the Scots fiasco, that costume pictures were his route back into the American market. He also, of course, had made the original *Scarlet Pimpernel* with Leslie Howard and Merle Oberon back in 1934, and therefore had a certain lingering affection for the property, especially as most of the rights in it were now his. He therefore acquired the services of Michael Powell and Emeric Pressburger who had worked so well with David in *A Matter of Life and Death* but were now a lot less optimistic: 'It never went right,' recalled Powell, 'because there were relics of the musical idea still in it; the result was a terrible mess and if you make a film between Goldwyn and Korda, you get ground to powder.'

This was discovered by David at an early stage. *The Elusive Pimpernel* took nearly six months to shoot, at a total cost of £450,000. Then there were the retakes, which cost another £27,000.

'How much?' asked a reporter at one Korda press conference.

'Two per cent of the total cost of the picture,' replied Korda.

'But how much was that?' pressed the newspaper man.

'One hundred percent,' responded Korda solemnly.

The film ended in a predictable lawsuit between Goldwyn and Korda and a lot more catastrophic reviews for David. It did, however, reunite him with Margaret Leighton and Jack Hawkins from *Bonnie Prince Charlie*, who again got all the notices. Quite far down the castlist was also to be found a young Patrick MacNee, who remembered: 'A rumour started around that time, and went on all the way through to *The Sea Wolves*, which was our last picture together thirty years later, that we were cousins. In fact, we had a more intriguing family connexion. My mother had once had an affair with David's brother Max, and to avoid embarrassment she used to introduce him to me as "your uncle Max". So if Max was my uncle, then his brother had to be a sort of cousin.'

David limped back to Hollywood from his second Korda calamity in two years more than ever determined that anything, even total unemployment or a lawsuit or possibly both, would now be a better idea than continuing to serve out his Goldwyn contract. In this belief he was encouraged by several local managers and agents who assured him that now was the moment to go freelance and capitalize on what was still an evidently well-liked if rather dated screen image. Even the worst of David's reviews, and there were enough of those around now to fill several of the scrapbooks that he always kept as a record of his work, were usually written more in sorrow than in anger. And now, told by Goldwyn that he was to be sent over to stooge for Shirley Temple in a bobbysoxer romance called *A Kiss for Corliss*, he decided that the time had come to call it a day.

Storming into his boss's office, he announced to the mogul that he would do the Temple rubbish but that on its last day of shooting he would no longer consider himself to be a contract player. One or two of those closest to him, not least Hjordis, thought this more than a little foolhardy

with a young family still in need of support; but the
professional advice was to go freelance, and David had in
any case slightly outstayed his welcome at the studio.
Goldwyn put up depressingly little resistance, indeed
seemed almost indecently eager to be getting rid of an
actor who for the last two years had meant nothing at the
box office and trouble around the studio. It was left to
Caroline Lejeune, writing a sad little review of *A Kiss for
Corliss* in the *Observer*, to provide a rhyming epitaph for
David's last few depressing and damaging Goldwyn years:

> 'I sometimes think that David Niven
> Should not take all the parts he's given.'

Chapter Eighteen

1949–1951

'Round the rugged rocks
The ragged rascal ran'

The Elusive Pimpernel, when it finally surfaced in America in late 1950 under what was presumably thought to be a fractionally more dynamic title (*The Fighting Pimpernel*), did not mark a promising start to Niven's freelance career as an actor. Indeed, the US distributors were so depressed by the whole overwritten, overcostumed and under-talented farrago that they decided it wasn't even worth paying for the printing of colour negatives; as the movie was so desperately old-fashioned anyway, they might as well release it in black and white, a Hollywood insult which even the British film industry reckoned was almost unprecedented. By now, they were definitely not seeking David here, there or anywhere.

This was more than a little unfortunate, considering that for the first time in his life he had cut himself free. Except for that very brief 1932–4 period of his first arrival in America, David had always been under the control of school or Army or studio. Admittedly he had often re-belled, but his whole working existence had been lived within the framework of an organization which had provided him with the kind of security and continuity he had never found in his home life. He had always, however much he cultivated the image of himself as a strolling vagabond, been protected by Stowe or Sandhurst, the regiment, the War Office or Goldwyn. Now he was entering his forties, feeling like a naughty schoolboy who has been finally expelled and therefore lost any kind of role. Just as it was no good being an officer and a gentleman in a movie capital suddenly full of the young Marlon Brando and the youthful Paul Newman, so it was no good being a studio rebel when you had no studio.

Indeed, his abrupt departure from Goldwyn, at a time when his employer still wielded considerable power in the small Hollywood community and a nervous new TV industry, meant that David immediately became largely untouchable elsewhere. The agents who had promised to look after him once he had achieved his freedom now began to fade mysteriously into the hills, all except one who actually went so far as to die the day after David had signed with him.

Even independent producers, who were still relatively few and far between, suddenly began to wonder whether it would really be worth incurring the wrath of Goldwyn, with whom they might well at some time want to do a studio or co-production deal, merely in order to hire an actor whose post-war track record had consisted of seven major flops in less than three years. The only variations in that dire catalogue had been two minor critical hits (*Enchantment* and *The Bishop's Wife*) which had both been Goldwyn-crafted products of the studio from which he was now barred for life.

While others were being blacklisted for rather more serious political reasons, Niven found himself simply ignored as an actor of no remarkable talent whose once-useful screen type had now been overtaken by an altogether different generation of home-made and generally downmarket screen heroes. This was a verdict which even David himself in his most confident moments would have found it hard to challenge.

Not surprisingly, he began to murmur to those few (mainly British) columnists still taking some sort of interest in what passed for his career that perhaps the time had come to stop thinking about acting and to start thinking about producing or directing; but as David had neither the money to produce nor the talent to direct, those options were never really open to him. Yet he managed, at least while there were journalists in earshot, to keep up a reasonably cheery façade. 'I have no intention', he told one in August 1949, 'of ending up out here as the kind of old actor who plays English butlers in other people's movies. My motto has always been, like the RAF's, "Press forward regardless," and that's exactly what I shall do. At least, if anybody does hire me now, the money will be coming to me and not to Sam Goldwyn. Certainly I've had a run of disasters, but nobody can be as lucky as I have forever. Sometimes I think I should just have run a whole-page ad. in *Variety* this year reading "Oops, Sorry, Niven".'

For a while after the Goldwyn bust-up, David seriously considered moving the family back to Britain where his boys still had places marked down for them at Stowe. The warmth of California still appealed to Hjordis, however, and if things were bad for him in Hollywood there was absolutely no guarantee that they would be any better in a British cinema still reeling from *Elusive Pimpernel* and *Bonnie Prince Charlie*. There, too, audience tastes were changing from the old preoccupation with clean-cut officers and gentleman. A new and sensitive, moody actor of the Dirk Bogarde generation was more likely to find work than a Niven still looking and sounding like Ronald Colman's renegade younger brother who had been inadvertently left over from the 1930s.

This change in David's professional fortunes was under-scored by a sharp alteration in his private life. With the coming of Hjordis, he had been keen to find them both new friends well away from what was left of the British colony in California – people who would not forever be comparing her to Primmie, or reminding him of an earlier life and marriage. Some surviving members of the Hollywood British, notably the Nigel Bruce family, felt quite rightly that David had begun to neglect them and turn his back on the whole English community in California, a community whose early generosity towards him in the 1930s had never really been repaid. These were difficult times for Niven and he did not want to be reminded of better ones. Ever a pragmatic man, it had also occurred to him that there was no longer much to be gained by being English in California.

The arrival of Hjordis also meant that, not surprisingly, Swedish was a language to be heard alongside English in the Pink House. Greta Garbo was the first nude woman David's sons ever saw in their pool, while another Swedish actress, Viveca Lindfors, remembers 'one or two hilarious dinner parties when Hjordis would suddenly decide to deal with the catering, only because of her broken English we'd end up with stuffed pigs and weird desserts. But they were evidently very happy and very much in love, though now I think back on it this was a low period in David's life because, like so many actors, he'd been allowed to rely on his charm instead of any real acting talent and now, when the demand for charm seemed to be very low, it was as though he didn't want to risk anything else. In that sense his charm was working against him, just as Marilyn Monroe's sex appeal always worked against her in the end. David had let himself become what people thought he was, just a charming man instead of an actor.'

Niven was finding other new friends around this time, equally far removed from the stalwarts of the Hollywood Cricket Club, as Lauren Bacall recalls: 'It was in the late 1940s that David and my husband Humphrey Bogart became very close friends. I think a lot of garbage has been written about Bogie being at the centre of a rat pack of cronies, when in fact he had very few real friends and David for the last few years of his life was one of them. They certainly might not have seemed to have a lot in common: Bogie was a very active Democrat, where David, if he had any American political leanings at all, would surely have been a Republican. But they both had a tremendous desire to work, and though David was never the star that Bogie was, he was intelligent and a realist, and Bogie responded to that. Also they both took their sailing very seriously. Usually when you have a boat in Hollywood the only thing they ask you is how many does it sleep? They want boats with waiters and decks that can take high heels and all that baloney. Bogie and Niven actually adored the sea, and they understood it. They were real sailors, and they'd go out together in Bogie's boat and that formed a great bond.'

Getting away on Bogart's boat was also of course a way of escaping career and financial problems that were becoming crippling: David's income tax was still not fully paid off, nor was the mortgage on the Pink House, and the only glimmer of any work on the horizon was the possibility of a small and thankless role as an opera-company manager in a Kathryn Grayson musical called *The Toast of New Orleans* that MGM were putting together to launch the career of their new star larynx, Mario Lanza.

This might pay off a few bills, but it clearly was not going to keep the mind alive or especially sane. It was just at this point, as Hjordis remembers, that David decided to set off on a new tack altogether: 'One morning, early in 1950 it must have been, he woke up and said, "All right, we have no money and nobody is going to give me a film. So what am I going to do? I am going to write." In the garden of the Pink House was a little rotunda, so he put a table in it and got a chair and some paper and sat down every morning and within about four months he had written a book.'

Published a year later in New York and London to remarkably little press or public attention, David's first book was a light comic novel called *Round the Rugged Rocks* which remains in my view the best thing he ever wrote. It has been out of print for nearly forty years, and David always told me that he was not bringing it back in his lifetime for the simple reason that it contains most of the best stories he used later in *The Moon's A Balloon* and *Bring on the Empty Horses*, but worked over as fiction.

The title quote was drawn casually enough from that old rhyme given to children having trouble in pronouncing their 'R' sounds ('Round the rugged rocks the ragged rascal ran'), but on that seemingly unpromising basis David constructed a jaunty escapade about an English soldier who comes out of the war and, after a series of extremely familiar American adventures in illicit pony racing, ends up rather to his own amazement as a Hollywood movie star. Written in a jocular, journalistic style that reads at times like an unholy alliance of Richard Gordon and Art Buchwald, the book starts with a ritual author's disclaimer: 'This, heaven help me, is not an autobiography. All of the characters who appear on these pages are unfortunately imaginary.'

In that case we should address ourselves immediately to one of the book's leading figures, a character by the name of Oglethorpe, 'a subaltern of thirty who looked fifty: six feet six inches in height, with a moustache which could be seen from behind (on a clear day), very thin indeed and his chin was non-existent'. Not only does Trubshawe come through this description as clearly as if it were a photograph, but Oglethorpe was the name by which David frequently addressed him. Oglethorpe was, in fact, a mythical military caricature first conjured up by them both during Army days in Malta. Clearly here is something rather more personal than David ever liked to admit, and there is, I would suggest, a good deal more to be learned about David himself through his descriptions of the character called John Hamilton in the book than there is through many of his first-person memoirs. The cloak of fiction allowed him to say things here about himself and those around him which could never have been said in an autobiography. *Round the Rugged Rocks* also leaves us with a few tantalizing identity problems. It would, for instance, were we not in fear of extremely well-trained libel lawyers, be interesting to speculate about who in real life is the actor described by David in the book as 'Ralph Ridgway, idol of millions, English actor who settled in California in 1938, took out American citizenship when the war was declared in Europe and then, after Pearl Harbor, appeared before an American Army draft board with a signed statement confirming homosexuality and therefore unfitness to fight'.

Round the Rugged Rocks (which in America was published as *Once Over Lightly*) gave considerable pleasure to David and the few who seem to have read it; but it was not an autobiography, and even if it had been was unlikely to have made him any money, given the state of his dismal box-office appeal in the early 1950s. As a comic novel it certainly wasn't going to make him any money, though it did attract one or two respectful reviews, mostly buried far down the pages of English literary publications in round-ups of 'new fiction'.

David himself seems in better times almost to have forgotten that he ever wrote the book, and it is never mentioned in either of his later autobiographies. Yet it made him an author fully twenty years before *The Moon's A Balloon*, and the experience of that first book and the discipline of writing it are what paved the way to the success of the second, as well as providing most of its best material.

For the moment it was back to an increasingly desperate and moribund movie career. The only thing worse than a Mario Lanza film musical of the early 1950s was a British film musical of the early 1950s and that was what David had to face next. *Happy Go Lovely* was a stunningly terrible attempt to crack the American market by flying Niven, Vera Ellen, Cesar Romero and an American musical director to the Edinburgh Festival and having them film there the usual backstage story about a show in romantic and financial difficulties. The critic of the *New York Times* thought he could faintly detect 'a certain limpid charm', though whether this was David's or the film's was not specified. The best that others could summon up in favour of David was 'unobtrusive' and 'immaculately dressed', thereby making it look as though he would at any moment be relegated to the ranks of the British butlers that so terrified him as a film career prospect.

Still, the Scots locations did at least allow Niven to renew a few local contacts and even to stand in that year's election for rector of Glasgow University, an honorary but prestigious post to which both he and the playwright James Bridie were narrowly beaten by the Scottish MP Walter Elliot. Before going back to Hollywood, Niven also spent some time with old English stage friends like the Oliviers and Noël Coward, all of whom urged him to think about the theatre if his film career was indeed in ruins. Coward did more than advise: he actually came up with a sort of offer. His long-time friend and partner, John C. Wilson, was about to present Gloria Swanson in a French farce by André Roussin called *Nina*, in which it seemed there might be a part for David, who would thereby be able to make his Broadway début and, if all went well, open up for himself a stage career. Once again, the old friends were rallying round. If indeed the willingness of such friends to help out in a crisis can be the test of a worthwhile existence, it has to be said that Niven comes out well ahead. Nobody actually wanted to see him fail, perhaps not even Goldwyn, who had never taken David's photograph off his piano.

Before Broadway there was one more Hollywood job to do. MGM, perhaps feeling guilty at leaving David standing around through so much of *The Toast of New Orleans* with nothing more to do than stare at Mario Lanza's admittedly remarkable tonsils, now offered him a light-hearted Kipling Indian adventure called *Soldiers Three* and apparently much more up his street. There was just one snag: he would have to accept third billing, not only to Walter Pidgeon, which might have been just about tolerable in view of Mr Pidgeon's senior age and distinction, but also to the English actor Stewart Granger, who had not arrived in Hollywood or achieved his first stardom there until fully a decade after David.

This clearly did not make for the easiest of relationships, as Granger later told me: 'What the hell David was doing playing a supporting part in that horror I shall never know – I suppose he was very hard up at the time. But I remember that extraordinary charm, and the great difference in our temperaments. David never wanted to tilt at the windmills; I was forever beefing and grumbling and groaning because I knew we were in what was going to be a disaster. Indeed, the only way that film worked was because it was so bad as an adventure that some people thought it was meant to be a comedy and just laughed at it happily enough. Now David also knew that we were making this disaster, and yet here was this cheerful, charming man being jolly all over the set and I kept saying to him, "How can you be like that?" and he'd say, "Well, it may be shit and not very good shit, but we have to go through it, so let's just be cheerful about it." I never knew how he could do that, but it was true of his whole character. He'd describe somebody on the set to me as an utter arsehole, and a moment later the man would be standing there and in almost the same breath David would be saying, "My dear old fellow, how are you?" without turning a hair, and I'd be left with my mouth hanging open, not knowing how he could do it.

'When I first came out from England around this time, he'd really hit the skids, but even when he was doing all right he was, like Cary Grant, very tight with the money. I was always rather jealous about the way that everybody seemed to love David, and the way that he managed to give the impression that he was loving every single minute of every single day. I don't think he was, I don't think anybody could, but he had an enviable knack of seeming to be happy and people liked that. He was also very good about seeming to be a star. If you look carefully, in most of his really good films with people like Olivier and Cary Grant he's always just the other man, but somehow he made you forget that. He played the Hollywood game very well – came over as a ladies' man, had the affair with

Merle, got himself established, always good with the wives of the Jewish moguls who ran the studios, knew exactly who to talk to at parties. So everything that he got was sort of free, whereas actors like me who were terribly bad at the social life around the studios had to work twice as hard to get anywhere. He always considered that the film business had been "nice" to him, whereas I don't really think it's been "nice" to me at all. But I'm not even sure that's what it's meant to be. David just knew how to stay in work, even if the work was terrible. I don't think he was really an actor, not in the sense that, say, Rex Harrison is an actor. David was just a very expert player of the Hollywood game.'

For all the awfulness of its script, *Soldiers Three* had certain advantages for Niven, not least the presence on the set of his beloved Coote-old-man, the actor who was then still living in the flat above his garage and had taken over Trubshawe's role as the bluff, military friend for all seasons. Further down that castlist were also to be found Robert Newton, already a legendary Hollywood drunk, and the Irish actor Cyril Cusack who recalls: 'One extraordinary night after the shooting Niven took Bob Newton and me out for a drink and said, "Now, look, you fellows know all about stage acting. I'm just going to make my début on Broadway – how's it done?" As though we were going to be able over that one drink to pass on to him our two whole lifetimes of theatrical experience! So we just told him not to worry and it would probably be a great success.'

It wasn't. David's first and last Broadway play went into rehearsal early in the autumn of 1951 with Gloria Swanson in the title role as Nina, Alan Webb as her jealous husband and Niven as the play's only other character, the traditionally suave lover of French bedroom farce. André Roussin, the author, was then at the height of his European success: *Nina* itself had been running more than two years in Paris, while another of his comedies (*The Little Hut*, which David was later to film) had just started a two-year London run with Robert Morley.

Nina on Broadway was an altogether different matter, as the producer Toby Rowland remembers: 'I was sent out from London on behalf of H.M. Tennent, which had an interest in the production, because they always did the Roussin plays in London; only before I arrived, the American managers had settled on Gloria Swanson, who couldn't act at all but was still quite a big name and had been doing a lot of touring in summer stock. And David, who was on his uppers in Hollywood, had been persuaded that a stage success would be good for his career; then there was a manic Hungarian director, Gregory Ratoff, and Alan Webb, the only real actor in the cast, who also had the only really good part as the wronged husband. When we all assembled for the first read-through it was immediately apparent that Ratoff was mad, that Gloria couldn't do it all, that Alan was going to be extremely good, and that David might just about get by on a wry sort of charm.

'Rehearsals were not easy. Gloria was already into the midst of a vastly complex health-food diet, and she also had her own clothes-designing business which was to make all her own gowns for the show including a vast black taffeta costume which seemed to kind of explode when David embraced her in the first act, thereby shooting whalebone supports right up his nostrils. That was about the biggest laugh we got: by this time the director had been barred the theatre, so a number of different people had taken over the production, including myself, the stage manager and Sam Taylor who had done the American adaptation. Gloria remained outrageously horrible, Alan managed to look sad and put-upon which was ideal for his part in the plot, and David just marvellously managed to stay cheerful and charming throughout the whole ghastly experience.'

Things were not helped during the pre-Broadway try-out in Philadelphia by Miss Swanson's decision to give an interview to a local paper outlining precisely how terrible she thought the play in general and her part in particular, thereby causing the *New York Times* to note, 'Now that actresses have taken to reviewing their own shows out of town, there is not much work left for a drama critic.' Nor was Niven in the most optimistic of spirits, since one weekend during a shooting party up in New England Hjordis had been accidentally hit in the face by several bullets, leaving David once again sitting by the hospital bedside of a beloved wife.

Happily she soon recovered, and early in December the *Nina* company reached New York where David and Hjordis, reckoning they were unlikely to be there for long, took an economical bedroom at the Blackstone Hotel just next door to one occupied by another Broadway hopeful of that season called Audrey Hepburn. Her luck along the Great White Way in a French boulevard comedy (*Gigi*, which opened just a few nights ahead of *Nina*) was to be considerably greater than his. Though he managed to get through the whole of the second act without any more corset supports rammed up his nose, that was about the most that could be said of a desperately uneasy evening, later relegated by Miss Swanson to just three lines in her 500-page autobiography. One critic was kind enough to note that David packed a suitcase on stage with quite remarkable elegance and aplomb, while another (assuming the usual inaccurate birthplace) reckoned that he had left his art in the Highlands.

Surprisingly enough the play ran for about three months on those reviews. Alan Webb even managed to get an award for his performance, and by the end of the run David had settled into a stage presence of considerable elegance, as Toby Rowland remembers: 'I still don't think he was really acting. He was just giving an impression of what a better actor might look like in the role, but by this time he had decided to cut his losses and enjoy himself, so he used to come in every night and say to Alan, "Well, what shall we do to her tonight?" and they used to devise these terrible practical jokes on stage. I don't think Gloria ever even noticed: certainly her performance didn't change by so much as a breath from the first night to the last. She just used to plough on through, while David tried to suppress his giggling. I remember Hjordis, though, being marvellous. David had no money at all then, and she used to go round in a wonderful rabbit coat dyed bright red. When I told her it was the most extraordinary coat I'd ever seen, she said she had decided to wear something flamboyant until David could afford to buy her the mink again.'

Other people managed to rally round. Rex and Lilli Harrison even braved Philadelphia. Some gave advice or copious notes on David's performance, though Rex's suggestion was as ever succinct: 'Leave.' Other friends like Coote and Jack Merivale decided to go later in the run, as Merivale recalls: 'The reviews and everybody who'd already seen it had warned us that we were in for a pretty terrible evening, but Coote said it would be extremely disloyal not to go, so we set off for the theatre and after the first act it was so bad that we repaired across the street to a bar and stayed there through most of the second. Then we went back and caught a bit of that, which was even worse than the first, so we spent the second interval and all the third act in the bar, and then went backstage and told David he'd been marvellous. I don't think he entirely believed us.'

It was left to Walter Kerr to write *Nina*'s epitaph: 'Miss Swanson has designed her own clothes for the production, and the extent of her misfortunes can be gauged by the fact that some of them came apart on stage. By that time, however, a similar fate had overtaken the play.'

Chapter Nineteen

1952–1953

'I smelt strongly of defeat, and Hollywood is like a bird dog. When things are going badly, it tenses and sniffs at you. It scrapes away at the camouflage. It knows.'

By the beginning of 1952 David was not only a failed film star, he was also a failed Broadway star. *Nina* limped to the end of a three-month run, and back at the Pink House his financial affairs were in such poor shape that he was trying to sell off some of its best Regency furniture. His career was fast spiralling down in a curiously vicious circle. The only films he was offered were rubbish, but he couldn't afford not to take them, even though by doing so he lowered his public and critical standing even further.

Yet he remained, as Hjordis and both his sons recall, remarkably resilient: 'My father seldom brought his troubles home,' says James Niven. 'He had to pay for us and the house and Hjordis, and if that meant making terrible pictures for a living, well, so be it. He always told us that if we were teased at school for being the children of a film star we were to say, "My father is a simply terrible actor but he enjoys doing it very much indeed and it's really all he can do." But we didn't see a lot of him: he'd get back from whatever studio it was around six, and by that time our nanny would be getting us ready for bed and we'd be brought down to watch him drink a scotch and soda and then we'd go upstairs.'

'For a while,' remembers David Jr, 'he went on to the gin and that was a great mistake because for some reason it made him truly horrid. Being highly articulate, and having this tremendous command of the English language, he would just destroy us verbally. It was never a physical thing, but we would sit there cowering with fear and trying to find any excuse to run up to our rooms. But then one day we just confronted him and told him how awful he got after a couple of gins, and he went straight back to the scotch and it was fine from then on. Just something about the gin, I guess.'

The boys' relationship with Hjordis was, in Doreen Hawkins' view, more akin to that with an older sister than a stepmother: 'She always made it very clear that she wanted children of her own, and that she was not going to be a kind of substitute mother trying to step into Primmie's shoes. I remember her romping around with the boys in the garden of the Pink House or leaping into the pool with them, but she never really looked on herself as their mother. She was very fond of them, and in the holidays she'd spend time with them, but in a way she always treated them as mischievous younger brothers rather than stepsons – it wasn't a maternal thing at all. The great disaster was that she and David couldn't have any children of their own. She was always trying, poor darling, and then having terrible miscarriages, and each time that happened she'd go into a deep, deep depression which used to upset David terribly. I remember his tremendous anxiety about her: "Got to keep Mum happy, you see," he'd say time and again. He was desperately keen on the idea of a happy family life, with a home where the boys could grow up secure.'

'My father', says David Jr, 'almost never talked about our real mother and somehow we didn't really think to ask about her until much later, when he did speak of her with great love and affection. He was a sensational father, took us on fishing trips, all the things that normal fathers do, but he came of a generation who were taught never to reveal their innermost feelings. His career problems were his own, and he didn't want to bore us with them or cry on other shoulders. He had that very stiff-lipped quality. He liked living well, and when we were young he wasn't always able to, and I think that worried him which was why he never said no to any job. All he would ask was: where and when and how much?'

'Because I was three years younger than my brother,' says Jamie, 'and had never really lived in England at all I became the all-American son, and Daddy would come home from the studio and hit baseballs toward me through the garden sprinklers. He loved doing that: the balls would create fascinating bouncers off the sprinklers and you'd get soaking wet. He never made me feel that he was a Hollywood star, and he never pushed us into the papers the way a lot of my school friends got pushed because they were actors' children. He kept a very strong sense of proportion about his work and our lives being two quite separate things, and I think that was terribly important, especially when you consider how many contemporaries and friends of mine died because they couldn't take that sort of showbiz pressure. We were always sheltered from that by Daddy, and I think in some ways his attitude to Hollywood was a very cool and clear one, because he'd seen it both as a success and as a failure.

'Hjordis was always more of a companion than a mother, and there were moments when we had a lot of fun together and other moments when it got very tricky, but I'm sure that's true of any stepmother– stepchild relationship. She didn't act like a mother and she made it very clear that she never wanted to be our mother. When she adopted her own two girls she became a mother to them, and that was when it got very tricky. There's no doubt that our relationship changed dramatically the day she adopted her first child.'

That was still some ten years ahead, and in the meantime

life went on much as before, with David lurching from bad film to bad film one step ahead of the creditors and the vulture columnists. By this time he'd abandoned all hope of sending his boys back to school in England, having estimated during one sleepless night that the air fares alone would set him back about $50,000 in the course of their educational lifetime: not even for Stowe could he find that kind of money, and his sons thus went to local Californian establishments while David tried to keep their increasingly American accents a secret from their Rollo relatives back home.

He was still, however, seeking out new American friends, in whose company he and Hjordis could avoid the crumbling community of expatriate British actors with their embarrassingly long and accurate memories of his early bachelor exploits and their lingering devotion to the memory of Primmie. Not only the Humphrey Bogarts but now William Randolph Hearst Jr and his wife also became constant week-end partners, as Hearst recalls: 'David had, of course, been a great favourite of my old man's up at San Simeon in the Marion Davies time, but then long after the war he used to come back up to the ranch with Hjordis and it was there I think that he started painting in the very early 1950s. He'd known that Churchill did it for relaxation and he kind of liked that idea, so he'd bring his brushes and canvas and sit around painting San Simeon. My wife said the result looked like something French, so he signed it "David de Niven" and gave it to us. He was also very good on wine: all those early adventures in the liquor trade had left him with a detailed knowledge of cellars, and he used to go down to the one at San Simeon and emerge cuddling four bottles of the very best French vintages. He couldn't have been more gentle with them if they'd been newborn babes.'

Soon after David got back to Hollywood from the dreaded *Nina*, he found himself in an even greater mistake. *The Lady Says No* gave him second billing to Joan Caulfield in a B-to-Z comedy about a photographer falling in love with a best–selling feminist novelist. Though it might be charitable to think of this theme as being about twenty years ahead of its time, it was in fact so ineptly handled that most reviewers simply ignored it altogether, assuming it had been a sort of aberration from which all concerned might recover if left in merciful seclusion. From that, Niven moved on to a fractionally better idea: *Appointment With Venus* (known in America as *Island Rescue*) was a Ralph Thomas–Betty Box comedy about a wartime attempt to smuggle a pedigree cow off the Channel Islands under the eyes of the Nazi occupying force, and it at least had the virtue of getting David and his family back to Britain for a while.

Not that he was altogether delighted by what he found there, as he soon noted in one of his periodic missives to *The Times*: 'During a long motor trip through the Midlands and West Country, I was appalled to see village after beautiful village ruined by clusters of disintegrating Nissen huts and by monstrous, rusting and decaying dumps of old ammunition boxes, aircraft tyres, tin cans and the like . . . we can expect many foreign visitors to the national bedside during the coming summer months – if for their benefit only, should the doctor in charge not bestir himself and freshen up the patient?'

Appointment With Venus was the first feature film ever made on the island of Sark, and the Dame herself gave it her approval, noting only that they had made the character of the German commandant rather too kindly. David played the commando major deputed to get the cow off the island, with Glynis Johns as the local girl who helps him, and though in the end the film fell uneasily somewhere between farce and melodrama, it was made with confidence and a certain style by the director, Gerald Thomas, who in later years was to go on with such success to the *Carry On* farces.

It was also the first film that really managed to establish the screen presence and career of an English actor who came in later years to reflect and even echo many of the

peculiarly English Niven virtues of decency and military
joviality, Kenneth More. A decade later it was to be More
who was the producer Carl Foreman's first choice for the
Niven role in *The Guns of Navarone*, but at this time, as
Kenny later recalled in his autobiography, 'David was very
much the star, and when he actually spoke to me I felt like
a million dollars. He had done all the pre-war stuff in
Hollywood and was an international name . . . One weekend during the shooting I went to stay with him and as we
walked through the hall of the house he'd rented, I noticed
a chair near the fireplace with a yellow-and-black harlequin
pattern on the seat. "Isn't that bloody awful," David
remarked . . . "it's terrible. We'll have to do something
about that, Kenny, no doubt about it. We'll have to deal
with it, dear old thing." We went into the drawing room
. . . after dinner and a good many Camparis, David told
me to burn the chair. With some difficulty I pulled off the
legs, took out the harlequin seat, and threw it bit by bit
into the fire. David did an Indian war dance around the
fire, seeming for some reason deliriously happy . . . I
staggered off to bed and slept like a stone. Next morning,
when I came down to breakfast, Hjordis was looking
worried. "What has happened to the chair?" she asked . . .
David, po-faced, said "Kenny burned it, darling. He got
high, and burned it." I couldn't deny it. That is exactly
what I had done. But on David's instructions . . . somehow
I couldn't tell her that, and I don't think she ever forgave
me. That was tactical lesson number one from Niven.

'Lesson number two came when I had my big scene
knocking out one of the German troops. When we were
to shoot it, the set was suddenly totally deserted and the
director came over to me. "Your scene is cut," he said
simply. "David is the star here, and if anyone is going to
be hitting Germans in this picture, it's him and not you."
And that was all there was to that.'

David still had more to worry about than a little competition from the up-and-coming Kenneth More. Back in
Hollywood, he had not had a real American studio success

since well before the war and work had dried up altogether. He had already tried the theatre with no more luck than the current cinema, and that left only one conceivable avenue of escape: television. This was, unlike Broadway, a high-risk alternative, simply because the film studios in their current paranoiac terror of the new medium were actually blacking any actors or directors who worked for it. To be seen on television was thus reckoned in 1952 to mean instant death to a film career.

Deciding that he had nothing to lose, David was thus one of the first real stars to go into the new medium. He began doing hair-raising live television dramas out of New York, the chaotic making of one in particular later being brilliantly if fictionally recreated by him as a chapter in his last novel, *Go Slowly, Come Back Quickly*.

Even though he had none of the stage training that was then taken for granted by most television actors, who tended to broadcast out of New York rather than Los Angeles and therefore to be theatre people rather than film people, something in David's quick-thinking military mind responded well to the panic stations of live TV drama and he scored a considerable success with Helen Hayes on the Schlitz Playhouse and then in a distinguished ABC production of *The Petrified Forest* with Kim Hunter and Art Carney. He got only $300 for doing it, but thirty million people saw it and liked it, which was a good deal more than could have been said for any of his recent movies.

The only trouble was that David was on at least two of the current Hollywood blacklists. Not only had he walked out of a Goldwyn studio contract, he had also gone over to the enemy and appeared on live television. All in all, he'd probably have done better in 1952 as one of the Reds under the bed. But it was precisely because no other film maker would now touch Niven with a 10–foot microphone boom that one maverick director–producer suddenly acquired an interest in him. As Otto Preminger explained years later, 'The more everyone told me I shouldn't cast

David, the more I wanted to have him in my film.'

The film in question here was *The Moon is Blue*, a light comedy of romantic mistakes stagily set in a New York bachelor pad – the kind of comedy which ten years later would instinctively have been ascribed to Neil Simon, but which was in fact the work of an old Viennese friend of Otto's, Hugh Herbert. Preminger had already had a considerable success directing it on the New York stage, and was now determined to return with it to Hollywood, but only on his own terms: no longer would he be the employee of some arrogant studio chief, but instead the head of his own film company working on a simple distribution deal with United Artists.

They, of course, still wanted to interfere, to the extent of telling Preminger that, though his central casting of William Holden and Maggie McNamara (in the original Barbara Bel Geddes role) was splendid, the idea of having David Niven play Holden's bachelor friend and rival was disastrous, as Niven was now 'all washed up'. Preminger did not agree: he'd been among the few who had seen David on stage in *Nina*, and something in his gay-bachelor (gay in its pre-homosexual connotation, of course) performance there convinced Otto that he'd be dead right for the film. First, and perhaps to convince United Artists of their mistake, Preminger told Niven to go to San Francisco for three months and play the role there on stage with his road company.

As a confidence restorative, that California stage run in *The Moon is Blue* (David's only other theatrical engagement ever) worked extremely well. In a part similar to the one he had already played in *Nina*, but in a vastly better play which he knew he might be getting the chance to film, David fairly blossomed as a stage actor and coincidentally during that brief run also hit upon one of the best career ideas of his entire life.

Playing at the theatre next door to Niven's in San Francisco at that time was Charles Boyer in *Don Juan in Hell* and, as both men were there without their families, they would often go out to a nearby restaurant after their curtains were down. One night the conversation turned to television. Boyer had, he said, started to talk to Dick Powell about the idea of forming a TV production company. Would Niven be interested in joining them?

David was not so much interested as ecstatic. He had always greatly envied men like Douglas Fairbanks Sr and Chaplin who had arrived in Hollywood early enough to control their own studios, and deeply resented the head-masterly power that a man like Goldwyn had been able to exercise over his own working and private lives. Despite the fact that he had moved so early into television out of desperation, surely his reward now would be in finding himself one of the inmates allowed to control the asylum?

It was not quite as easy as that. In the first place Boyer, Powell and Niven, having decided to call their new company Four-Star Playhouse, were quite unable to find their fourth star, since everyone they approached was still far too terrified of movie-studio reprisals. They did, however, manage to work out a deal with CBS whereby they would make twenty-six half-hour dramas for television in their first season (1952–3) and fifty-two the next. 'It is wonderful', David told an English reporter at this time, 'to be a producer at last and in television. The schoolgirl jealousy of the film industry will have to end and we can, with a little intelligent planning, actually help each other. Certainly it means a lot more work for actors and writers and directors, and as television is clearly not going to go away, now it's here we should all make the most of it.'

Although no other star would actually join Niven, Boyer and Powell on the Four-Star masthead (Joel McCrea and Ros Russell both considered it), three such long-standing and well-liked Hollywood figures were able to call on a lot of old friendships, with the result that guest stars on their dramas during that very first season included Merle Oberon, Ronald Colman, Joan Fontaine and Ida Lupino who later became a regular member of the team as both

actress and director. The idea was not, of course, that
Niven or Boyer or Powell should appear in every single
one of their half-hour productions: they simply worked on
them as and when film commitments allowed, though
because David was at this time the least in demand of the
trio, it was he who made the sharpest initial impact. As
Lauren Bacall recalls: 'David had gone into that Four-Star
deal out of sheer desperation at the way his film career
was moving, or rather wasn't; he asked me to join them,
and like a jerk I refused, which shows you how lousy my
professional instincts were. But anyway Bogie and I began
watching their shows out of interest and one night Bogie
said, "My God he can act," and it was true. David's dramas
were always the best acted and the best written of the
season, and he remains the only leading actor I have ever
known whose career was totally revived and turned around
as a result of television. He really did begin to do some
very good work there.'

The Four-Star company went rapidly from strength to
strength. In their later season they were producing not just
one-shot dramas but also such continuing series as *Zane
Gray Theater*, *The Rifleman* and *Wanted Dead or Alive*.
One of their most remarkable achievements is recalled by
the actress Neile Toffel: 'Four-Star was the company which
virtually invented the spin-off, whereby you take a character out of one successful series and star him or her in a
series of their own. At that time Bob Culp was doing a
show for them called *Trackdown* and in it there was this
character of a bounty hunter, and Boyer and Niven and
Powell decided to take him away from that and set him up
on his own in *Wanted Dead or Alive*. That ran for three
years and 117 episodes: the man who played the lead in it
was my husband, Steve McQueen.'

McQueen was probably Four-Star's most impressive
discovery, but the other actors who became established
there are no less impressive: David Janssen, Chuck Con-
nors and Jack Lemmon all did some of their earliest screen
work for Niven's company, and though at first the finances

were very shaky indeed (David remembered having to draw what savings he had out of a bank one Friday in order to pay the weekly technicians' wage bill), the fact that he was now a producer and the part-owner of a television company did wonders for his confidence as an actor. It also meant that he had somewhere to work whenever he chose to do so.

Thus, almost ten years after the war, David's luck at last began to turn again. Preminger took him straight back from the San Francisco stage into his film version of *The Moon is Blue*, which duly opened to a clutch of good reviews for Niven as the ageing rake (a performance which looked all the better up against William Holden's somewhat leaden attempts to play light comedy) and a storm of extremely welcome publicity and controversy caused by a refusal to give the film the then all-important seal of approval by the Motion Picture Production Code. Preminger had decided that the idea of a code like this was in 1953 both censorious and morally indefensible in what was supposed to be a free society; he had also, I suspect, decided that to challenge the code's authority would give his fairly innocuous little sex comedy some welcome attention. Because the script made free use of words like 'virgin' and 'seduce', he chose not to submit it to the code office in the knowledge that they would demand minor cuts he had already decided not to make. Without that approval, it was left to individual censor boards in local areas to decide whether the film was unsuitable for screening, and even though some did take that view, the attendant publicity and the fury of critics like Bosley Crowther (who noted that the censors were merely 'handing a pretentious, foolish and tedious picture a prime publicity gimmick') meant that it was assured a wide showing. Admittedly one cinema manager in Jersey City did manage to get himself briefly arrested for screening this so-called 'indecent, immoral and obscene' picture, but a judge rapidly overturned his $100 fine and it was left to the Catholic League of Decency to ask Oscar voters not to give their ballots to

the movie's title song. They didn't, though whether out of
obedience or simple good taste we shall never know.
Meanwhile Cardinal Spellman, the Roman Catholic Arch-
bishop of New York, denounced *The Moon is Blue* as 'an
occasion of sin' and it was left to David to enquire tactfully
of His Eminence why, in that case, he had allowed the
play to run for more than two years in his own diocese?

On the other side of the Atlantic, critics determined to
point up the greater lunacies of American officialdom in
one of its periodic fits of morality hailed the picture as
delightful, and Beverly Baxter even went so far as to
compare it quite favourably to *The Importance of Being
Earnest*. The film also managed to open simultaneously in
German, since Preminger had brilliantly hit on the notion
of flying Hardy Kruger and an all-German cast to Hollywood and having them shoot a Teutonic version of the
script on the same set every night after the American actors
had gone home.

Chapter Twenty

1953–1955

'When I tried to reason with her, she sat on the landing alternately sobbing like a child and snarling at me through the banisters like a caged animal.'

Given that it took an average of between six and nine months in the mid–1950s to get a film from studio to cinema screen, it was about a year before the sharp improvement in David's movie fortunes signalled by *The Moon is Blue* began to be apparent in the class of role he was offered, but in the meantime he was back to the usual rubbish. Indeed it is a rule of thumb, for Niven's post-war career, that any good film he almost accidentally stumbled into (and there were less than half a dozen across thirty-five years) was immediately followed by about half a dozen terrible ones.

At a time when actors were at last managing to exert more control over the shape of their careers, David had long since abandoned any attempt to impose any kind of structure at all on his. He seldom refused work so long as the money looked reliable, and on those few occasions when he did turn down a role on image or moral grounds, such as the one eventually played in *Lolita* by James Mason, it almost invariably proved to have been the wrong career decision. Niven was a working actor whose only real plan, intention or ambition was to stay in work as regularly as possible. Years of Goldwyn Studios' control had robbed him of almost all independent ability to analyse or shape his own career constructively. Few star careers in the entire history of the cinema have ever been so prolific, amorphous, anomalous or disorganized as David's.

Two dire English comedies therefore followed *The Moon is Blue* in rapid succession. For the first of these, Harry Kurnitz's *The Love Lottery*, Niven was well enough typecast as an elegant but fading Hollywood star who, in order to win back the lead in the box-office polls that he has lost to Fang the Wonder Dog, agrees to be the star prize in a romantic contest.

Immediately after that David went to Ireland for *Happy Ever After* (known in America, though no more success-fully, as *Tonight's The Night*), a bizarre attempt to do a John Ford comedy of Irish folklore without Mr Ford him-self. Barry Fitzgerald was there, sure enough, and a dis-tinguished English support team led by A. E. Matthews and George Cole, but the notion of casting Niven as a villainous squire trying to evict lovable locals badly alien-ated those who had come along to witness his usual one-man charm school, while the best of his reviews merely noted that he 'maintains dignity in trying circumstances'.

Back in London, David and Hjordis took some pride in hosting small parties at their rented flat for Bogart and Lauren Bacall, who were also over on film business. One night, David later recalled for Michael Parkinson, 'John Huston and the Bogarts and Hjordis and I were having dinner in a restaurant when in walked one of our tallest dukes, a man not too fond of me because once, years earlier, I had been out shooting with him when it was quite clear to me that, by mistake, he had shot down a carrier pigeon. So as it landed, I couldn't resist asking, "Are there any letters for me?" and that was the end of that weekend. Anyway, that had been years ago, and this night the duke very graciously came over to our table and, after I'd introduced him to the Bogarts and Huston, said, "You must come and shoot with us again." And I said, "Any time." And he said, "The fourth week in February." As the duke went off to his own table Bogey said, "Hey, get a load of you, shooting with a duke." And Huston, who knew a lot about shooting, said, "Well, actually it's not all that great a compliment, because the last week in February is the very end of the shooting season, when they ask the drunken local butcher and just a few other locals and go around shooting the cocks only." Bogart was furious, and went over to the duke and said, "Whaddya mean, insulting my old pal with cocks only?"'

Now that he seemed settled back in London, David took on his third English film in succession and at long last came up with, if not a winner, then at least a film of which he had no need to feel ashamed. *Carrington VC*, known in America as *Court-Martial* because it was feared that VC might be mistaken over there for some new and terrible venereal disease, had been a long-running West End stage play about the military trial of an Army major accused of theft. Though this was not a role to compare with that of the manic Captain Queeg in *The Caine Mutiny* which his friend Humphrey Bogart was filming in that same year, there is no doubt that Major Carrington proved extremely useful to Niven as a warm-up for that other major in trouble who was to win him an Oscar only four years later. Though Niven's performance lacked some of the subtlety that Alec Clunes had brought to the original stage role, his playing had an integrity and a dignity which harked back to *The First of the Few*, *The Way Ahead* and *A Matter of Life and Death*, rather than to the tacky Hollywood comedies of more recent years.

For one of the surprisingly few times in his post-war career, David was working with a first-class director. Anthony Asquith had chosen him for Carrington mainly because he needed a name on which to sell what was to be an extremely English film in America and his choice was to open the door for David to *Separate Tables*. As the square jawed hero determined to conduct his own defence in front of the court-martial David had, thought *The Times*, 'just the spontaneous decency of reaction and the temperamental mix of lightness and dash of which heroes are made; though he may seem on the face of it miscast, he gives in fact one of the best performances of his entire career'.

Yet the film failed to make much impression in America, where it was indeed heavily cut because the Production Code, which had objected so strongly to *The Moon Is Blue*, now also took against a scene in which David, though married to the neurotic Margaret Leighton, is seen having a brief affair with Noelle Middleton of the Women's Royal Army Corps. The only real trouble with *Carrington* was that it remained a resolutely stagy court-room drama, which not even Asquith's considerable cinematic ingenuity could adequately lift out of its original theatrical setting.

Back in Hollywood after *Carrington* VC, with no prospect of any immediate film work there, David went back to the Four-Star Playhouse. 'By now', he told Cecil Smith, 'we were becoming one of the best television companies in the business, but I was still finding it hard to be a producer. The auditions would make me a nervous wreck: I'd sit there looking at these poor devils trying to get work and then remember what it was like for me in the 1930s, and I'd think there but for the grace of God and a lot of luck went me. But we simply couldn't hire every actor who turned up at the door, much as I'd have liked to, so I finally worked out a system. When an actor or actress came to read for a part, I would have my secretary hear them while I stayed in the inner office and watched them through the keyhole. Then I could telephone through and say yes or no without having to get into embarrassing confrontations. The plan was supposed to be that Dick and Charles and I would do one show each every month during the season, and then we'd have a guest star in for the other week; often that broke down, of course, if one or other of us was off doing a film or something, and very often it just depended on who got to the office first and read the script. I remember once finding in the mail a marvellous half-hour drama called *The Answer*, about a bum in a Bowery bar who convinces all the other derelicts that he has found the answer to life itself, and I was so desperate to do it that I quite literally hid the script from Powell and Boyer until it was my turn to make a show.'

But away from the Four-Star studios, David found himself involved in a real-life drama which was to haunt him for the rest of his days, one which he could only bring himself to write about twenty years later after he had changed the name of all those involved. It began one morning in the summer of 1953 with a call from the nearby Paramount Studios. Vivien Leigh was there, starting to work opposite Peter Finch, with whom she was then living, on a film called *Elephant Walk*. Vivien was at this time in one of her manic phases and after screaming at Finch, whom she insisted on calling Larry, turned on her bemused director, William Dieterle, and began shrieking at him entire speeches from *A Streetcar Named Desire* in which she had triumphed on stage and screen as the mad, alcoholic Blanche duBois, forever depending on the kindness of strangers. By now the 'strangers' on the *Elephant Walk* set had decided that something must be done to restore Vivien to sanity. Finch was obviously unable to be of much help, because of the already tormented state of their affair, and although Olivier, her husband, had immediately been sent for, it would take him two or three days to reach California from Ischia, where he had gone for a brief holiday with William Walton and his wife.

In the meantime, someone on the spot in Hollywood had to be found to cope with Vivien, get her off the set and, if possible, into a clinic or asylum where she could be kept for a few days far from the ever-watchful gaze of gossip columnists like Louella Parsons, who had actually been on the *Elephant Walk* set that morning. It was at this point that Niven's long-standing friendship with the Oliviers was remembered, and he was duly asked to come and take Vivien away. What happened over the next forty-eight hours can be found in a chapter of *Bring on the Empty Horses* which David called 'Our Little Girl'. As Stewart Granger remembers it: 'David took her back to the house she had rented, and then he called me and the two of us spent most of a day and one whole night trying to get her to swallow a couple of pills that would sedate her enough to allow a couple of nurses to come and take her into a clinic. Vivien was fiery and very cunning and absolutely determined not to be taken away by people in white coats, and she brilliantly managed to get an entire bottle of pills one by one into the swimming pool, so that in the end it's five o'clock in the morning and we still haven't got the pills down her, and Vivien is now watching all-night television stark naked, and David says let's make her breakfast and slip the pills inside the scrambled eggs, so we cook this enormous breakfast and then Vivien says she's on a diet so to avoid suspicion David has to eat the eggs, and of course passes straight out on the sofa. So then I'm left alone with her and in the end I had to hold her down on the bed while the nurse stuck the needle in her arm to sedate her, and Vivien just looked up at me very calmly and said, "I thought you were my friends." In a way, I think we were.'

The next day Olivier arrived and, amid a blaze of precisely the kind of publicity that Niven and Granger had been trying so hard to avoid, took Vivien back on a stretcher to London. As they carried her aboard the plane, it was David on the tarmac who had his arms around her almost uncontrollably shaking husband. Before the plane even took off, it had been announced by the studio that Elizabeth Taylor would be taking over in *Elephant Walk*.

After all this it must have been almost a relief for David to escape into the costumed, swashbuckling farrago that was his next picture. *The King's Thief* had been constructed, though none too well, as a romantic vehicle for two of MGM's biggest current contract properties, Ann Blyth and Edmund Purdom. Further down that castlist, and looking embarrassed at being caught in it, could be found not only Niven doing a remarkable impersonation of Basil Rathbone as the villainous Duke of Brampton, and George Sanders as a world-weary Charles II, but also a young Roger Moore, then at the start of his film career and a long friendship with Niven.

'I was just out from England and David was extremely generous to me,' he recalls. 'We already had a rather curious connexion which not many people know about. When David's first novel, *Round the Rugged Rocks*, had been published in London about five years earlier, the serial rights were bought by a woman's magazine. Now, in those days they liked to have lots of illustrations, and quite often between acting jobs I used to work as a model. One day an artist friend of mine called me up and asked if I would pose as the hero of this new story about a young soldier going to Hollywood and becoming a film star. So, in a way, before I ever met David, I had already played him.

'When I first arrived in Hollywood there were still three quite distinct social sets, the As and the Bs and the Cs, and which one you belonged to depended entirely on the terms of your studio contract and how much you were getting paid and what sort of parts you were getting. The three groups never intermingled socially, and as David belonged to the As and I was in the Cs we never used to meet except on the set where he always took a lot of trouble to remember my name, which was more than anybody else ever did. Niven always said later that this film was one of the lowest points of his career, and certainly it cannot have been much fun taking third billing to Edmund Purdom and Ann Blyth, but he never let that show. He just did the job and made sure he was pleasant to everyone on the set, and then went home to Hjordis and the boys as soon as he could.'

By now, largely thanks to Four-Star, David was at least out of immediate debt and managing once again to pay off the mortgage on his beloved Pink House. However, he still had virtually nothing in the bank and two sons to educate, which was why he found himself going straight into yet another picture he shouldn't have been seen dead in – the remake of an old Preston Sturges script. As rewritten by Sidney Sheldon, this was now to be a Mitzi Gaynor romance called *The Birds and the Bees*, and its main aim, so far as one can be detected at all, seems to have been the introduction to the wide screen of a television comic called George Gobel, who had suddenly become very big indeed on the small screen. David was hired to play Miss Gaynor's father, a military cardsharp who sets his daughter off in pursuit of Gobel in the hope of acquiring his family fortune, and he gave that now-familiar performance of embarrassed reticence.

After *The Birds and the Bees* David was at last able to afford a holiday and he took Hjordis to stay with Noël Coward at Blue Harbour, the house Noël used as a winter home in Jamaica. The visit was not a success, as Noël's diary records: 'Nivens arrived on Tuesday. David was feeling rather ill and the next morning he burst out into a flaming attack of chickenpox. This, combined with a sun rash he got the first days he was here, has laid him very low indeed. His temperature has fluctuated between 100 and 104, and he has hardly slept at all owing to violent itching. Everything has been tried but so far nothing has relieved it. This means that they will have to be here for three weeks instead of one. Oh dear.'

Coward was, like Niven, not a man to waste any experience and on this occasion it was he who beat Niven to the typewriter. Noël's one and only novel (*Pomp and Circumstance*, published in 1960) has as one of its central plot themes a man suddenly and surprisingly confined to bed by an unexpected attack of chickenpox in middle age.

For both Coward and Niven, whose careers were still in deep doldrums, this was to prove a miraculous summer. As soon as David's spots had vanished the two men returned to California, where Noël went into rehearsal for the triumphant cabaret season at Las Vegas that was to restore his fortunes both financially and critically, thanks in no small measure to an opening performance at which a ratpack of friends, including the Nivens and the Bogarts, flown down to Vegas by Frank Sinatra, cheered him to the echo. A few days later David was back home by the pool at the Pink House when the phone rang: it was a call from a man called Mike Todd, who was thinking about filming *Around the World in Eighty Days* and was in search of a Phileas Fogg.

Mike Todd was not really at this time a film producer at all, at least not in the conventional mogul mould. His main claim to fame had in fact been the perfection of a technical wide-screen process known as Todd AO, which had just been successfully used in the filming of *Oklahoma*! and was now all set to rival CinemaScope, Cinerama and VistaVision in Hollywood's increasingly desperate chase after a gimmick which would get audiences away from their still-tiny television screens. In order to capitalize on the invention, Todd needed to make a film of his own, and casting around for suitably gargantuan properties he remembered that a decade earlier, back in 1946, he and Orson Welles had briefly considered a stage musical version of the Jules Verne travelogue. Before that project was abandoned, largely because of Welles's failure to come up with a script that was feasible for the stage, Todd had as a precaution purchased film rights that were still partially his; and now, everything that had been wrong with the project as a stage show fitted it perfectly for the wide-screen extravaganza he needed to make in order to exploit the wonders of Todd AO. All that he lacked was a star to play Fogg.

This was, admittedly, something of a problem. Fogg was to be one of the longest parts ever played by an actor on the screen, and in three full hours he was seldom to be out of the shot. But Todd had already decided that this was to be his film rather than the property of any single star, and that to underline the point he was going to have fifty world-class stars all playing cameo roles. Fogg thus became the straight man who had to go through the whole picture having scenes stolen from under him by guests who were only in for a day's shooting. Moreover, he would have to share the billing with the three other principals – the

manservant Passepartout, the Indian Princess they meet
along their travels, and the English detective who sets out
in hot pursuit.

So what Todd was looking for was a star, but not too
big or charismatic a star: somebody who would anchor the
picture and keep it afloat without ever imposing too much
of himself on it. He also had to be English, charming and
in his middle forties, though even with all that to go on
Todd still never thought of Niven. The idea came to him
from an old flame of David's, Evelyn Keyes, who was now
living with Todd: 'It just seemed such an obvious idea that
I mentioned it to Mike and he agreed. Another of my
ex-boyfriends was a partner of Cantinflas, who was then
cast for Passepartout, though on the set all that had to be
kept a secret from Mike, who was extremely jealous, so
David and I used to pretend that we had hardly ever met
before, which was of course rather an understatement of
our relationship.'

Chapter Twenty-One

1955–1957

'Nothing is impossible: I engage to be back here in London, in the card room of the Reform Club, on Saturday the 21st of December at a quarter before nine pm. And now, Gentlemen, I believe diamonds are trumps?'

Shooting *Around the World in Eighty Days* took David through the rest of 1955 and well into the spring of 1956. Billed not unjustly as the most fantastic and elaborate screen epic of all time, its statistics were at least as impressive as some of its landscapes. The film featured the greatest number of stars ever cast in character roles rather than as themselves; the most people (68,894) ever photographed in separate worldwide locations; the greatest distance ever travelled to make a film (four million air passenger miles); the most camera set-ups ever used (2,000, some 200 more than *Gone With The Wind*); the most sets ever used (140 actual locations plus interiors on sound stages in London, Hong Kong and Tokyo as well as six Hollywood studios); the most costumes ever used (74,685) and the most assistant directors (33).

This was also the first film made by Cantinflas outside Latin America, the first film directed by Michael Anderson for the United States and the first (and last) film made anywhere by Mike Todd. It was not without its problems: one director (John Farrow) was replaced after an hour's shooting on the first day; Shirley MacLaine did not take kindly to being cast as 'a campy Indian princess'; Robert Newton took to the bottle; and at least one of the fifty guest stars (Gregory Peck) had, according to Todd's son, to be replaced for 'not taking his role as a cavalry major seriously enough'.

Todd paid most of his major guest stars about £5,000 for an appearance on screen of often less than five minutes, and where possible he tried to do some sort of contra-deal. Thus, for his immortal performance as the head of the employment agency who first despatches Passepartout to Fogg, Noël Coward was given £100 plus a small Bonnard worth £4,600. As he wrote in his diary after that one day's shooting, 'Mustn't grumble.'

Other inspired casting ideas included Fernandel as a Parisian cab driver, Marlene Dietrich as a saloon hostess, Buster Keaton as a train conductor, Bea Lillie as a revivalist leader, Peter Lorre as a Japanese steward and Hermione Gingold as a London prostitute.

Niven had never worked with a cast like this, indeed no one had. Even his old hero, Ronald Colman, was making a farewell appearance as an official of the Great Indian Peninsular Railway, and other old friends from Charles Boyer through Evelyn Keyes to John Mills and Frank Sinatra were also in there somewhere, leaving David with the distinct impression that he was being not so much overshadowed as often obliterated entirely. It was like being a candle in the midst of a firework display.

Yet to his considerable credit he managed to turn in a performance of sustained charm and elegance, never better than when he is up with Passepartout in the air balloon, cooling his champagne in the snow as they fly over the Alps. That, rather than any single moment with a guest star, was the quintessential image and memory of *Around the World*, and it belonged entirely to David. He was daunted by some of the competition: I remember watching him in London shooting the scene very early in the film where he has to come into the Reform Club to make the famous wager that will get him round the world in less than three months. Lined up there to greet him were my father as the governor of the Bank of England and Trevor Howard, Finlay Currie, Ronald Squire, Basil Sydney, A.E. Matthews and Harcourt Williams as other members or servants of the club. Niven had, ranged across the room from him, a cross-section of the best and most experienced character actors in the whole of the British theatre and cinema, and their serried ranks made him so nervous that he would stumble over quite simple lines for most of that first morning. Then, suddenly, he seemed to get his confidence back. It was as if he'd realized that, with the fixing of the wager, he was the one who was going on with the film while they disappeared into the background to await news of his worldwide adventures.

As more and more guest stars joined Todd's bandwagon, the more there were who were eager to get on. John Gielgud remembered being persuaded to take part simply on Todd's promise that he would share a scene with his old friend Noël Coward, who had already signed for it. By the time they got to Spain and wanted to have the millionaire bullfighter Dominguin take part, Todd said to him, 'What about money?' and Dominguin simply asked, 'How much do you need?'

Often he needed a good deal just to get through the next's day's shooting. Todd was no stranger to bankruptcy, and the filming would frequently grind to a halt on one continent or another while he went chasing off in search of yet another loan. Something of the adventurer in him appealed hugely to a corresponding quality in Niven. Here was not just another of the old studio bosses to whom David had taken such a great and often anti-semitic dislike: here was a showman-cum-entrepreneur who wanted only a few months of his time instead of a life contract. Todd would even refer to his film as a show, and the whole affair had a considerable theatricality about it.

'Todd was simply a genius,' David later told a reporter. 'When we had to shoot that Alps balloon sequence, cavort-

The Other Side of the Moon

ing in a wicker basket at the top of a crane 180 feet above the Universal back lot, he realized there was a problem. I'm allergic to heights. At home I almost pass out if I have to stand on a chair to fix a lightbulb. So Todd suspended operations while we discussed my ascent, using imported champagne to neutralize the heat and dust of the location. The bottle and a reserve supply accompanied us aloft. It was just another case of Todd being there with the goods.'

This was despite the fact that earlier in the shooting David had very nearly managed to get him arrested. 'As I was about to fly to London to start the club sequences,' he recalled, 'Todd wired me from there asking me to bring a number of things over for him. So half-way through the flight I had the captain radio to Heathrow where Mike was to meet me: "I have your suits, your cigars and your radios as requested. The only thing I couldn't get was your heroin." When we landed in London, the airport was swarming with Scotland Yard detectives, and Mike was completely surrounded at the gate by narcotics men. It took several hours of extremely fast talking to explain that gag, and relations on the set were more than a little strained for a day or two.'

Yet the huge risks that Todd had taken on *Around the World in Eighty Days* paid off magnificently in the end. The film took more than $21 million at the time of its first release, and one print of it played at a cinema on Broadway for more than fifteen months. 'Oh, well,' Niven cabled Todd the morning after an ecstatically reviewed New York premiere, 'better luck next time.'

If *Around the World in Eighty Days* was not quite Niven's best film, it was certainly his biggest. During the shooting, in response to Todd's keen instinct for publicizing himself rather than any of his actors, David had taken on his first-ever personal press representative, and as a result lengthy feature articles now began appearing in most American magazines retelling the usual myths about his first arrival in California. Niven's fortunes were now definitely looking up, and his publicist was able to promote him as the star of one of the most expensive and ambitious movies ever made. Though Todd had in fact been able to acquire his services at a knock-down rate of little more than $100,000 (so keen had David been to make the film that at one point his horrified agent heard him telling Todd he would do it for nothing), it undoubtedly put up his price for subsequent work. Moreover, he was still getting comforting cheques from Otto Preminger, who had persuaded him to take a small percentage rather than his usual cash deal for *The Moon is Blue*.

Suddenly, people were even beginning to think of films that could one day be built around David. There was much talk at this time and later of a film biography of Baden-Powell, which in fact never happened, but Todd's epic had at last given him a kind of critical respectability.

Bernard Levin, film reviewing at that time for the *Manchester Guardian*, wrote of Niven 'dominating even this gigantic screen with as fine a performance as he has given these many years', while Milton Shulman in the *Sunday Express* remarked on his 'imperturbable aplomb as he meets every crisis knowing that all is still well with the Empire so long as tea is served sharply at four'. For C.A. Lejeune in the *Observer*, 'Niven, dry as the very best club sherry, plays Phileas Fogg to perfection. Such a man, one feels, could go imperturbably around the world with a top hat, an umbrella and a carpet bag, scooping up an Indian princess on the way.' Yet Todd, in his determination to make his film rather than any of its participants the real star, was to have the last word: at the following year's Oscar ceremony, it won the award for best picture. The award for best actor went to Yul Brynner for *The King and I*.

From a film with a cast of several thousand, David now moved to one with a cast effectively of only three. For no other reason than quick cash, he had agreed even after the Todd marathon to take third billing to Ava Gardner and Stewart Granger in a catastrophically sanitized screen version of André Roussin's *The Little Hut*. His experience on

Broadway with the same author's *Nina* might have been expected to teach Niven that Roussin tended to die a terrible death in American hands, but David was not a man who learnt much by experience, and he blithely set off for Rome to find Ava Gardner already nearing the end of her tumultuous affair with Walter Chiari (an Italian actor whose small role in the film was really the only reason Gardner had agreed to do it) and Granger desperate to get shot of the film as soon as possible so as to get back to a heavily pregnant Jean Simmons in California. Added to all of that, the script had been heavily castrated in order to qualify for even an X certificate in a still-prurient American cinema, and Niven and Granger, though charming enough, were no match for the original stage team of Robert Morley and David Tomlinson. Nor was there any real way of opening up an extremely claustrophobic one-set story for the screen.

Apart from that, *The Little Hut* had few problems as a film, though, as Granger recalls, 'it got off to a really terrible start. I was only doing it because Jean wanted me out of the way while she was being pregnant, and besides I didn't want another studio suspension; Ava was only doing it because she was having an affair with this funny little Italian who was in the film, and God knows why David was doing it. Anyway, we all arrive in Rome for the shooting, and they have a press conference to launch it and the three of us, David and Ava and I, line up to be big stars and suddenly we're all shoved out of the way as the press stampede to photograph Ava's little Italian, who turns out to be a huge star locally. So that makes us laugh a lot, but then Ava takes to having very long lunches with him and that annoys David, who is already in cahoots with the writer Hugh Herbert because he's also done *The Moon is Blue*. Eventually David and I decide that if we are ever to get home to California alive we have to lodge some sort of formal protest against the length of Ava's lunch breaks. So David says, now look, we simply go to the director and tell him we are not standing for this. So I agree, and together we set off across the studio in search of the director, Mark Robson, and I start saying, "Er, David and I have been discussing this and we feel that we really have to . . . ," then suddenly I look beside me and there's no David. He's vanished back to his dressing room, leaving me as usual to be the heavy with the reputation for complaining on the set.

'That was typical of Niven: he never liked making trouble if he could get somebody else to make it for him, and you never really quite knew where you were with him. He'd vanish, leaving behind that grin just like a Cheshire Cat. Even on the set you didn't always know really where the man was: acting with David was like playing the straight man to a moustache. He was always playing with it, or twitching it on other people's lines. You couldn't win against that bloody moustache.'

From Rome, David took Hjordis back to Sweden for what had become an annual holiday with her family, and then stopped off in London on his way back to Hollywood to do a job for his old friend Doug Fairbanks Jr who now had a film and television production company. This was *The Silken Affair*, a dire romantic comedy based on a short story by the film critic of the *New Yorker*, John McCarten, though that proved to be no kind of insurance as his colleagues on both sides of the Atlantic tore into the film with the traditional venom that journalists reserve for attacks on friends. Niven played a bowler-hatted accountant who starts fiddling the books when he falls in love with Geraldine Page, and though the *Observer* commented that his charm was still lethal, the *Daily Express* regretted that yet again 'a brilliant comic performance has been totally submerged by the fatuity of the script'.

Undaunted and apparently blissfully unaware that he was rapidly undoing any critical or commercial good that had been done to his career by *Around the World in Eighty Days*, David once more returned to the Pink House and to a couple of increasingly American sons heavily into baseball. These last months of 1956 were a sad time, as

Lauren Bacall remembers: 'Bogie was now very ill, and David would come by almost every day on his way home from the studio. He never missed a day and Bogie was very keen to see him, in fact he was one of the few people Bogie did want to see right up to the end because he knew he'd make him laugh. As long as Bogie was well enough I went on working to show that nothing was really wrong, and it was around this time that David and I had to do a live television show for David Selznick. It was his only ever TV production, to mark something like Edison's centenary, and we were supposed to be doing an Irwin Shaw play called *Girls in Their Summer Dresses*. We were both still terrified of live television, but somehow we got through the dress rehearsal and were feeling quite pleased with ourselves when Selznick came down from the control room and said, "I just want you to know one thing: I have never in my life seen two such terrible performances." Well, that just about finished us. David had to have his lines written on cuffs, tablecloths, scenery, the walls, everything: he was just so shaken because of what Selznick had done to him. I wasn't all that delighted either.'

Back on the wide screen, David was now committed to playing the psychoanalyst in *Oh Men! Oh Women!*, a role that Franchot Tone had been playing on Broadway with considerable success for the past two seasons. Getting Niven for a film was in those days not difficult, as the screenwriter Nunnally Johnson once noted: 'You ring the Pink House and he usually answers himself. You ask how he is. Fine. Then you ask how Mrs Niven is. Fine too, why? Then you ask if he'd like to read a script. Love to, old chum. Then you send it round, he reads it and does the film. Unless, of course, he's busy.'

This time he'd have done better to be busy. Nunnally Johnson's script was a leaden reworking of the Broadway original by Chodorov which made only one real concession to the new medium. In the interests of CinemaScope, all Niven's patients were to be seen lying full-length on his psychiatrist's couch. But somebody must have thought the title would look good on a poster and David was in starry company (Ginger Rogers, Dan Dailey, Tony Randall), though there does not seem to have been any safety in those numbers.

Nor was there much in his next project, a weary remake of *My Man Godfrey* with Niven in the role created by an earlier and still more debonair founder of that same Hollywood charm school, William Powell, and David now not even the first choice for the repeat, as the director Henry Koster recalls: 'We started out with an Austrian actor called O.W. Fischer who was really terrible in the part: he was then a very big star in Germany, apparently, but utterly humourless and his idea of playing comedy was to go ho-ho at the end of every line. So after about a week of that I resigned, and the next morning the studio called me and said they had let him go and hired a new actor and I said who? And they said, well, would I be happy with David Niven, and I said would I ever? I'd known him since we did *The Bishop's Wife*, and he still couldn't resist a practical joke, so the first day on the set he played a whole scene just like Fischer with all the ho-hos; he'd taken all that trouble just to find out what it was about Fischer that was so impossible and then imitate it. After that we got along fine, and I think I worked as closely with him as any colleague could, but one never really got very much further than that. I don't think in all the weeks I worked with David I ever heard him have a heated discussion about anything: he was an unpolitical man who just liked telling jokes. Some good, some not so good: but he told them pretty well.'

June Allyson, Niven's co-star in that picture and the wife of his Four-Star partner Dick Powell, is not so sure: 'On the set he was always very businesslike, but at home with Richard one began to see a very different man, curious about all kinds of things that didn't really have much to do with work. I think I was the one who first suggested David as a replacement for Fischer, and you have to remember that he was always very popular out here.

Whereas Rex Harrison and some of the other English stars always seemed a little bit reserved, David always had that twinkle in his eye and I think it was that, rather than his Englishness, which one remembered and liked about him. He took a lot of trouble to be friendly, to make a film set a good place to be while he was working there. He never made any kind of trouble, which was why the studios all liked him. He delivered his performance as quickly and pleasantly as he could, and that's more than could be said of a lot of actors at that time.'

But those critics who wanted something rather more than merely brisk efficiency did not find it here: the *New York Times* noted sadly that 'June Allyson and David Niven are just not Carole Lombard and William Powell'. In any case, by 1957 the vogue for high society comedies of upstairs-downstairs life had all but disappeared even from as nostalgic a town as Hollywood, so the sight of David as an Austrian count having to masquerade as a butler failed to touch many hearts or indeed funny-bones. Studio posters were now advertising him as 'the impeccable Mr Niven' in the rather forlorn hope that he had at last found his place amidst that group of debonairs (William Powell, Adolphe Menjou, Herbert Marshall, Robert Montgomery, Melvyn Douglas) which had always proved so stylishly useful to a director in trouble with a script; but Niven was ten years younger than the youngest of them, and had got there rather too late. By the end of the 1950s all those careers were either over or else translated like Douglas's into craggy character roles. There was not much point in being the toast of the debonairs if people had stopped going to debonair movies, and the box-office returns on the remake of *My Man Godfrey* certainly bore this out.

David had not spent twenty years learning the ways of Hollywood, however, just to fall into the has-been trap. Financially he was now more secure than at any time since he had abandoned Goldwyn, and indeed after *Around the World in Eighty Days* he had even taken a few months off to show Hjordis around the world in the footsteps of, though in considerably more luxury than, Phileas Fogg. After *My Man Godfrey* he went cheerfully back to the clutches of his recent saviour, Otto Preminger; at least with him one never knew what was going to happen next, and whatever it was tended to be rather more intriguing than yet another remake of an old 1930s comedy.

What Preminger wanted Niven for this time was the filming of *Bonjour Tristesse*, a headline-grabbing first novel by Françoise Sagan about jet-set life on the French Riviera. It was to Mlle Sagan's considerable credit that she had managed to establish herself while still only eighteen as a heady mix of Juliette Greco and Jackie Collins on the typewriter, and Preminger saw here a natural winner, especially as the book had already sold over a million and a half hardback copies in the USA. The story of a teenage girl incestuously in love with her widowed father and trying therefore to pair his mistress off with her own boyfriend was bound to have something for everyone, and Preminger saw this as the film that was to save himself and his discovery Jean Seberg from the recent fiasco of their *Saint Joan*. To add a bit of class he also cast Niven as the father and Deborah Kerr as his former mistress, thereby bringing David together for the first time with the actress who was to become his screen partner in four more films towards the end of his career and one of the last great influences on his private and public life.

She remembers: 'I loved David very much. Our relationship was one of total fun, because every disaster on the set or off was always met by David as some kind of elaborate joke played on him from above. He never let that mask slip in public, and it was only after years of working with him that I began to see a darker, sadder side to his nature. Most of the time we were like two children in school, crying with laughter over each other's jokes; but there was a terrible insecurity about him when we got near the end of a picture. If he didn't know exactly what film he was going into next, he got terribly neurotic about not being in work. He had to keep working, working, working all the time and I never in all the years I knew him found out why. Was he really so worried about money, or was it an escape from the family, or just that he liked the life of a film studio more than any other? He couldn't bear life if he wasn't actually working: a lot of actors are like that. David didn't have any other life until he started to write again: at this time, the films were really everything.'

Even if they did sometimes go very wrong. On *Bonjour Tristesse* there was quite a lot wrong, not least the script which was first of all the work of Sam Behrman and then heavily revised by Arthur Laurents. Mlle Sagan did not take kindly to what she saw as the 'Hollywoodization' of her work, nor to the fact that she had sold the film rights before publication for a fraction of what they were now thought to be worth.

Preminger did not take kindly to Miss Seberg, with whom he had been fighting all through *Saint Joan*, and even David found himself in the midst of an uncharacteristic shouting match with Preminger on the Champs Elysées one day when there had been a mix-up over the shooting schedule and David had gone off to join a Loel Guinness party in Deauville under the misapprehension that his services were not required. When he finally got back to Paris, Preminger's screams of rage could be heard across several boulevards. 'Otto,' murmured David through the shouting, 'I have to talk to you privately. I have this terrible handicap. Whenever anyone shouts at me, I forget all my lines. It's been that way since teachers shouted at me in classrooms. If people shout at me now, I find I have to go to my dressing room and lie in the dark for several hours.' Otto never shouted at him again: he did, however, note what a pity it was that a man who always seemed so charming on the screen could not always manage it in real life.

David and Deborah did their best to protect Seberg from the noisier sessions with the flamboyant director, but it was clear from the beginning that they were all on to a loser. As Derek Granger of the *Financial Times* later noted: 'One can only hope that *Bonjour Tristesse* will bring a quick, grey smile of Left-bank derision to the pinched little face of its gilded authoress . . . Mlle Sagan's story may not have been great literature and may quite possibly have been thought trashy, but at least it conformed to a good French tradition of being short, spare, lucid and philosophically misanthropic. Mr Preminger's film, which aims at French sophistication in the little Midwest person of Miss Jean Seberg and the hefty Anglo-Saxon ones of Mr David Niven and Miss Deborah Kerr, manages with positively superhuman persistence to seem long, untidy, muddled and mushy. The effect is hardly less depraved than a CinemaScopic carnival-time presentation of high living in Bournemouth. In roles that call for Edwige Feuil-lère and Pierre Brasseur, Miss Kerr and Mr Niven manage a determined tennis-club glitter.' So much for *Bonjour Tristesse*; but it was remarkably perceptive of Mr Granger to suggest, even as part of an insult, that Niven and Kerr belonged to the tennis-club world of Bournemouth, for that was precisely where they were now to score the greatest success of their entire careers.

Chapter Twenty-Two

1957–1959

'David and Hjordis Niven have been living apart for several weeks. They say no divorce is contemplated. They are trying to work out their very personal problems as quietly and privately as possible.'

With Humphrey Bogart dead, and Mike Todd killed in a plane crash only a few hours after he had opened up his house in Palm Springs to the Nivens for a weekend together, David began to get the feeling that Hollywood was crumbling to dust around him. Though still only in his late forties, he had come of a much earlier generation of movie stars than the one presently in charge of the capital, and that generation was now fast disappearing. Of those David had started out with before the war, Ronald Colman died in 1958, Errol Flynn in 1959, Clark Gable in 1960, Gary Cooper in 1961. In the late 1950s studios were already being sold off to real-estate men and such stars as there were belonged to an altogether different and more laid-back world, the world of Newman and Brando and Dean. It was no longer David's world or generation, which was why more and more he began to find himself drawn back towards Europe where actors like him still found work, indeed still had scripts written for them by craftsmen such as Terence Rattigan.

During 1954–5, Rattigan had enjoyed tremendous London and Broadway success with *Separate Tables*, two inter-

linked one-act plays set in the Beauregard Private Hotel
near Bournemouth. The first, and weaker, of these plays
concerned a drunken political journalist and his meeting
with the fashion model who several years earlier had ruined
his life; the second was about a bogus Army major charged
with molesting young women in a nearby cinema, but
finding some sort of redemption through the love of a
repressed and ungainly spinster living in the same hotel.
The plays were originally and wonderfully directed in the
theatre by Peter Glenville, and what held them together
and made them a coherent evening instead of just a random
double-bill was the convention whereby one actor and
actress (on stage Eric Portman and Margaret Leighton)
would double as the principal characters in each play,
while around them the rest of the cast of other hotel guests
remained the same throughout the evening.

When *Separate Tables* was bought for the screen by the
Hecht–Hill–Lancaster company, that important convention was soon to be destroyed, much to Rattigan's fury.
The original plan had been to film the plays with Laurence
Olivier and Vivien Leigh doubling the leading roles (as
Portman and Leighton had done on stage) and with Olivier
also directing. Then the film company seems to have decided that a more 'bankable' star was needed for the box
office, at which point it was suggested that Burt Lancaster,
himself one of the company's three directors, should play
the drunken journalist. At this juncture Olivier and his
wife pulled out of the project altogether, and it was decided
that Rita Hayworth, then about to marry another of the
company's directors (James Hill), should play the fashion
model; but a merciful sense of their own Thespian limi-
tations, or perhaps just a determination not to be seen by
the fans as a repressed spinster and a bogus major, made
Hayworth and Lancaster decide not to go forward into the
second story. Instead this was now to be played by two
quite different actors, David Niven and Deborah Kerr,
casting which had the inevitable effect of making the first
half of the film look totally American and the second half

deeply English, though that had all been signed and sealed before the director, Delbert Mann, came on the scene.

'My first instinct', he recalls, 'was that I was quite the wrong kind of director, and I'd never even been to Bournemouth or experienced that totally British small-hotel life; but Hecht sent me there to research it, and within half a day I'd found prototypes of all the characters that Terry had written about, all living there in retirement homes – the old schoolmaster, the little lady who played the horses, the retired Army man. Terry knew them all: his mother had once lived in a private hotel just like the one he was writing about.

'Our main problem was getting a screenplay which would turn the two original plays into just one narrative line, and we had about five attempts with different writers, including Terry himself, before we finally got it right. Even then I still had great reservations about David: the role of the major was so different from anything I'd seen him do before.'

David, however, who had seen Eric Portman in the play when it first opened in London almost three years earlier, was certain that here was something he had to have: a rare chance to prove himself on the screen in a part that might have been created for him. He knew that major almost as well as he knew himself. He had been to Sandhurst, and to Malta, and later, through the war, with men like the major, failed soldiers desperately living on the invention of past glories. There was something else about the character too: his determination to lead a double life, to invent for himself an identity far removed from his own, made a lot of sense to a man who had spent his life as an actor. The grin and tonic man had come into his own at last.

'There was', says Doreen Hawkins, who happened to be staying with the Nivens when shooting began on *Separate Tables*, 'a new and desperate seriousness about David when he came back from the studio at night and went off to learn his lines for the next day. He hardly talked about the film at all, but when he did there was none of the usual jokiness about "just another job": this was something he really wanted to work on, and he was determined that he should do it well. It was, I think, his one real test as an actor, and this time he wasn't going to allow the schoolboy in him to fail it. *Separate Tables* was where he grew up as an actor.'

'David was very different on the set of *Separate Tables*', remembers Deborah Kerr, 'from the David I'd been with a few months earlier in France for *Bonjour Tristesse*. Now he kept saying, "God, this is the real stuff, isn't it?" and I think he caught that major because in so many ways he understood him. I don't mean sexually or anything like that, but as a character and as a person David felt that he was on familiar ground – that he too in his own life had always been acting and pretending, "dressing up for the grown-ups", as he used to say.'

'David and Deborah', says Delbert Mann, 'worked gloriously together in that film, both of them realizing that they were taking wild, wild chances with those two roles. If we had slipped or missed, those relationships would have been laughable with Deborah playing the hysterical woman who is frightened of the word sex and David as the emotionally crippled man hiding behind this façade of the blustering wartime major. And when he's unmasked, David perfectly caught that anguish and pain behind the eyes. There's a moment at the end of the picture when the major enters the dining room of the hotel after some of the guests have asked him to leave because of the scandal of his court case. The proprietor of the hotel, played by Wendy Hiller, says that she'll support him if he wants to stay, but will understand if he wants to go and then the next thing we see is everyone at breakfast with the major crossing the room in an absolute, shocked silence all the way to his little separate table and sitting there, burying his face in a menu which he's known by heart for ten years. And gradually, one at a time, the other guests start to speak to him to show that all is forgiven. Even Deborah, over the horrified protests of her mother, Gladys Cooper, who had led the campaign against him, finally talks to him. We shot this scene over about four days to get all the reactions and finally we had to get a close-up on David registering all the emotion of that scene and he said it was panic time. There was this whole line-up of the British stage, Wendy Hiller and Gladys Cooper and Cathleen Nesbitt and Felix Aylmer all staring at him and when he'd finished they all applauded. I think that was maybe the best moment of his whole acting career.'

'Tried by a jury of my peers,' was David's own recollection of that scene, 'and found wanting.'

This was to be almost the last great stand of the Hollywood English, and Wendy Hiller was to recall a sharp Anglo-American split on the set: 'We outnumbered the Americans on the film by nine to two, which was just as well because Gladys never seemed to know a line and it was all Burt Lancaster's own money that we were using up with the retakes. As soon as he and Rita Hayworth started to do any of their scenes, Gladys used to remove her glasses and fall into a deep sleep at the side of the set, which I did think was rather naughty and certainly used to unnerve Rita, a poor darling dancing girl who was already rather lost in the film.

'It was David who saved that situation. After it had happened for the third time and Gladys's snores really were a little loud, he said, "Lunch, I think," and that gave them time to recover. He was always one of nature's ambassadors: dear God, what charm.'

As soon as the film was in the can, David followed his usual policy of not hanging around for a reaction. He went straight back into television for Four-Star and also did a memorable guest spot on a live Robert Montgomery show for which he locked his jacket and some crucial props inadvertently in the dressing room, a problem he discovered only about thirty seconds before air time and which led to a performance of some confusion. He also now found a lucrative sideline in magazine advertisements for the more distinguished airlines and whisky distillers, and then moved rapidly into another trio of undistinguished light comedies. In the quarter-century that was to pass between the release of *Separate Tables* and David's death in 1983, he went on to make thirty-five more films, of which only five (*The Guns of Navarone, Paper Tiger, Murder by Death, The Pink Panther* and *Death on the Nile*) could be considered in any way worthwhile. The case for David as a major screen actor really ends with that great closing scene of *Separate Tables* and it was with this, suitably enough, that he won his only Oscar.

If he thought that meant an escape from twenty years of typecasting as the kind of man who could hold a cup of tea in one hand and a duchess in the other, Niven was in for a nasty shock. His next film, *Ask Any Girl*, reunited him with his Indian princess from *Around the World*, Shirley MacLaine, but did neither of them any good at all and indeed left David right back in the critical doldrums. Still, there was at least the Oscar ceremony to await with trepidation: David had to beat Paul Newman, Spencer Tracy, Sidney Poitier and Tony Curtis and had to do so in the knowledge that the previous year's winner had been Alec Guinness and therefore the Academy voters were unlikely to go for two British actors in two consecutive years. In fact, they very nearly didn't. A few days before voting took place, the influential movie critic of the *Washington Daily News* ran a syndicated story saying that David didn't deserve to win because his performance was a carbon-copy of Eric Portman's on stage, one which Niven had seen 'at least forty times'. Reacting swiftly to this, Niven cabled Portman in London and got him to issue a statement that David had only seen his performance once, very early in the London run. Armed with that denial, David then got an apology out of the Washington paper and made sure that it was widely spread around Hollywood.

Even so, he sat on Oscar night next to Hjordis convinced that he was going to be beaten to the statue by one of the Americans. When Irene Dunne finally called out his name, he stumbled up the steps to the stage and, by way of an explanation, started to say that he was so loaded down with good-luck charms as to be off-balance. He got as far as, 'I am so loaded', gained the laugh that inevitably followed this, and decided not to go on with what would have been an anti-climactic explanation. The next day, among the congratulatory telegrams was an invitation to dine with Sam Goldwyn. The rebel son had made good at last, and Sam had lived to see it.

Then it was back to the routine of terrible comedies. After *Ask Any Girl* came *Happy Anniversary* with Mitzi Gaynor, billed unreassuringly as 'a comedy of premarital sex', and then *Please Don't Eat the Daisies*, a screen version of Jean Kerr's autobiographical pieces about her life as the wife of Broadway's leading drama critic. By the time that started, however, in the summer of 1959, David had his own marital problems to worry about. Hjordis had left him.

'How does one know why these things happen?' asks Hjordis now. 'The marriage just broke. I moved out of the Pink House for a while. To live on my own.'

David blamed himself for the break, saying that he had been too tied up in his work, his Oscar and all of that to be a good husband to her. Other observers found other causes, ranging from Hjordis's inability to have children of her own to her desire for a career other than that of being 'Mrs David Niven' at Hollywood parties. One friend even reckoned that there were only so many times you could hear David going through the same repertoire of old anecdotes before anyone would want to leave home; but, as Lauren Bacall said, 'You show me a couple who say their marriage hasn't at some time come close to breaking point, and I'll show you a couple of liars.'

Friends rallied round, some at considerable peril to themselves. Stewart Granger, for instance: 'One night he turned up suddenly at the house where Jean Simmons and I were then living in Hollywood and said, "Could I have a Scotch, old chap?" And then he said, "She's left me. Hjordis has left me." He didn't exactly say why, but I got the impression it was at least partly because for years she'd been told she was the most beautiful woman in Hollywood, and she now wanted to see whether she could make it on her own as a model. She wanted to be the star for a while: I think that's understandable. It's very boring being married to a star and not being one yourself. Anyway, David and I got rather pissed that night, and I began saying that I really thought the split was a very good thing and that he'd be a lot better off without her. I was really just trying to cheer him up and make the best of it; so then what happens? A few months later they get together again, and David tells Hjordis all the awful things I've been saying about her, and she never speaks to me again. You really can't win in cases like that.'

'David was terribly broken up when Hjordis left him,' says Deborah Kerr. 'I remember him being very stunned and not knowing what to do about the boys who were in their teens. He said he thought he'd take them shooting in Canada and Peter, my husband, said, "Why not take them to Hawaii where all three of you will have these gorgeous girls to look at instead of a lot of old Canadian bears?" So that was what they did.'

During that Hawaiian holiday, David crashed a surfboard into a rock and was delighted that Hjordis phoned to enquire after his safety when she saw a newspaper picture of him covered in blood. Yet there was still no thought of a reconciliation, and back in California he went to work with Doris Day on the film about Jean and Walter Kerr. Niven was actually very good in this, managing to give a fair impression of a Broadway drama critic with domestic problems, and with Doris Day then hot from the commercial triumph of *Pillow Talk* the film should have worked rather better than it did. With them in it was the celebrated English actor and fish mimic Richard Haydn, who remembers 'a rather distraught David on the set. It so happened that we were both called for the first day of shooting but he was terribly nervous and that whole day's work had to be done again later.'

Joe Pasternak, who was producing David here for the third time (after *Ask Any Girl* and *The Toast of New Orleans*), found a unique way to deal with his insecurities: 'David used to keep asking me why I'd hired him when there were so many better actors around so I said, "Look, I'll tell you what I'll do. Every day I have to look at the rushes, and if you're any good I'll give you a quarter." So every morning he used to hang around like a schoolboy waiting for his 25 cents and some days I wouldn't give it him and then he'd act a bit better the next day. But I don't think he was very happy: certainly he and Doris Day never spoke except on the set, and David seemed much more turned in on himself than he had been before.'

'At first', said Richard Haydn, 'I thought this must be something to do with Hjordis having left him, but it really wasn't that at all. He said he was always quite terrible on the first day of shooting, always convinced that this was going to be the picture where they finally found out he couldn't act at all and sent him away. In fact, he was often a very touching and moving and effective actor, but he had this crippling sense of his own inadequacy. Yet at the same time he managed to make you feel that while you were with him he had never enjoyed being anywhere so much in his life as with you. When he and Hjordis were together I used to see them quite often, because we all lived on Amalfi Drive and were dead-keen gardeners, so we used to go out shopping for plants in Glendale. She was wonderfully decorative and always smelt gorgeous, but there was something odd about her. She always looked like a perfectly decorated house in which nobody ever actually lived, and David treated her rather like a precious toy that might get broken if you were too rough with it.'

It was during the filming of *Please Don't Eat the Daisies*, in the early autumn of 1959, that the Nivens got back together again. Hjordis recalls: 'I think it was David's sense of humour that got us back. I really did miss him, and I wasn't very good about living alone. I am not a very practical person, and it never occurred to me to lock a door because after being married to David for 900 years he was always the one who locked up at night. So he knew the little house I'd rented would never be locked, and one morning on the way to the studio he just walked into the bedroom carrying his own breakfast on a tray, as though he'd been living there all the time. I realized then how much I'd missed him, and quite soon after that I moved back into the Pink House.'

David duly issued a press statement, this time to Louella Parsons: 'When we separated a few months ago, Hjordis and I told our friends we hoped to be given the chance to work things out as quietly and privately as possible. This was respected by everyone without exception, and we are truly grateful because we have worked things out in the happiest possible way.' Miss Parsons added an almost regal footnote: 'I am sure', she wrote, 'that David and Hjordis have been miserable since their parting, and they are to be congratulated on this mature and happy solving of their problems.' She might have continued: 'And, of course, on giving the reconciliation news to me instead of Hedda Hopper.'

With the return of Hjordis, David's life was to change more drastically than at any time since their marriage ten years earlier. Within the next few months he was to leave Hollywood for Europe, and to become the father of an adopted girl. Somehow the few months of separation from Hjordis had been a breaking point in almost every other way; it had given David time to think about the life he really wanted to lead, and about where he wanted to lead it. Hollywood in 1959 was no longer even faintly recognizable as the place where he had started work as an actor in 1934; it wasn't even the town to which he had returned from the war in 1946. True, it had just given him its highest award, but *Separate Tables* had been a film written and almost exclusively played by the English, and it was not likely to lead to any sort of a sequel. As far as Hollywood was concerned, David was still the light comedian you threw into shaky comedies in the hope of getting a bit of class. The major had been courageous and unusual casting for an actor with Niven's light track record, and there was no sign that a part would come along like that twice in his life-time.

In the winter of 1959 a neighbour of David's a few doors down Amalfi Drive was brutally murdered by burglars, and he suddenly found himself asking, for the first time in his life, why he was living there instead of in the Europe to which both he and Hjordis belonged. Moreover, if they were really going to adopt children, which was what Hjordis now most wanted, would it not make more sense to adopt Swedish children and bring them up on their own continent rather than in an America to which he felt less and less attached?

At this time, Niven believed that most of his work would still come from and be done in Hollywood, but did that mean he actually had to live there? A number of his greatest friends, from Deborah Kerr through Peter Ustinov to Noël Coward, had now bought houses in Switzerland; more and more international films were now being made on locations around the world; Switzerland was still offering good tax breaks; from there, he could be back at the club in London or Hjordis with friends in Stockholm within a matter of hours instead of days. The boys could finish their education in Europe; London had just started to swing. What was Niven doing now in California, apart from watching by the graveside as the old studios faded into extinction? He had enjoyed the best of Hollywood from the 1930s through to the 1950s – the time had come to get out before the worst overtook it.

Oddly enough, what made him finally decide to leave California at the beginning of 1960 was that the outside of his beloved Pink House needed repainting. David suddenly found that, on the verge of his fiftieth birthday, after a quarter of a century as a leading player, with fifty-five films and one Oscar behind him, he actually could not afford to get the job done.

Chapter Twenty-Three

1960

'The islands of the Aegean have given birth to many legends of war and adventure. In the last war 2,000 British soldiers lay marooned there, doomed unless they could be evacuated. What happened next became the legend of Navarone.'

One of the many curious facets of David's long career as an actor is that he only ever made real money by writing about it, and then only in the last ten years of his life. Fifteen years of original Goldwyn contract playing had been followed by a largely unsuccessful freelance decade in which he had really enjoyed only three hits: *The Moon is Blue* (1953), *Around the World in Eighty Days* (1956) and *Separate Tables* (1958). On the first of these, which did modestly well at the box office, Preminger had allowed him a small percentage of the profits in lieu of more immediate payment. For the other two, he had been on a flat salary of between $100,000 and $200,000. Good money, certainly, but not the kind of cash that was making millionaires of the stars around him who had gone into real estate, financial investment or their own movie production companies. Four-Star was certainly now beginning to show an annual profit, but he was only in for a third of that and their studio production costs were still high.

So Niven's constant worry in post-war California, and the reason he often seemed to friends so oddly tight-fisted, was that he had never really managed to save anything against the day when his acting services (which consisted largely of a certain youthful charm) would no longer be required; and he knew very well that he was not the kind of craggy theatrical player who was going to flourish as aged senators. Certainly he and Hjordis and the boys were living well enough up on Amalfi Drive, but always at the upper limit of his annual income. David's major financial achievement since the war had been in keeping out of serious debt, and somehow that no longer seemed quite enough for a man of fifty who had managed to stay in near-constant film work for almost three decades. The tax haven of a Swiss Alp therefore began to seem like a very good idea indeed, especially if he and Hjordis were now to adopt and embark on a whole new round of school and college fees.

David, according to Jess Morgan, who was for many years his American business manager, suffered all the problems of insecurity between jobs that are known to actors, and he was always trying to create capital. He wanted the freedom to say no to the parts he did not want to play, and until this time he had never really enjoyed that. He knew enough not to wait around for another *Gone With The Wind* in the way that some actors did, and he had a shrewd understanding of the business, which meant that he knew enough to realize that an actor only gets work by staying in work. David saw at once what *Around the World in Eighty Days* could do for him, and he fought hard to get that part. Once he had it, there were weeks when he never knew if he were going to get paid, or if Todd would come through with it, but he stayed with the film because he knew it was a wonderful part. Niven ended up with less money than he could have got for making almost any other movie that year, but he knew it was the right one to be seen in. When he won the Oscar he gained a lot of confidence, but he still was not getting anything like superstar money, even though he had been farsighted enough to go into television at a time when most screen actors were still terrified of it.

When David decided to live in Europe, Jess Morgan
went to Switzerland to set up various financial arrangements, which meant that effectively Niven was going to be
better off: 'But I don't think the decision to move was
solely financial; I think emotionally he felt that his roots
were in Europe and that he'd be happier with the life
there. It was where he had come from, after all; his wife
was Swedish and his sons were English. He was just going
home again.'

He was not, of course, returning to live in England,
where the tax situation was considerably tougher even than
California. Switzerland was his destination, and his first
guides there were Deborah Kerr and her husband, the
writer Peter Viertel. The chalet that David bought at
Château d'Oex in 1960 was the one where he died twenty-
three years later, and it was in many ways the favourite of
all his homes. Ideally placed for the ski slopes that now
became his greatest delight, with friends like Elizabeth
Taylor and Richard Burton twenty minutes north of him
in Gstaad and friends like Noël Coward twenty minutes to
the south in Les Avants (and Geneva airport less than an
hour away, which meant that he could be on almost any
film set in the world within a day or so, he had now at last
found the best of all possible worlds. A couple of weeks
later the Pink House was sold to David's friend, the agent
Phil Kellogg.

The question of whether David should stay in Hollywood
or move back to Europe was in some ways a tricky one,
as Kellogg saw it, because a lot of Americans felt that this
was where Niven had been given all his real breaks as an
actor and that he therefore owed the Americans some sort
of loyalty. But David was not an American citizen and he
really had no reason to stay now that the boys were almost
out of high school. The moment he got to Europe he never
looked back. He started working there as soon as he got
off the plane, though that was largely accidental. 'I was in
London just about that time,' said Kellogg, 'meeting with
Carl Foreman who was just starting work on *Guns of*

Navarone, and he had a role for which David would be wonderful. But when they'd put in the enquiry it looked as though David would still be on *Please Don't Eat the Daisies*, so they decided to go with Kenneth More instead. Then More proved unavailable and Foreman came back to me, and I said I think we might be able to get you David after all.'

Ever since Alistair MacLean had, in 1957, published his best-seller about a group of veteran English, American and Greek commandos scaling impossible cliff-faces on an Aegean island to immobilize German wartime guns and thereby free some 2,000 trapped British soldiers, Carl Foreman had realized that here were the makings of a splendid all-star wide-screen action adventure. Quite who those stars were to be was, however, open to some doubt. Originally Foreman announced that they would be Hugh O'Brian, Trevor Howard, Alec Guinness, Marlon Brando and Cary Grant, a remarkable castlist made all the more remarkable by the fact that not one of them ended up in the finished film. William Holden, Jack Hawkins and Gary Cooper were later also announced, though none of them was in it either. Eventually, after a couple of years of negotiation and recasting, the group settled down as Gregory Peck, Anthony Quinn, David Niven, Anthony Quayle and Stanley Baker.

'The first night we met on the location in Athens,' recalls the director of *Navarone*, Lee Thompson, 'David was very cheery but a little anxious that, with all those other stars around, he was just going to be left standing about a lot. He felt that his character wasn't as well developed as some of the others, and he wanted to be convinced that I'd look after him and try and bring out the comedy in the role, which he knew he was good at. He felt, maybe rightly, that all the characters had been written as supermen without very much depth. But you have to remember also that he'd just won an Oscar, and so there was a certain amount of rivalry on the set between him and Peck and Quinn, all eyeing each other warily and wondering which of them was going to come out ahead. There was nothing really unpleasant there, but you could sense the tension, the rivalry, until Quinn brought out a lot of little portable chess sets and they all got hooked on those and more or less forgot their rivalry.'

The Guns of Navarone was to cost an unprecedented $6 million to film, and to take just over twice that in the first year of its American release. It also undoubtedly started a vogue for all-star international action adventure pictures which was to last for the next twenty years, though ironically, when in 1977 Foreman went back to the mother lode to make a sequel (*Force Ten From Navarone*, with Edward Fox in the Niven role and Robert Shaw in that created by Peck), the genre was a spent force and the sequel barely recouped its costs.

Even the original was not without its problems. At least one director (Alexander Mackendrick) was sacked before he had even got a foot of film in the can, and the plot went through so many twists that Gregory Peck finally submitted his own version to Foreman: 'David Niven really loves Tony Quayle and Gregory Peck loves Anthony Quinn. Tony Quayle breaks a leg and is sent off to hospital. Tony Quinn falls in love with Irene Papas, and David Niven and Peck catch each other on the rebound and live happily ever after.'

Playing the 'lean-limbed, laconic mountain climber', Peck was to emerge as the film's leader, partly as a result of the plot and partly because he was always just that much bigger a star than any of the others. He also had a capacity for sobriety which even Niven had to admire: 'By the time filming was over for the day, some of the team would be paralytic because, working in a tank of ice cold water, the only way to stay warm was with a steady supply of brandy. But Greg would match anybody drink for drink, and never so much as stagger or muff a line. Really quite disgusting to see a man able to handle liquor like that.'

Peck was in no doubt that the film was treading a tricky tightrope: 'We played half-a-dozen commandos somehow able to perform miracles, outwitting a whole German regiment, getting right into the middle of them, stealing their uniforms and masquerading as Nazis. Well, to do that you'd have to do with the Nazis what Mack Sennett did with the Keystone Cops. There were 550 chances for them to kill all of us before we even set foot on the island, but we had to do it all with total and utter conviction, even though we were aware that the whole film was flirting with parody.'

That conviction paid off. *Time* magazine reckoned that *Navarone* was 'the most enjoyable consignment of baloney in months' and other critics were quick to join in the praise for Foreman's gun-blasting epic, one which seemed almost literally to widen the screen at a time when it had been confined to a lot of close-up domestic dramas.

Navarone also brought Niven together for the first time with Tony Quayle, the actor who was later to spearhead the campaign to raise funds for research into the disease which killed him. He recalls: '*Navarone* was a very long film and we were a very mixed bunch of people, some like Tony Quinn not always easy to get on with. But Niven was always this wonderfully extrovert character: "Hello, old bean, how are you?" and all of that. I think he made a tremendous contribution to the film, though he was the only one who really suffered for it. Towards the end, when we were shooting in the water tank, he got a cut lip which became infected and led to general septicaemia, and for a while they thought he was going to die and there were endless meetings called to decide what would happen and whether we'd reshoot or finish the picture with a double or what. In the end, after about four weeks in hospital, he recovered totally but I remember even when he was very ill I went to see him in bed and he was still grinning and I said, "David, why are you always so abominably cheerful, is it something in your nature or what?" and he said, "Well, old bean, I think that life is such a fucker, it really is so bloody awful that if you've got any energy at all then it's your absolute duty to try and be chirpy and keep people lively and amused and happy."

'To him life was a total game of chance. I remember once asking him whether I should agree to do some terrible film and he said, "Of course, old bean. You'll be seen by 60,000,000 people. How many saw Larry do his *Othello*? Probably not even 60,000." And I said surely the whole thing was about quality rather than quantity, but I don't think David ever understood that. Whether it was the Army, or Hollywood, or the women, or his writing, the whole thing was just one great big adventure. He didn't think acting was any kind of an art: he thought it was all a great treasure hunt for the girls and the caviare. He had no comment to make on the world, and after a while it became almost unbearable to hear him telling the same stories time and time again. He wasn't really an actor: he was a man who presented himself to the world over and over again.'

Navarone started filming again shortly after David came out of hospital, where, he claimed: 'One man produced an immense hypodermic and with a loud animal cry plunged it into my bum and started pumping away like a mad garage mechanic.' The film reunited him for the first time in ten years with his oldest friend, Michael Trubshawe, who had a small part in it. Something about their friendship had now gone terribly wrong: 'David never really wanted me to become an actor, and he had never gone out of his way to help me. But now that we were together, purely by chance, he seemed almost embarrassed.' Part of the problem was that, just before leaving Hollywood, Niven had given an unfortunate interview to a gossip columnist saying that in his view there was nothing more boring than old friendships, and that every six months everyone should start all over again and make new friends, and forget all about the others. This found its way back to Hugh Williams, who sent Trubshawe a copy. David was quoted as saying, 'It must be awful all getting old together, decrepit together and finally dying together. One must change chums.' For a while Trubshawe had it framed in his bathroom, because somehow it seemed to him such an extraordinary example of David's 'heartlessness and thoughtlessness'. Then, when Trubshawe got a bit part in *Navarone*, he wrote telling David what flight he would be on and where he would be staying in Rhodes, which was the main location. However, on arrival, he was surprised and disappointed when his old chum was not at the airport; nor had David even left a note at the hotel. 'In fact I didn't see him at all for forty-eight hours and then it was only for a quick drink. My scene was with Peck, so David and I hardly spoke the whole time I was out there. As he said, nothing more boring than old friendships.'

Trubshawe did two more films with Niven (*The Best of Enemies* and *The Pink Panther*) and gradually their friendship returned to a more even keel, not least because during *The Best of Enemies* it was Trubshawe's turn to be quite seriously ill and it was Hjordis who nursed him back to health. 'David kept saying, "Are you all right, old bean?" and when it was patently clear that I wasn't, he moved me into his hotel room where there was some air conditioning in the middle of the bloody desert where we were filming. But the friendship was really over. In the thirty years after the war, I think he came down to lunch in Sussex maybe twice, bringing with him a bottle of whisky and a pot of caviare. There'd be a few brief reminiscences and then he'd be off back to London and that was that. A few letters, more towards the end when he began to get ill, but no real contact. I think he began to regard me, probably rightly, as rather a dimwit who could only talk about the past and somehow he didn't want to think about our past, only the Hollywood past which I hadn't shared. I think our past meant Primmie and the war, and he really wanted to forget all of that: his was now a quite different life.'

David was still hacking around for work. The move to Europe was an expensive one, and although domestically things were a great deal better since Hjordis and he had managed to adopt the first of their daughters, Kristina, professionally David was now a man of fifty starting out on a second fatherhood with no more job security (indeed, rather less) than when he'd first gone back to Hollywood with Primmie and the boys just after the war. It may well be argued that constant job insecurity is the lot of any actor; but most actors know why they become actors and what sort of actors they really want to be. David had no such knowledge, and consequently suffered the constant film starlet's fear that the passing years might do him considerable harm at the box office, as his increasingly lined face reminded his audiences that they too were not getting any younger. Equally, although he now began to ski and paint with a vengeance, he was only really happy doing that when he knew he had a job to go to in a week or two.

Thus began the most prolific and depressing period of David's life as an actor. Between *The Guns of Navarone* in 1960 and his death in 1983 he made thirty-two films, most of them so terrible that they are not even shown on daytime television in Nebraska. He made them because he needed the money, and because by the time he'd stopped needing the money, the girls had already begun to grow up and he needed the companionship of the film sets that were always his favourite clubs.

'He was extraordinary with those little girls,' recalls Hjordis. 'He was totally besotted by Kristina, and by Fiona, whom we adopted two years later. If ever I said no to them, they would go to Papa and wriggle their little bottoms and get whatever they wanted. He loved to take them out in the snow. When I was a child in Sweden I had been forced to ski and as a result absolutely hated it but now, in Château d'Oex, I came to love it and these were really very happy times for us. I think since the separation we had both become more secure in ourselves because we realized that both of us could function perfectly well without each other, well maybe not perfectly, but we could at least lead our own lives if we had to. And then somehow it became much easier to share these lives.'

'I think', says David Niven Jr, 'that the great difference between my father with his first family and my father with his second was that when Jamie and I were young he really didn't have a great deal of money, whereas by the time Kristina and Fiona were growing up he was able to give them some of the luxuries that we never had. Not that we had nothing, but they had everything and that was the difference; also he had always wanted daughters and unfortunately got stuck with two sons, so I think adoption was the ideal solution. It made him and Hjordis very happy and the girls were fabulous; they were always told from the very beginning that they were adopted, so it was never an ugly word and there were no surprises. I remember once, one of my sisters saying in an argument with me, "Well at least I was chosen; Daddy got stuck with you."'

For Jamie, though, the adoptions did mean the end of one relationship: 'My father was very sensible about treating the adopted girls exactly as if they were his own, but at the same time never shortchanging the love he had for my brother and myself. He was always a very fair man, and he just felt that now he had four children instead of two. He never played favourites; I think having a stepfather himself made him very conscious of the dangers. But my relationship with Hjordis really did change the moment the girls came along; she just wouldn't talk to me, and some days it really got very bad indeed. Other days we'd manage to make a joke of it.'

The short, golden period of 1955–60 in which David had made three of his best films (*Around the World, Separate Tables* and *Navarone*) was now already at an end.

Though most of its stars would try again sooner or later, *Navarone* proved an oddly unrepeatable triumph. Something about the format ('an elderly gang goes to war', as Derek Monsey uncharitably summarized it) endeared itself to cinema-goers all too used to their war films being played by clean-limbed young Americans. Here was a rough-and-ready bunch of Greek (Quinn, by screen image if not birth), English (Niven and Quayle), Welsh (Baker) and American (Peck) middle-aged men embarking on a cartoon adventure but in deadly earnest. It was Quinn who best summed up the gang chemistry when he gave them all their chess sets: 'Look how it reveals their characters. Niven, the Errol Flynn of the chessboard, barging around it crying, "Idiotic move, what? Well, never mind, on we go." Peck, calm like Lincoln, contemplating every move, deep in thought. Baker highly competitive: great glee in victory, terrible fury at defeat. When Carl Foreman loses there are whole centuries of persecution in his face. And Quayle moves like a general, planning his strategy across the board way ahead. Me? I just throw the board at them when I lose.'

Chapter Twenty-Four

1961–1963

'What a beautiful day. I wonder who's on my rocks?'

Central to David's character were two curious contradictions: he was a natural loner who yet badly needed the camaraderie of the film set, and a passionate family man who yet relished the occasional affair. ('Here in London on business,' he wrote gleefully to a friend in the late 1960s; 'the business is both film and monkey.') He was also, for all his affirmations of great good luck, a man who never quite seemed to find himself in the right place at the right time. Now that he had a restored marriage, two enchanting new babies and a Swiss chalet, the one thing he lacked was the ability to stay home and enjoy any of it. From *Navarone* he went straight into four other movies almost back to back, presumably to finance the Swiss chalet and a house that he and Hjordis were also thinking of acquiring as a summer home on Cap Ferrat in the South of France.

Now that he was a resident of Switzerland, Niven reckoned the time had come to move into the co-productions that were being set up all over Europe as more and more stars left Hollywood for better tax climates. The advent of direct over-the-pole flights made California in any case rather less than nine hours away, just one more stop-over on a busy actor's travel schedule instead of a vital permanent base. Niven did not, in fact, make another feature film there until 1963, when he was back in California on Four-Star business, but in the meantime he was careful to keep up his Hollywood connections, giving lengthy interviews to American magazines in which he would now quite shamelessly rewrite his own past, firmly denying to one columnist that the affair with Merle Oberon back in the 1930s had ever taken place. He also outlined to a Los Angeles reporter some of the hazards of taking up summer residence at Lo Scoglietto, the Cap Ferrat villa just above the harbour at St Jean which the Nivens were renting and soon to buy.

'I know this is hard for an outsider to understand,' he said, 'but you see I rented this beautiful villa overlooking the sea. When I rented it I understood that the sea front belonged to me, that I could enjoy it in privacy and get the vacation I so richly deserved. But in France the law says the public is entitled to use the sea front, and they've been squatting in front of my villa every day. They've made me into a shaking, gibbering idiot. But they're my rocks, old boy. Look at it from my point of view. I wake up in the morning and I see the sun streaming in. I say to myself, "What a beautiful day. I wonder who's on my rocks?" And I dash out in a rage. Sure enough, there are six people squatting on the concrete slab I had made, with a chain which says "Private" on it. I say to them, "I'm sorry, this is private." Then they say, "You're a foreigner, aren't you?" I admit I am. Then they say, "You don't know the laws of France. The sea here is for everyone." Then I tell them, "Well, get off my land and into the sea." "Aha," they sneer, "three metres of the land bordering the sea also belongs to the people. So we're entitled to sit here." But the worst is lunchtime. While I'm lying there, they take out large loaves of bread, cheese and bottles of wine. I'm starving, but I can't show it. Cries from my own villa announce that luncheon is served, but honour won't permit me to leave. They offer me food through the chain, like I'm some awful animal in the zoo. The French won't let foreigners near my rocks and old-timers, squatters of three weeks or more, resent any newcomers on the rocks. I've more or less gotten to know the old-timers and I probably would be friendly with them by now, but that would be acknowledging defeat and my regiment would never forgive me. But I think that the biggest heartbreak of all is my sons who, brought up in the traditions of Gibraltar, just refuse to fight for the rocks and would rather go to the public beach and meet some pretty girls. My wife, a Swede brought up in the traditions of neutrality, also refuses to fight for the rocks. So I'm alone in the knowledge that all the time, out there, there is someone on my rocks having a helluva good time.'

It was not easy being a film star, especially in a business that David saw crumbling round him. Asked why he had done some heavy promotional tours for *The Guns of Navarone*, he replied simply, 'Because nine-to-six actors who do nothing to help sell a film once it is in the can are not only selling the industry short, they're also helping to dig their own professional graves. It's a star's duty now to get out on the road and sell the film on radio and television and in magazines, even if he doesn't have a percentage of the profits. The lush days are over: now every actor has a stake in the success of every film he makes, simply because he has to make it work if he's to work again.'

'Having two houses now', he told another American reporter, 'means that I have to work all the time to keep them going, so I don't see either very much. Nobody loves money more than I do, but I've no set price for a picture. If it comes in the middle of the skiing season I'll charge more, if it's for an old friend then I'll do it for a lot less.'

By now his price was averaging around $250,000 a picture, which meant that if he did four in a year he could just about claim to be a millionaire except that, as he himself said, the cost of the houses and the new family still did not leave a lot in the bank. Financially and artistically insecure as ever, he went straight from *Navarone* to a long and punishing location in the Israeli desert for an Italian film called *I Due Nemici*, which was released in Britain and America as *The Best of Enemies*. He started work on this (opposite the Italian star Alberto Sordi, who took top billing in several European countries) in the knowledge that he had lost the one film job that might have seen him gracefully into a perfectly-cast old age.

An old friend in London, the former foreign editor of the *Sunday Times*, had just sold the film rights in a sequence of snobbery-with-violence thrillers. Asked to suggest his ideal choice of leading actor, Ian Fleming unhesitatingly named Niven. The producers thought about that, decided reluctantly that David, at just past fifty, was already over the hill for the start of what they hoped was going to be a long series, and gave the role of James Bond to thirty-year-old Sean Connery. Ian Fleming went to his grave three years later still complaining that Bond was really far more like Niven than Connery, a suave Englishman rather than a raw Scot. Six years later Niven did once get to play 007, but in one of the only two Bond films that stand outside the Saltzman–Broccoli mainstream, *Casino Royale*.

Back in the Israeli desert, Niven slogged on through *I Due Nemici*, convinced in his more sandswept moments that across every dune he could see Peter O'Toole as Lawrence of Arabia. Both Niven and Olivier had, in fact, been offered roles in *Lawrence*, and had even been sent off for a weekend on producer Sam Spiegel's yacht to think about it. Spiegel did not mind the drinks bill or the wages bill for a crew of nineteen, but what he did mind was that both David and Larry cabled their regrets at being unavailable for the film over his yacht's ship-to-shore telephone system.

In *I Due Nemici*, David was once again playing what he was always best at, the Sandhurst major determined to treat desert warfare against the Italians as an extension of school sports. Michael Wilding and Harry Andrews also went into bat on his side, and the result was a quirky satire on Anglo-Italian national characteristics which never quite got the attention it deserved, largely because most critics in Britain and America assumed it was a war film somehow gone adrift instead of a more ambitious attempt at social comedy under fire.

While he was shooting the interiors in a Rome studio early in 1961, David also took part in what remains to this day the least known of his films. Called *The Shortest Day*, it was an elaborate attempt to satirize *The Longest Day*, Darryl Zanuck's epic of the Normandy landings, using some of the few working actors not already involved in the other project. Since many critics were later inclined to treat *The Longest Day* as near-comedy, however, the idea of a comedy about it fell on stony and mystified ground, and the film was relegated to curiosity status only.

Niven nevertheless grew to like the Rome studios, handy as they were for both the South of France and Switzerland, and while the work was there he grabbed it. Next came *La Città Prigoniera*, known in England and America as *The Captive City* and yet another wartime caper, this one to do with the liberation of Athens and a secret ammunition dump needed by the partisans. Having perfected his swaggerstick-major performance over at least a dozen films, David could give it almost automatically, regardless of the slightly changing circumstances of each individual script. Sandhurst was belatedly proving to have given him the best possible training, if not actually for the Army then certainly for a whole sequence of army films that required him to do little more than stand around looking military, decent, British and probably damned brave under fire.

By then David had grown so accustomed to filming in Rome that he was even reported to be thinking of investing in a new $7 million studio complex there. In the event he thought better of it, and went back to the South of France, where there were now three females in his family.

'David's home', says Hjordis, 'was really wherever the family was, but he did seem terribly happy once we'd got the two girls and the homes in Switzerland and France, and he could ski, sail and fish whenever he wasn't working. He was a very funny man, you know. Once in France, when we'd had some terrible row, he simply got out of bed and went into his dressing-room and came back stark naked except for a top hat. You really couldn't stay angry for very long at a man who behaved like that. Like all Pisceans he was a worrier, but he also had that marvellous gift of being able to look at life objectively. He didn't take it as a personal insult to himself if things didn't work out the way he wanted. He could always act his way out of a paper bag, and he had a kind of nostalgia for the old Hollywood, which he'd seen more or less disappear with the death of friends like Bogart and Flynn. There were certain things about the post-war world he really didn't care for: he couldn't bear excesses of any kind – smoking, drinking, pills all worried him. If I took a sleeping pill he used to worry. He never even took aspirins. And of course as Kristina and Fiona grew older, he began to worry about who they were out with and what time they'd be home. In that sense he was a very traditional father.'

David's next film (unless you count an uncredited appearance in the last of the Crosby–Hope pictures, *The Road to Hong Kong*, in which as a favour to his old friends he turned up for one shot only as an improbable Tibetan monk) was an intriguing if none-too-successful attempt to break the military mould in which he had been cast since *Navarone*. John Mortimer, who was to become one of the last great friends of Niven's life, had turned a novel by Francis Clifford into *Guns of Darkness*, a screenplay about an ageing playboy in Latin America who becomes a hero in spite of himself during a saga of revolution and murder. The director was to be Anthony Asquith, who had already got an unusually strong performance out of Niven ten years earlier for *Carrington VC*, and with a supporting cast led by Leslie Caron and James Robertson Justice this tale from Greenland should have worked out rather well. In fact it didn't, as John Mortimer recalls.

'I'm afraid that was a terrible little film, though it did lead to a wonderful friendship with David. We shot it in Spain, where we both developed a great liking for the local brandy, so from then on I was always known as Fundador. The whole experience of being with him was infinitely preferable to the film that came out of it; it really wasn't a very happy experience, and David didn't much care for Leslie Caron, but we used to go up into the hills with this manic Spanish driver who David always said had a thing about headlights. If he saw a pair of them coming at him out of the darkness, he used to try to drive in between them shouting, "*Yipes!*" I suppose we were lucky to live through that film, but I do remember David then being an enormous delight to be with, and totally unpretentious, although he came of that Hollywood generation who were instantly recognizable all over the world by their faces, and he used to love being recognized in very small Spanish villages. I think it gave him a kind of confidence, reminded him that he still had an audience and therefore was still useful at the box-office.

'I suppose another reason we got on so well was that we both loved telling stories, and the fact that we told the same stories over and over again only made them better. In a way he reminded me very much of my father. Both men had these wonderful set-piece anecdotes that they'd begin to tell and then start laughing at themselves, so in the end they were totally unable to finish them but tears of joy were pouring down their cheeks. And I used to tell him all my courtroom stories of murder trials and malign dwarves, and sometimes years later I'd hear the same stories coming back to me in David's faintly garbled versions of them. He really was a genius as a raconteur: he could do wonderful accents, had perfect timing, and he had this tremendous dinner-party technique of starting a story very quietly and then gradually bringing it up to full volume once he'd got the whole attention of the table. I don't think his acting ever quite achieved the brilliance or the polish of his dinner-party conversations.'

Gradually, through the 1960s, as the stories got better and the films got worse, David began to realize that perhaps the former were his true métier and the sooner he got them down on paper the better. Since the first novel more than a decade earlier, his only writing had been long, long letters to friends and/or journalists from whatever location on which he happened to find himself, but now like all actors he had begun to think about the possibility of a book of memoirs – one that in his case might happen rather sooner than usual since it had become all too clear, as he approached his middle fifties, that such distinction as he had achieved as an actor was already virtually over. From here on in, he was to do very little more on screen than warm over various earlier performances, only now for rather better money.

Late in 1962 he was back in Spain again, this time to play the British envoy to China in a $7 million Samuel Bronston epic called *55 Days at Peking*. Niven had some reason to be grateful to Bronston, the maker of such other epics as *El Cid* and *King of Kings*, because when an earlier blockbuster had somehow failed before the cameras started rolling, David had collected a $100,000 pay-off. Now he was to get rather more than that for looking controlled and English while the Boxers attacked Legation City, though his main recollection of a lengthy and somewhat turgid shoot was the morning when he suddenly found himself having to address a four-eyed empress of China because, in the studio heat, Flora Robson's contact lenses had slid down to either side of her nostrils.

55 Days at Peking was not by any definition a happy picture. Its stars, Charlton Heston and Ava Gardner, did not exactly hit it off, the director had a heart attack mid-way through the shooting, whole teams of writers disappeared even before the first shots were in the can, and one of those who stayed to see the action through (Philip Yordan) later confided to Miss Gardner's biographer, John Daniell, that 'all through the picture she would remain locked in her dressing room terrified by the thousands of extras, and her double appeared in endless over-the-shoulder shots. In many scenes Heston begged her to join him, but she again hid, drank and sulked. The real reason was fear: she was terrified of the competition from the two major British stars, David Niven and Flora Robson.'

So the old *Wuthering Heights* team were back in action, while further down the castlist could also be found another of Niven's off-the-set cronies, John Ireland. 'We first met in Hollywood way back,' he recalls, 'and we used to sail occasionally together. Then, when I was working in Europe and David had just bought the house on Cap Ferrat, he proudly took us all around it, even though the shutters were cracked and there was paint peeling everywhere. But he said, "Don't worry, old bean, Hjordis will get all that fixed in no time," and sure enough the next time we called in there it all was looking fabulous. When we got to Spain for the picture I told him I was a friend of Larry Harvey, and that seemed to reassure him, except that he knew none of my costumes fitted, so whenever we had a scene together with Ava he'd make me stand right next to her until she finally said, "I really can't act with a man who has things sticking out all over him," because my trousers were far too tight. That was a very happy morning for David. The picture didn't really work, but we had a lot of fun.'

This was more than could be said for its major star, Charlton Heston who, as he now recalls, disliked the whole experience: 'David was an enchanting man, witty and a joy to be with. We spent a lot of time together on that film after our families had gone home. We were living very close together, and I remember the first night I went to dine with him I didn't have the address so I had my driver come all the way out from Madrid to pick me up and we left my house and drove about three houses down the same road and there was David's. It really wasn't a good film, though, and you should be able to make a marvellous one about the Boxer Rebellion. Both David and Ava had stop-dates in their contracts and we kept overrunning them so it all got very tense, but David remained marvellously good-humoured and constantly plotting elaborate practical jokes. Once we were shooting a night sequence where we had to go and blow up a powder magazine by racing across about 150 yards of open ground. So as we were crouching in the ditch from where we were supposed to start, David said, "Now, old chum, please don't embarrass me here. I'm a good ten years older than you, and I really need a head start." So, feeling magnanimous, I said, "Sure thing, David, I'll wait till you're clear of the ditch before I start." So they call "Action" and of course David is out of that ditch like a bloody rabbit. I couldn't have kept up with him even if we had started level. So we get to the end of the shot and the director says, "Jesus God, Charlton, lumbering along there behind, it looked ridiculous. You really must try to keep up."'

The Bronston epic sometimes seemed, to participants and observers both, more like *55 Years at Peking*, but by the time it finally ground to a halt David had something more to worry about than just another set of unenthusiastic reviews ('Mr Niven now gnaws his moustache to denote deep thought'). But it wasn't only the future safety of Peking that he was thinking about. During that long shoot, word had come through from Hollywood that Dick Powell was dying of cancer; this meant a good deal more to David than just the loss of a friend and partner. Since he had ceased to reside in California three years earlier, almost all his money there had been tied up in Four-Star, of which he was still a large shareholder. Like Boyer, also in Europe, he had inevitably become a sleeping partner, leaving Powell to run the television company, which he had done most expertly. With his death, the company was suddenly in real danger unless Niven and Boyer were prepared to return to the fold and do something about retrieving their investment.

Niven was on a plane to California the moment he got out of *Peking*, and within a couple of days after that he was in the Four-Star studio planning a major new series in which he and Boyer would both play major roles and with which they would be able to set their company back on its feet. David had, ever since *Raffles*, always wanted to do something else on the screen about a gentleman crook; better yet, what about a whole family of them?

Towards the end of 1963 Gladys Cooper, who had been with David from *The Bishop's Wife* to *Separate Tables*, was coming to the end of the filming of *My Fair Lady* and thinking that the end had also come to her Californian life. All her other Hollywood friends seemed to have either died or gone home to an English retirement; even David was now resident in Europe, and she was on the verge of putting her Napoli Drive house on the market when Four-Star sent her a cable: 'Can offer three-year deal for series to be called *The Rogues*. Guarantee you appear in not less than half the episodes each season. One thousand dollars for first day's work then three thousand if it goes beyond six days. Co-stars Nivan Boyer Robert Coote Gig Young. Please say yes.'

Gladys said yes. It was the best television deal she had ever been offered, and in my admittedly biased view the best crime-caper series ever made for the small screen. Because Niven and Boyer were effectively the executive producers as well as the stars of the series, they made sure of the best scripts and sets and supporting players in the business, and the result was precisely the kind of high-class comic work that David should have been doing on the wide screen but somehow hardly ever had. *The Rogues* was to television exactly what *The Thin Man* series had been to the cinema thirty years earlier. Gladys played the matriarch of a family of crooked sons (Niven, Boyer, Coote and Young), each of whom would handle one of the weekly capers, and over the next three television seasons they shot thirty hour-long stories, all hallmarked by a kind of care, style, charm, elegance and wit that were not in ready supply elsewhere in American television then or later. When I once asked Gladys, at the end of a long and varied stage and screen life, whether looking back across eighty years she had any real regrets she said, 'Only one: I wish they had never stopped *The Rogues*.'

Chapter Twenty-Five

1964–1966

'Casino Royale *is either going to be a classic bit of fun or the biggest fuck-up since the Flood. I think probably the latter.*'

One *Rogue* very soon led Niven to another: no sooner had he finished his tele-films in the first season of that series than he was offered by Blake Edwards the top billing in a wide-screen caper comedy to be called *The Pink Panther*. David would be cast as Sir Charles Lytton, an aristocratic and notorious jewel thief known as The Phantom, with Robert Wagner as his nephew and Capucine as his accomplice. There was to be one other character in the leading quartet: playing Capucine's husband, a bungling police inspector, would be Peter Sellers.

If Niven was supposed to be the master thief, it was of course Sellers who stole the film from under him, though initially the role had been planned for Peter Ustinov with Ava Gardner instead of Capucine as the glamorous wife. When that casting proved unworkable, Edwards sent for Sellers as a last-minute replacement and then fell so in love with his characterization of the manic French bungler that the film immediately became a Clouseau farce with David and the others desperately trying to keep some sort of coherent plot going around his stunning pratfalls. Niven was later and uncharacteristically to admit to me a deep disappointment about the way this first *Panther* film turned out. After a long run of multi-national rubbish in the early 1960s, he had found his stylistic mark again with *The Rogues* and was hoping now on the wide screen to re-establish himself in what could turn out to be a series of latterday *Raffles* adventures of the kind he had always craved: at last he would get his *Thin Man*.

It was not to be, and David was the last to argue with the kind of success that Sellers's erratic genius gave *The Pink Panther*. He turned in a performance of wry elegance and left the rest of the series, all save the last, for Sellers alone. Among the critics, it was only Penelope Gilliatt for the *Observer* who noticed that something had gone wrong with the Niven character along the way: 'Sir Charles has the basis of being a marvellous send-up of all the classy cads in fiction, but neither the star nor the director seems to have quite the energy to do it . . . it's the sight gags that work best, and they all belong to Sellers as the hopelessly inefficient detective.'

The Pink Panther did, however, bring Niven together with Robert Wagner, like Mortimer and Bill Buckley one of the three great new friends of his last years. 'I suppose we first met way back at the end of the 1940s on Bogie's boat,' says Wagner now, 'but I didn't really get to know him as a friend until we began working together, and then I went skiing with him and he would talk about his family and the way that he really wanted to end his life writing and painting rather than acting. He was very realistic about the movies: when they were over they were over, and although he kept albums of every picture he made with photographs of all the cast and crew he never really talked about the films, just the people he'd met on them. I think he really liked being around movie people, and people liked him because there was never any competitiveness. He was just there to have a good time in the hope that maybe the audience would too. Whatever you wanted to do, ski or swim or fish or sail or climb mountains or ride horses, David had always done a bit of it. The same way that wherever you were, in a Swiss village or a French restaurant or a London street, he always knew a couple of people not just by sight, but to ask about their wives and kids. He always said to me, "Keep the circus going inside you, keep it all going, don't take anything too seriously, it'll all work out in the end." He'd do a totally professional job on a film and then just walk away from it and on to the next.

'That first *Panther* really was supposed to be his picture, and when they suddenly brought in Sellers instead of Ustinov he could see it being taken away from him scene by scene. He just sat back and watched Sellers take it from him, because he knew there was nothing he could do; he was very realistic about film, he knew that in the end it was a director's medium and that an actor could only do the job, maintain a kind of dignity and the rest was out of his control.'

Blake Edwards had first met Niven when he was writing and directing television films for Four-Star: 'He was a man who always had his light bulb on: he always took a lot of trouble to shine and I think even Sellers behaved especially well on that film because of David's example.'

All the same, David knew when he'd been robbed. A couple of years later, Henry Mancini, who composed the famous theme music for *The Pink Panther*, had to lead the orchestra during an Academy Awards ceremony at which David was making an appearance: 'To play him on I decided to use the theme from *The Pink Panther*. After the rehearsal David came over and very quietly said, "Hank, I don't think I can quite claim that as my music. Would you mind awfully playing *Around the World in Eighty Days* instead?" So we did.'

David had never had the easiest of times at Academy Awards ceremonies. A few years after he'd won his own Oscar for *Separate Tables*, he was hosting a section of the show when a man named Bob Opel managed to get on to the stage behind him stark naked. 'Isn't it fascinating', said David to several million television viewers gaping aghast at a streaker on their screens, 'that probably the only laugh this man will ever get in his life is by stripping off his clothes and showing his shortcomings.'

Back in the South of France, David's summer life had settled into a pleasant routine. With Lo Scoglietto extensively redecorated, he and Hjordis began to entertain such distinguished neighbours as Prince Rainier and Princess Grace of Monaco; she, as Grace Kelly, had been a friend of the Nivens since the very early days of their marriage when Hjordis remembers her as one of the few members of Hollywood royalty prepared to welcome the new Mrs Niven openly and eagerly to California at a time when the others were still wrapped up in memories of Primmie. Then there was the legendary story of a dinner in Monaco at which Rainier had asked David who, of all the Hollywood stars he had been romantically involved with, was his absolute favourite. 'Grace,' said David without batting an eyelid. 'Gracie. Gracie, er, Fields.'

Prince Rainier, as he recently told me, regarded David as 'a very dear friend. He and Hjordis had come to our wedding with Cary Grant and Ava Gardner, and before they bought their house on Cap Ferrat they would often come down to see us both. He was somebody you could always rely on; ready to give advice but never to impose it. He had a very nice attachment to old chums, took trouble always to stay in touch. In the winters we sometimes used to ski together; I don't think he ever thought much of himself as a skier; he once said that the great thing was to stay upright until you had got past all the girls' schools that surrounded his chalet in Château d'Oex. After that he didn't mind falling over in the snow, but he was determined not to have all the little girls laughing at him.

'He never really took himself very seriously, certainly not as an actor, but he really enjoyed the greater lunacies of showbusiness. One of the happiest times I saw him was when he'd just been paid hundreds of thousands of dollars for appearing as a British colonel in a commercial for underarm deodorant that was to be shown exclusively on

Japanese television. Something about the bad taste of all that really appealed to him.

'We only ever had one real argument, and oddly enough it was about medals. In spite of his Army background and his war service, he said that he now thought they were totally idiotic and that nobody should wear them or receive them or indeed give them to other people. Well, as I have to spend a certain amount of my time giving out medals, that became a very lively argument indeed. But apart from that one night we really got on very well, and Grace and I used to love going over to Lo Scoglietto. David was very houseproud, you know, and Hjordis took a rather Swedish view of housekeeping which is very different from the English one. So David was always terribly keen to get the house running well and with the proper staff. In Switzerland he had a wonderfully eccentric Swiss handyman and butler and cook who sadly died just two days before he did. When we went there once for supper David had told him that he had to wear a white jacket, so the man found this kind of blouse and came in looking like a laboratory attendant.

'David and Grace both shared a nostalgia for the old Hollywood studios, and a certain regret for the glamour of the days that had totally gone from California in the 1960s. She and Hjordis always got on very well together, but David was one of the very few men I could simply ring up and say, "Come over for dinner tonight." We both had teenage daughters, of course, and worrying about them creates a great bond. But David had no real age, he never looked as old as he was and he kept himself in very good shape, never smoked or drank very much and was keen on the outdoor life, though he often had to ski in secret, far from any photographers' cameras. He was usually under contract for another film, and the contracts always specified that he was not to risk breaking a leg. As a friend, though, David had that most remarkable and rare quality of being always available but never actually in the way.'

The good life in Monte Carlo, on Cap Ferrat and among

the mountains of Gstaad did not come cheap, and David was still in no position to turn down work, however unpromising. Late in 1964 he therefore went back to Hollywood to stooge around with Marlon Brando (who took top billing) in what was unreassuringly billed as Brando's first comedy, presumably by publicists who had forgotten his hilarious appearance as Mark Antony in *Julius Caesar* ten years earlier. He and Niven were this time cast as a couple of Riviera con-men out to fleece wealthy women in a plot which at one point required Brando to appear as a lovelorn paraplegic. *Bedtime Story* was shot (though, as Penelope Gilliatt said, 'unfortunately not fatally') by Ralph Levy. Its female star was Shirley Jones who remembers: 'One Sunday, David rang and said he wanted to take me to Amalfi Drive, where he used to live, and so we walked around up there and he talked about his first marriage. He said that when Primmie died he really didn't think he'd be able to go on with his life; he said that when she walked into a room you felt you'd been touched by an angel. I think there had been a lot of sadness and loss in his life, but he never made anything sound too heavy. Most comedians turn to comedy because they've had sad lives: I think that was true of David, but now he said that at last with the girls and Hjordis he'd found a kind of happiness again. He said he had always loved the American way of life because it was so much more open and honest than the English; but I think by now he'd settled for another kind of life in Europe with the family, and the career really no longer mattered to him so very much. Acting was just what he did to pay for everything else.'

While his professional life sank back into sustained mediocrity, David's social life was fast improving. Not only Prince Rainier and Princess Grace of Monaco but also Jackie Kennedy and her surviving family had become firm friends, and away from Hollywood the Nivens were able to slip easily and gracefully into the high society which his screen image had always conjured up. As Hollywood studios grew daily tackier, David cheerfully withdrew into a world of older and more gracious European and East Coast American living. Indeed, after *Bedtime Story* and the wrapping up of *The Rogues*, he was to make only three more films in California as against twenty-one in Britain or on other non-American locations.

The first of these was a doomed attempt to do a favour for an old friend. Peter Ustinov had been working on a screenplay derived from a Romain Gary novel about an eighty-year-old widow looking back on her picaresque life and loves; called *Lady L*, it had been set up originally by MGM and Carlo Ponti as a European co-production to star Gina Lollobrigida, Tony Curtis and Ralph Richardson under the direction of George Cukor. All four of those originals then pulled out, leaving Ustinov himself to try to retrieve a production which he really had only undertaken to write on condition that he did not have to read any of the earlier drafts. He had also agreed to direct, with Ponti's wife Sophia Loren now in the Lollobrigida role and Paul Newman and David standing in for Tony Curtis and Sir Ralph. The result was not a happy one, though the film did manage to introduce to the screen a new star in Castle Howard, the palatial Yorkshire country house later to achieve more lasting fame as the location of *Brideshead Revisited*. Filming there among the Yorkshire gentry who were doubling as extras, Ustinov was asked by one local squire precisely what he was doing as the director. 'Well,' replied Peter, 'I put the camera where I think it ought to be.' After a pause the squire enquired, 'Do you put it there yourself, or do you have a man do it?'

The squirearchy was still not entirely clear about the nature of an actor's life; when David a few months later had sadly to attend the funeral of his former father-in-law, Bill Rollo, who had been killed at the age of seventy while hunting with the Quorn, he was asked by the Duke of Beaufort if he would be staying the night with the widow. 'Alas not,' replied David, 'I am shooting in Spain tomorrow.' 'Ah,' said Beaufort, 'I hear they have a nice lot of birds down there this year.'

In the mid–1960s, the vogue for the glossy spy thriller had emerged from Bondage and was now already into self-parody, so when James Leasor began publishing his *Jason Love* capers it seemed once again possible that David might be presented with the perfect screen role for his own brand of wry, self-deprecatory performance. Jason Love was a country doctor who happened to have served his country well in MI5 during the war and was therefore inclined to be sent off to the Middle East when pro-British local rulers were in imminent danger of assassination.

Where The Spies Are did not work out well, though as Alexander Walker noted in the London *Standard*, 'a vintage star as engagingly witty and implausibility-proof as Mr Niven is worth any Bond-man's arsenal of booby-trapped accessories and machine-made death traps. I welcome Niven as a flesh and blood transfusion into a kind of film that is now tottering under the weight of its own gimmickry.' That transfusion had, however, come rather too late. Cinema-going audiences, or what was left of them, were rapidly tiring of spy spoofs and, though billed as the first of a series of Jason Love adventures, *Where The Spies Are* also proved to be the last.

By the middle of 1965 David's career was really on the skids. Within the previous five or ten years he had witnessed the collapse of entire film industries in Hollywood and Rome, and come home to an England where the cinema had turned to an entirely new breed of angry young stars into which David fitted neither by age nor character. More and more his career seemed to depend on a few old friends using him either out of nostalgia for a shared Hollywood past or simply because they were as out of touch as he was with the demands and charact ristics of the contemporary cinema. In the mid–1960s nostalgia had yet to be discovered as a potent box-office force, style was unfashionable and glossy comedies remarkably thin on the ground, all of which left David stranded high and dry on those rocks outside Lo Scoglietto, though at least he had some distinguished company there. A little old man was frequently to be seen on a camp stool just on the edge of the Niven property daubing away at a canvas. After a while David suggested to the staff that they might perhaps get him to move along a bit, since the family were forever falling over him as they left the garden. The little old man, it then transpired, was in fact Marc Chagall, intent on painting one of the more picturesque houses around St Jean.

It is not easy to explain the alacrity with which David agreed to join such old friends as J. Lee Thompson and Flora Robson for a gothic chiller called *Eye of the Devil*, about which all the *Sunday Times* could say was that it was 'quite hilariously bad'. The project had perhaps promised better than that, but if ever a film was jinxed then this was surely the one. They started out with Kim Novak in the lead, but she had a riding accident after several weeks' shooting and had to be replaced by Deborah Kerr at the head of a castlist which also featured Sharon Tate, later to come to a gruesome end in a celebrated Hollywood mass murder. No fewer than three directors (Arthur Hiller, Michael Anderson and Sidney Furie) were at various times involved in the project on which the final credit was taken by J. Lee Thompson.

'If just for the sake of argument', noted John Russell Taylor in *The Times*, 'you were required to cast the role of a brooding, mysteriously obsessed French aristocrat who has chosen to fulfil his family's destiny by sacrificing himself to the dark gods in return for a good grape harvest, who is the very last Hollywood star you would choose? It is a nice decision, but on the whole I think my vote would go to suave, debonair David Niven, an elegant parcel secured with an old school tie. It is some index, therefore, of what we may expect from *Eye of the Devil* that faced with just such a casting problem the makers have plumped unerringly for David Niven, busily simulating a gleam of crazed dedication . . . it is, however, undeniably something different in entertainment.'

As indeed was David's next picture. When the James

Bond novels had been bought for the screen by the Saltz-man–Broccoli team, an odd contractual quirk of pre-selling left the very first of them, *Casino Royale*, outside the main package. This then became available to rival producers, although intriguingly it had already turned up once on the screen in America, as a little-known TV drama of 1954 starring Barry Nelson as the very first James Bond. Now a full-scale feature film was to be made by Charles Feldman and, as Broccoli and Saltzman understandably refused to loan him Sean Connery, Mr Feldman decided to turn this one into a kind of parody 007 – though, God knows, there had already been enough of those, including David's own *Where The Spies Are* just a year or so earlier.

Nevertheless three writers were set to work on the project (Wolf Mankowitz, John Law and Michael Sayers) and they were soon joined by Ben Hecht, Terry Southern and Billy Wilder. To that mishmash of widely varying draft screenplays Feldman then added another element: he had just seen and much enjoyed a film called *What's New Pussycat?*, so Woody Allen and Peter Sellers were drafted in to help on the Bond, which had by now reached such unmanageable proportions (and a budget of $8 million, considerably more than the 'regular' Bond films were then costing) that no less than five directors were brought in to handle different sequences of it: John Huston, Ken Hughes, Val Guest, Robert Parrish and Joe McGrath.

A film that already had five directors and eight writers was clearly going to need more than one James Bond. Thus Niven played Bond, but so too did Woody Allen and Peter Sellers, all apparently under the misapprehension that the audience would be dying to find out which was the real 007. By the time shooting started, two more directors had been brought in (Richard Talmadge and Anthony Squire) and the whole ghastly shambles had also ensnared Orson Welles, Deborah Kerr, Ursula Andress, Joanna Pettet, William Holden, Charles Boyer, George Raft, Jean-Paul Belmondo and a young Jacqueline Bisset. All were used as if making personal appearances at a convention of autograph hunters, and the result was a shameful travesty of Fleming's original novel; so far from being a coherent thriller, *Casino Royale* looked like an all-night party of Bond freaks photographed by a surveillance system; and there was, as Andrew Sarris noted, something very depressing about watching 'the director John Huston flaunting the hardened arteries of David Niven and Deborah Kerr in a Scottish castle'.

By this time nobody could possibly have blamed David for wondering whether, in his middle fifties, the time had come to start thinking about a new career. The problem was to find out what that career might be: most actors in his perilous and fast-declining situation had either turned to television, which David had liked well enough during *The Rogues* but where he was now getting no offers at all from American or European networks, or the stage which he had always loathed. It was Hjordis who reminded him what he had done during a similar crisis just after he had left Goldwyn fifteen years earlier. He had become a writer.

Chapter Twenty-Six

1967–1969

'If I wasn't an actor I'd be unemployable, or at best the secretary to a golf club somewhere. Nine holes at that, and blue in the face with port.'

For a while after the débâcle of *Casino Royale*, it looked as though David's screen career might at last be going to take a turn for the better. John Frankenheimer, the director of *The Manchurian Candidate* and *Seven Days in May*, had decided to film for MGM a zany but intriguing tale of a group of American seamen (Alan Alda, Mickey Rooney, Jack Carter) coming across a ghostly British lieutenant-commander who, having fallen dead drunk at his first engagement, has been sent back to earth by his outraged ancestors to redeem the family honour by sailing round and round the world until he can successfully sink an enemy ship. He does finally, with some American help, manage to sink a Japanese cruiser but by that time the war is unfortunately over and he is therefore doomed to sail on forever like the Flying Dutchman.

It was a wonderful role for Niven but alas not a very good film. Frankenheimer's determination to counterweight it with actual newsreel shoots of everyone from Winston Churchill to Van Johnson made it look a little confused, and the critical reaction was often hostile when *The Extraordinary Seaman* did finally get a delayed US release two years after it had been made. By then Niven's main recollection was of an extremely rough location shoot in Mexico: 'Frankenheimer', he told a Hollywood reporter at the time of the film's eventual American premiere, 'wanted me to fall off a 20-foot mast into waters that might well be shark-infested. I was keen to use a double, but he wouldn't hear of that so finally, teeth chattering, I went through with it. After I got out of the water, a large dorsal fin appeared a few feet from where I had been. "Sharks!" I cried. "Dolphins," said Frankenheimer, "nothing but dolphins." I still maintain they were sharks.'

Back amid the comparatively safe waters of South-ampton on Long Island David was able to preside proudly over a happy family event. His two sons were now well into their twenties: the elder, David Jr, was to become by turns an agent, a London restaurant proprietor and a Hollywood producer, while the younger, Jamie, had settled for an altogether non-showbusiness life and was about to marry Fernanda Wetherill, the daughter of a wealthy American department-store family.

'Originally my father had wanted me to go to Trinity College, Cambridge,' says Jamie, 'because all my mother's family had been there. But I'd grown up in America and I was keen to study there, so I wrote to Harvard to see if they'd accept me on my English "A" levels and when they said they would, I rang my father who was on a film set at the time. I heard him put down the phone, go over to the crew and say, "My son's just been accepted for Harvard. Is that a good thing?" and when they all cheered he let me go there instead of Cambridge. He always expected the best of his sons, always to be on time, always to be polite, and if you were failing in any way he let you know that very clearly. He couldn't bear slovenliness or rudeness or people not doing their best.

'David, my brother, decided at a very early age to go into the movie business, but I was always expected to go to college. For a while I vaguely thought about the Army, and I remember telling my father once that if England went to war I would want to sign up just as he had. He was furious. He said he'd spent twelve years of his life in the Army and that was enough for our family.' In the event, on leaving Harvard, Jamie went into banking and thinks his father was quite relieved, because he had always said that there was a better world somewhere out there than the movie business and the last thing he wanted was a showbusiness family.

'My father was just taking films that fitted into his lifestyle and his skiing and his family and all of that,' continues Jamie, 'instead of necessarily doing the work that would have been best for his career. He used to say that the first thing to find out about a film was when it was, because he didn't want it to interrupt the holidays when the girls were home from school. Then the second thing to ask was who was in it, because some people were just awful to work with, and the third thing was where it was being shot, because some places are just awful too. Then, if all that looked good, the next thing to ask about was the money, so he could go on enjoying his life, and only after all of that was OK would he even begin to think about asking for a script.

'Of course, he began to regret that the good roles weren't coming in any more, and that might have been his fault for not working harder at getting them. But you have to remember that he never regarded himself as a great talent. He just thought of himself doing a good job.

'My father was also very uncertain now about his feelings for England. He had no desire to go back and live there, even though so many people thought of him as essentially terribly British. The war affected him in a way that very few people realize: he felt it had all been a horrible mess, and he loathed the government for getting so many people into it. The fact that he himself had had to choose people to go on bombing raids from which he knew they could never return affected him very deeply for years afterwards, and it gave him a loathing of all politicians. So he had no particular country which he could now regard as his own: he just associated various places with various old friends who lived there and as increasingly they began to die off, because my father's friends so often seemed to be older than he was, he could never really go back.'

David did manage to have a highly enjoyable time at Jamie's society wedding, one also attended by such Niven supporters as William F. Buckley and Lauren Bacall. Arriving at the hotel in Southampton with Hjordis and the girls, David sent down to room service for four tomatoes, four bananas, four plates of salami and two triple Scotches. 'The food is to feed the children,' he explained; 'the Scotch is to anaesthetize myself.'

For the reception, Niven stationed himself in an Edwardian cutaway morning coat at the head of the receiving line and announced to each guest, 'I am here to tell you three things: a) I am the father of the bridegroom, b) the drinks are over there and c) there are not enough toilets.'

David was by now developing a keen eye for social farce, never more so than when it immediately concerned himself. Soon after his son's wedding, inspired by who knows what intimations of mortality, he decided that, as he was now looking remarkably like a lizard with a chin that cascaded straight down into his collar, the time might conceivably have come for a discreet facelift. He was duly recommended to a Harley Street expert, only to find on arrival in his office that this was a surgeon who believed in plastic surgery only for those who had been seriously injured on the roads or in other accidents of war or peace. Once he had gathered the man's views on the subject, David then didn't dare to admit why he was in his office. Pointing in desperation to a perfectly innocuous scar on the back of his neck he muttered something about having that removed instead, only to find himself in hospital for a painful and totally unnecessary operation.

Once that was over, he went back to work on a film called *Prudence and the Pill*. Niven was now, in the view of Kenneth Tynan, 'the unchallenged seigneur of the comic domain that lies between a smile and a wince', but his ability to choose the wrong script with unerring regularity was unimpaired by the passing years. Fast approaching sixty, an age that might be thought to bring a certain mellow dignity, he lurched into a plot about birth-control pills which not even the serried ranks of Deborah Kerr, Edith Evans, Robert Coote and Keith Michell could save from being one of the most tasteless and unfunny sex comedies of the late 1960s.

'Somehow', said Judy Geeson, who was also on that film, 'I had expected both David and Deborah to have a certain coolness, but together they were forever giggling like schoolchildren. They really were a very funny couple and quite obviously devoted to each other from way back. They both had a very strong sense of the ridiculous. There was one wonderful day when we were doing a shot under very hot lights with Dame Edith who was then on the verge of her eightieth birthday, and when it came to her turn to speak there was just this very gentle snoring sound from her and I'm afraid all David had to do was look at me with that raised eyebrow and the two of us were quite literally under the table with laughter. He was never an unkind man, but I think more than any other actor I ever knew he saw the sheer silliness of the film business and thought that on occasions it really had to be laughed at very hard indeed. He'd been strengthened by the tragedies in his own life, and he just knew that in the end nothing could be taken too seriously, least of all himself.'

From *Prudence and the Pill* David went straight into another ghastly comedy of the generation gap, *The Impossible Years*, in which he was cast as the father of a secretly married teenage daughter. It was at just about this time that I began to meet David again in Switzerland with Noël Coward and, though he would hardly ever talk about it, his career seemed then to have struck a particularly disastrous patch: to have made within a two-year period *Eye of the Devil*, *Casino Royale*, *Prudence and the Pill* and *The Impossible Years* suggested at best an advanced career death-wish. Yet privately his life had seldom looked better. The move to Europe had given him a financial stability he had never enjoyed in Hollywood, he was now collecting huge cheques for random appearances on American television aspirin commercials (indeed, he was one of the first big stars to make such appearances respectable), his marriage was once again on an even keel, he was passionately devoted to his two adopted daughters, and he vastly preferred the Swiss-French life to anything he had known in California since Primmie's death.

Yet, as he now approached his sixtieth birthday, there was still no escaping the fact that his central working life as an actor was catastrophic. Indeed, he could often not bring himself to recall even the title of the film he was due to make next, and the old refusal to read scripts until the money had been guaranteed was now not so much a joke as a safety measure to avoid a total rotting of the brain cells.

To an unintelligent actor, none of that might have mattered much. To David, who had himself already written in *Round the Rugged Rocks* twenty years earlier a rather better comedy than any of those he was now being asked to do, the situation was almost unbearable. How could a man sell himself on charm and elegance and taste when they were the three ingredients most conspicuously lacking from all of the films he was currently appearing in? The only thing he really enjoyed about filming at this time was the post-production promotional tours, where he would drift around English and American radio and television studios chatting to journalists not so much about the film then on release (since there was always precious little to say about that) as about his memories of a better film industry. Almost accidentally he had, therefore, started to become one of the best of the Hollywood historians; not always one of the most factually reliable, perhaps, but certainly one of the funniest and most evocative of a fast-growing bunch. If he could dig up and refurbish all those old memories in front of a microphone or a note-scribbling journalist, why shouldn't he do it for himself on paper? That way there might even be money in it.

It was a series of meetings during the 1960s in London and Los Angeles with the *Sunday Express* and later *Los Angeles Times* columnist Roderick Mann that finally crystallized David's ambitions to write about himself and his career. 'He always said I nagged him into it,' says Mann, 'and I suppose in a way I did, because I'd always listened to these marvellous stories and after a while I began to wonder why I was always writing them down and he wasn't. David was a great mental gymnast in that he could take some quite ordinary anecdote and spice it up: it wasn't ever total fiction, but it was certainly improved. Occasionally I'd do things with David and then years later I'd hear him telling someone the story and I'd think well, that wasn't quite how it happened, but it was certainly much better the way he told it. In many ways he was a very sentimental man, you know: he used to fantasize about what his life might have been like if Primmie had lived, if things had worked out differently. He hardly ever talked about his work as an actor, except that he used to admit privately he really hated seeing himself in films. He'd say, "I have this vision of myself as a young man of twenty-five, and then I see this old poop prancing about on the screen and I really can't bear it."

'Eventually, in longhand, he began to write down some of the old Hollywood stories, and although as Cary Grant says a lot were borrowed from other people, David really did manage to tell them very well. His writing just got better and better, and the more I read of it the more I knew we had to find him an agent and a publisher.

'Even when he was broke, which when I first knew him just before *Separate Tables* he really was, David remained the most generous man I had ever met. He never let you pick up a bill, and of course that was part of his charm. He created for himself the character of the cheery storyteller. I don't think his life was always a very happy one, and there were times when his marriage seemed (from where I was standing) to be a bloody disaster, and certain friends seemed sometimes to love him rather more than his own flesh and blood. He had a guilt complex about not having been a very good father to the boys, and I think towards the end he hoped that sending them money might make up for that.

'There was also something about David that the camera never quite managed to catch. When you were with him, there was in real life a sense of something hidden, the kind of iron core that had got him through the war but which he now took trouble to hide because it was no longer required in the life he led.'

Encouraged by Mann, David started to write whenever he could. On film locations, in hotel bedrooms, on aeroplanes, in a little house in the garden of Lo Scoglietto overlooking his beloved and still jealously guarded rocks, he would set down the stories of his Stowe schooldays, his Army capers with Trubshawe, the whisky selling in New York, the pony racing in Atlantic City and the arrival in Hollywood. David had already realized that if the book of his life were to be made to work, it would have to contain a lot more than just studio gossip. All through his writing, as in *Round the Rugged Rocks*, there ran the constantly jovial strain of the Englishman in foreign troubles, whether fending off Mafia men at the pony-track or being caught by an old friend in the men's room of a chic Cortina hotel sinking his private parts into a glassful of brandy in the hope of thawing them out after a particularly frozen skiing session. Niven had, on the verge of his sixties, already arrived at the anecdotage that was to make such a triumph of his last working years.

Chapter Twenty-Seven

1969–1973

'I make two movies a year to take care of the butcher and the baker and the school fees. Then I try to write, but it's not easy. Acting is what's easy.'

There was as yet nothing to indicate that David was ever going to make any real money out of his writing. Even in the 1960s actors' memoirs rarely sold very well in hardback unless they were, like Errol Flynn's, of a scandalous nature. Not only had David's life not been of an especially scandalous nature, but even if it had been he was not the kind of man to write that sort of thing for publication. His memoirs were to be discreet without ever looking especially discreet, yet another of the remarkable conjuring tricks on which his entire career had been based.

As yet, writing was certainly no reason for giving up acting. Early in 1969 he therefore signed to play yet another British Army major, this one in a film called *Before Winter Comes*, which had been written for the screen by the novelist and critic Andrew Sinclair. Originally it had been a story in the *New Yorker* called *The Interpreter*, but as that role was to be played by Topol, David said he would not appear as the major unless the film was given a new title. It was Sinclair's first important screenwriting job and he was surprised that the script went straight into production – at that time a rare occurrence. It also launched John Hurt's career. Sinclair remembers that the first time he went to see David in Switzerland about the film he had left his passport at home in London and Niven managed to get him through the Geneva customs on a day pass, which he found most impressive. Walking around with David, he was amused to see that, if anybody stopped Niven for an autograph or recognized him, he would always complain mildly, but if they didn't notice him he really minded a great deal more.

'We shot the film south of Salzburg,' says Sinclair, 'and the director J. Lee Thompson liked to have me on the location to make instant script changes, but David couldn't bear that because he never managed to say the lines quite the way I had written them. In the end we compromised and I would only come down to the location for tea every day at the end of the shooting. I think David appreciated that, because one night at my hotel there were four marvellous trout with a note saying, "Love, David."'

The film was about a refugee camp at the end of the war. This led one night after the filming to a discussion about the way that, in 1945, there had been deconstruction camps where men who had been trained to kill on reflex had now to be taught not to do so in peacetime. David told Sinclair that when he got home from his war, there was a huge pile of post, most of it fan mail from Hollywood, but at the top was one letter which he opened; it was from one of his own men who was up on a murder charge because of just such a reflex killing a few weeks after the war. David said he had managed to get the charge reduced to one of manslaughter.

On the very first day of shooting David had to play a scene where he had to open a door, enter, descend a flight of stairs and start to speak. The cameras began to roll. He opened the door, came downstairs, opened his mouth, but not a word emerged. 'Sorry,' he said, and went back upstairs and out. The cameras began rolling again, he opened the door, came downstairs, but the same thing happened, and then a third time. Half-way back up the stairs he turned and quite shyly admitted to co-star Chaim

Topol, 'This is my eighty-second film but I'm afraid it still happens. Every time I come on the set for my first day's shooting I get butterflies in my stomach and my mouth dries up. The problem is that my upper lip sticks to my teeth.'

Though it opened to a mixed critical press, *Before Winter Comes* had a welcome touch of class and dignity. David had, as Dilys Powell noted, 'had some pretty shaggy roles of late; how good to see this beautiful actor here given a chance to extend his range. He subdues his natural charm in the portrait of military correctness, but gradually lets you see the man becoming involved, shaken by the possibility of making mistakes; at last you recognize his loneliness, trapped in the intolerable position of command.' In New York, Judith Crist voiced a similar feeling: 'Niven here reveals that the fine actor within has not been totally slaughtered by all the inane roles he has filled in recent years; he creates the Army Mind in all its manifestations in an unforgettable manner.'

Whatever good might have been done for his ailing career by *Before Winter Comes* was immediately undone by David's next venture, a multi-national comedy of sorts called *The Brain*, which badly needed several transplants and never got them. David was meant to be a master criminal who, having organized the Great Train Robbery, was now planning to snatch the military funds of NATO and transport them to New York in a giant replica of the Statue of Liberty; but though the film co-starred Bourvil, Jean-Paul Belmondo and Eli Wallach, and was directed by the most successful French comic-film maker of recent times, Gérard Oury, the result was a multi-lingual international disaster.

That sense of professional failure was to be increased by the complete cancellation of Niven's next film. At the end of 1969, in the distinguished company of Peter Finch, Liv Ullmann and Max Von Sydow, he went into rehearsal under Fred Zinnemann's direction for what was to be an ambitious $5 million filming of André Malraux's novel,

Man's Fate. At last David seemed to have got himself back among the élite of the cinema, working on a project of intellectual and critical stature. And that was precisely the moment when there was a change of executives at the top of MGM, with the result that the entire film was cancelled after three weeks' pre-camera rehearsal.

It was at this low point in his career that David went back to France determined to finish his memoirs: at least there he would have something which could not be cancelled, reshot or altered by other hands, something that was for once in his life all his own work. Early in the spring of 1970 he showed Roderick Mann the handwritten manuscript of an autobiography which was at that time entitled *Three Sides of a Square*. Mann immediately introduced him to George Greenfield, his own literary agent in London.

By this time David had already promised the publishers Hamish Hamilton Ltd that they could have a look at it. David and Jamie Hamilton were old friends, and years earlier Jamie had written to him suggesting that he should do a book but on no account was he to make it anything to do with Hollywood. Then, according to Greenfield, when what eventually became *The Moon's A Balloon* was such a runaway success, Jamie wrote to him again and said he'd like another book but begged Niven not to make it about Hollywood; and that of course was *Bring on The Empty Horses*.

Says Greenfield: 'David threatened to send out Jamie's letters to him as Christmas cards, with all his hardback sales figures printed underneath them, but of course he never did. I think Jamie finally agreed to pay an advance of £7,500 on *The Moon's A Balloon*, but I was convinced that we were going to do much better than that with it in America. So I told David that, to separate the men from the boys when it came to auctioning the American rights, we should set a minimum figure of $35,000, which David agreed.'

Greenfield therefore took the manuscript over the

Atlantic and the first person he went to see was Michael Korda at Simon and Schuster; David had, after all, worked for his uncle Alex on two films, and there was also the Merle Oberon connection, so that seemed the right place to start. But Korda literally pushed the manuscript back across the desk at Greenfield, saying that Niven was a ham old British actor and nobody in America would want to read about his life. 'So I asked if, as a favour to me, he would just read the first hundred pages; maybe not even that, may be just fifty. Korda refused: he said nobody gave a damn about Niven, and that was that.' Two months later Greenfield had an offer of $250,000 for the paperback rights alone, and in fact they eventually went for $350,000.

Before that, however, Greenfield had had a difficult time selling the American hardback rights. Norton and Morrow grudgingly offered $10,000 each, Atlantic Monthly Press went to $15,000 and finally Putnam offered $20,000, which was still way below what David and he had agreed as a minimum. Then the paperback deal changed everything, and Greenfield estimates that in the end David must have walked away with $500,000 from that book in America alone. Despite the American deals, in England people were still very uncertain about it. Pan Books told him that the Army stuff was all right but that it really fell apart once he got to Hollywood, and that the first half alone might be worth a paperback advance of about £500. Eventually Coronet bought the UK paperback rights for a mere £750, and when their sales had passed the first million they were so embarrassed by the modest terms on which they had bought *The Moon's A Balloon* that they offered retrospectively to improve the royalty rates substantially, a most unusual occurrence. A lot of newspapers turned down the serial rights – even the *Sunday Express*, because they said that Roderick Mann was always writing about Niven. Eventually Niven got £10,000 from the *People*.

Not many people realize even now that David's book changed publishing history. Before that no English actor

had ever written a really successful autobiography, one
that became an international best-seller, and although a
lot of others have since tried, very few have succeeded.
Eventually *The Moon* sold more than 5,000,000 copies
worldwide, and one of the reasons was the way that David
travelled many thousands of miles to promote it. He took
trouble everywhere he went to meet the people who were
involved in selling, publicizing or even binding his book.
He was, apparently, charming to all the packers, typists
and switchboard girls in all the offices, and in New York
that really paid off because at about 5.30 one evening the
television show *Today* rang and said they would have
David on coast-to-coast next morning if they could have
copies of the book down at their studios right away. In
fact the Putnam office had closed at five, but some of the
packers went back in and found the copies and took them
round to the television studio by hand that night.

'Over here', recalls George Greenfield, 'Hamish Hamilton gave him a party at the Savoy with all their editorial
staff, but David knew very well that once a book was
published they didn't matter at all. The people he took the
trouble to go round the room meeting individually were
all the sales staff, and the people from W.H. Smith and
the big bookshops. He used to sidle over to them once I'd
pointed them out and say, "Look, you don't know me,
and I'm sorry to interrupt your conversation, but I'm David
Niven and I've written this horrible little book which
nobody really wants, so do please try to sell it for me,"
and of course that worked wonderfully.'

In the midst of all the negotiations on *The Moon's A
Balloon* (the title had been changed from *Three Sides of a
Square* when David found the poem of the same name by
Cummings) a terrible discovery had been made. When
David had written *Round the Rugged Rocks* all those years
earlier, he had signed an option contract with his original
publisher and forgotten all about it until Greenfield had
signed and sealed these lucrative new paperback deals.
These deals were technically in breach of the original

arrangement with his first publisher, even though twenty years had elapsed since publication of the novel. So, according to Roderick Mann, David dictated a letter to his original publisher, saying in effect, '"I am a very old English actor who has written this volume of memoirs which is I fear deeply boring; but as you have a contract with me, I will of course have the 3,000 pages sent over to you unless you would rather just release me from that original contract," which of course was what they were only too eager to do.'

If David had only known the eventual size of fortune that lay in store for him from *The Moon's A Balloon*, he might possibly have had the sense to avoid his next three films. The first of these, known as *The Statue*, may indeed mark the nadir of even his screen career. He played, with a fixed grin of utter despair, a Nobel-prizewinning linguist whose sculptress wife produces a nude statue of him on which the private parts are so exaggerated that he decides her lover must have posed for it. A picture of truly breathtaking awfulness was then followed by one that was merely a curiosity: the highly regarded Polish director Jerzy Skolimowski cast Niven opposite Gina Lollobrigida in a moody black comedy shot on location in Germany and entitled *King, Queen, Knave*. Going to interview Niven on that set in Munich for a BBC 2 film programme of the early 1970s, I remember thinking it was rather like visiting a prisoner in some reasonably comfortable open jail who was about to get his release for good behaviour when the shooting came to an end.

By this time the reviews were starting to come in on *The Moon's A Balloon* and they were vastly better for David as a writer than any he had received as an actor since *Separate Tables* thirteen years earlier. The *New York Times* hailed 'a juicy all-day lollipop of a book', and the *New Yorker* even began to fantasize about a Niven school of textual criticism: 'Over the years', wrote Ian A. Frazier in a wonderfully tongue-in-cheek review, 'it has been the custom of literary critics to regard Niven as a lonely monument, self-created, almost as much a fiction as one of his own characters, magnificent in the uniqueness of his achievement. While I realize that this is a doctrine from which one of our number strays at his peril, I have always believed that such a view of the man and his work removes Niven from his historical context and neglects consideration of the author as a product of the turbulent intellectual climate of his time.'

Joking apart, the success of *The Moon's A Balloon* did help to move Niven out of a world of actors and into the company of the writers he had always much preferred: along with John Mortimer, Bill Buckley and Gore Vidal now became the friends of his last years, for Niven always went for the best. There was indeed a fame-loving side to him that could prove unattractive. For many years before Noël Coward fell ill at the beginning of 1973, it had become a custom on Boxing Day for him and his two devoted, lifelong companions, Graham Payn and Cole Lesley, to travel up by the mountain railway from Les Avants to Château d'Oex for a celebratory day with the Nivens. A few months after Noël's death David made it very clear to Cole and Graham that, without the Master, the Boxing Day celebrations would no longer take place.

The fact that David was a best-seller also opened up for him in America a new world of lucrative lecture tours. Being careful not to get too close to New York or Los Angeles, where he reckoned he had too many friends who might drop into his lectures and barrack, he travelled cheerfully around the Midwest. 'I drive into the town, and am met by the sponsor. His wife has just been to the hairdresser to get her blue rinse, and his daughter wants to be an actress. They greet me and take me to my hotel room. It's the Holiday Inn, usually the Bamboo Suite. Same in every town. I tell dull stories about my life in Europe. Then I tell dull stories about my life in Hollywood. Then I mention Gable and Garbo and Bogart. Then I finish up with a joke and move on to the next town. I can do twenty-seven different towns in thirty-one days like that. And all with the same stories.'

He was also much in demand for television chat shows, where he would give much the same urbane, reminiscent performance either for a large cheque or for free if he happened to have a film or book to promote. In bookselling he had, as he was the first to note, an unfair advantage: 'Because they happen to know this old face from the movies, they let me on television to sell my books while better authors who happen not to be actors are starving in garrets.'

Away from that sales circuit the Niven of the mid-1970s was becoming a rather more reflective and tranquil figure, as William F. Buckley recalls: 'When we first met back in the 1960s with Jackie Kennedy and Kenneth Galbraith during one Gstaad winter he seemed to me very much the David Niven one knew from all those movies. But then gradually we got to know each other much better because we shared an interest in painting (I must have about thirty of his just now) and sometimes he would talk about his writing. There was one wonderful occasion when he told us he was going to call his first autobiography *The Moon's A Balloon* and Ken Galbraith said, "Don't you know anything? You can't possibly sell a book with a title like that." And I agreed.' They were just 5,000,000 copies wrong. Buckley remembers David as always self-effacing about his writing, at least in the company of other writers, even when *Bring on The Empty Horses* was number one hardback best-seller in Britain and *The Moon's A Balloon* was simultaneously number one in paperback. Few non-fiction authors have ever achieved that double before or since.

'He was a man of extraordinary generosity,' says Buckley; 'indeed, I think as a father he spoiled his girls terribly by never, ever saying no to them; but as a friend he was forever bringing presents, and whenever we arrived at our house in Switzerland near his, our entire liquor supply for the two months we stayed there was already waiting as a gift from David.'

Before Niven's last, terrible illness Buckley could only once recall seeing him really worried, and that was just after the publication of his second book of memoirs. His publishers had asked Buckley for a quote, and so he gave them a line from his *New York Times* review which read: 'Probably the best book ever written about Hollywood.' A year or so later when Buckley's own first novel was about to be published in England, and the publisher told him to get a quote from David, who was busy filming at the time, he just told Buckley to use any line he liked and put his name under it. 'So I did that, and a few months later we were talking and I said, "About that quote you said I could have to advertise my novel. Well, I put: 'Probably the best novel ever written about fucking the Queen. David Niven'." I think that was about the only time I ever saw him really caught off balance. For about half a second, which for him was a long time. Then he started to laugh.'

David was soon to have his revenge. 'My chum Buckley', he said later, 'must be the worst amateur painter in the world. I can say that because I'm the second worst. He was staying with us once when Marc Chagall came to visit, in his eighties – a wonderful man. I begged Bill not to show him any of his paintings. He knocks off nine a night and they all look like the bottom of Lake Erie. But the moment they were introduced, Bill buttonholed Chagall and brought out his latest ghastly effort. Chagall studied it for a minute or two and then just shook his head and murmured, "Poor paint."'

Niven's interest in modern art led him to write a long and pained letter to *The Times* of 24 July 1973:

Sir: I write this not as a cynic, I honestly want to learn. Twelve years ago, I had an urge to own a painting by Miró and I took the advice of Swiss friends, the possessors of outstanding collections. All were agreed upon two things: a) the intelligence of the urge and b) the name of the best dealer in Switzerland. I visited this man and he produced exactly that I thought I was looking for in size, colour, humour and movement. When he named the price it was smelling salts time, but I am not the greatest actor in the world and the dealer took one look at my face and knew that he had made a sale. Then he pressed his luck. 'The fascinating thing about this picture', he said, 'is that when Miró finished it, like many artists he turned it to the wall and didn't look at it again for six months. When he turned it round again, he could not remember what he'd been painting in the first place so he reversed it and finished it upside down. Isn't that amusing?' Well, it was so amusing to me that my heart turned to stone. If the artist didn't know which way up his original idea should be, then I didn't want to fork out my hard-earned cash to buy it. The picture, needless to say, was snapped up by someone else and now is valued at ten times the original figure, which makes my Scots blood boil. I console myself by feeling that my integrity is intact. Is it? I'd love to know.

Three *Times* readers replied in varying states of disagreement, including one who noted sharply that 'Miró was a Surrealist, and one of Surrealism's most significant contributions to modern art was the notion that chance or accident can play an important and positive part in the process of creation.' In which case, David's own career as actor and author was itself a Surrealist creation.

Chapter Twenty-Eight

1973–1979

'Old age has got to start creeping up on me one day soon, and frankly I'm very scared. I don't want to be old. I've always felt so young. And I want to stay that way.'

The unexpected, runaway success of *The Moon's A Balloon* in the best-seller charts on both sides of the Atlantic meant that David would soon have to start thinking about another volume of Hollywood memoirs, though he did not exactly relish the prospect: 'I will do anything to avoid writing. First of all, I only do it when the weather is bad, so that writing doesn't interfere with living, and in the South of France I don't get too much bad weather. If a Boeing 747 flies over, that's worth at least ten minutes to me because I go out into the garden and look up at the sky. Then I'll take a look around the garden, check the boiler, anything not to go back and get on. If you're lucky enough to be able to polish a minimal talent into a career, then you should maybe write some of it down to encourage the others. But when I get really stuck on a chapter, I wander along Cap Ferrat to the old Somerset Maugham villa hoping for a whiff of inspiration. Only the summer house where he used to write is now mostly full of Algerian workers putting up some new buildings nearby, so there's not much inspiration to be had there.'

When the inspiration really dried up he could always go

off and make another film, though that generally proved to be a mistake. His 1973 offering was *Vampira*, a horror spoof that never even got an American release and left English critics in their usual state of regretful bemusement. There was, mercifully, better to come. Early in the following year David gave what was to be the last and still the leastknown of his half-dozen really good performances in a film called *Paper Tiger*. Its director was Ken Annakin, who had known David socially for years and always hoped to make a picture with him: 'When this one came up I knew he was the ideal casting. The part was in some ways a throwback to the one he had played so brilliantly in *Separate Tables* – an English teacher on an island in the Pacific who pretends that he's been a war hero and then has to live up to that pretence when he and his pupil are captured by guerrillas. This was a very tough picture for David to do, a lot of clambering over rocks in Malaysia, and he was already in pain with a bad back, but he was now one of those Hollywood veterans like Henry Fonda or Robert Ryan, who were always so wonderful to work with because of their assiduous professionalism. He gave a most brilliant performance and helped me get another one out of the little boy: some actors hate working with children, but David made a great friend of this one and even taught him to play cricket and billiards in the evening.'

There was one sequence in the film that was supposed to be a large diplomatic party at the Japanese embassy in Kuala Lumpur, and in order to round up enough suitably dressed extras, David and Annakin had to go round all the banks and British businesses in town inviting people to the party. By and large the wives were all keen to take part and be photographed with David, but the husbands apparently all wanted to get away to their golf in the hills. And all the time they were filming, David was laboriously writing the start of *Bring on the Empty Horses*.

Critics later hailed Niven's 'battered charm' in the role, but the film was not a huge success, though in retrospect it will, perhaps, be seen as his only real screen achievement

in the quarter-century that separated *Separate Tables* from
his death; this is by any standards a major film performance, and one that maddeningly indicates the kind of actor
David could have been if he had fallen more often among
good directors and good scripts.

Then it was on to a desperately lame Walt Disney
comedy called *No Deposit, No Return*, in which David
played a twinkly grandfather who quite rightly refuses
to pay out a cent of ransom money when his ghastly
all-American grandchildren are kidnapped, and back to
the memoirs that were now occupying more and more of
his time. He was now really past caring about his life as
an actor, simply grabbing whatever work came along when
he thought he might need the money. Thus he would turn
up in unlikely television commercials, or do voiceovers for
distinguished television wildlife films, or appear as the
'host' of horrendous American comedy shows like *The
Bluffers*, or even play the old Charles Laughton role in a
lacklustre TV version of Wilde's *Canterville Ghost*, all with
the same blithe disregard of quality control he had
exhibited forty years before when drifting around Hollywood in search of movie roles.

'David had by now decided', says his London agent
Dennis Selinger, 'that he really wanted to be a working
actor rather than a superstar. So, although he didn't get
the enormous salaries that a lot of giant stars were getting
in the mid–1970s, he always kept himself above the title
and in work. He wasn't bankable, nobody could hang a
picture on his name alone, but we were still managing to
get him around £300,000 for every picture he made in the
1970s, and there were a lot of them – certainly a dozen,
and then four more before he died in 1983. His attitude
was: "Find me the job, and so long as the money and the
billing are right I'll do it." He loved to work, and he had
a real horror of being idle. When I got him $150,000
for that Japanese deodorant commercial he was really as
thrilled as a little boy with a new toy, and I think he took
as much trouble about doing a coffee ad. to perfection as

he did over entire films. I got him £100,000 for that, which ten years ago was very good money; then he got a whisky ad. in Brazil which also paid very well. He was never short of money in these last years, but he really loved earning it; he saw films as a sort of club where he went in the morning and left at night with the cheque.'

David was also lucky in that, even when the pictures were terrible, his own reviews were never too personally wounding. He just moved on to the next, and if there wasn't one lined up, then he went back to writing. When the Michael Caines and the Steve McQueens came along, David had to face the fact that his Hollywood world was really over, but in Europe people still wanted him because he was reliable and always brought a touch of class to whatever he was doing. He was always great fun to have around on a set too, and never made any trouble, so people loved casting him and if there was a choice between him and perhaps a slightly better actor who was known to be moody or difficult on the set, David often got the job because producers knew he would make their lives easier instead of more troublesome. He always gave good value for money; and by these last ten years of his life, he was established not as an actor called David Niven but simply as David Niven. As Selinger says, 'You were buying a personality. If he had come on with the parrot in *Treasure Island* it would still have been David rather than Long John Silver that came across on the screen. In that sense he was much like C. Aubrey Smith towards the end of his career, when he too had given up playing parts and was really just there to be English and charming in an old-fashioned sort of way. Even when things weren't going too well with David's marriage, he always kept that twinkle in his eye which people recognized and liked. He was always familiar. You knew exactly where you were with him, and what you saw was what was there. Who is the biggest box-office star in the world today? Probably Harrison Ford on his 1980s track record; yet if he were walking down Bond Street, nobody would have the faintest idea who he was. Everyone always knew who David was; that was his business and in a way his career.'

At home, his marriage was coming under considerable emotional strain, and closer friends sometimes noticed a certain coolness in his relations with Hjordis. Robert Wagner remembered one evening 'walking into the Connaught Hotel in London and seeing her there, so I went over and said, "Isn't it wonderful that David has had this tremendous success with *Moon's A Balloon* and that people are enjoying it so much?" and she said, "I haven't read it."'

Niven was now living, when in London, with the wife of a journalist on *The Times* and, when in New York, with another married woman of equal discretion and charm; but he was determined that his marriage was not going to end. He was still fond of Hjordis and passionately devoted to their adopted teenage daughters, the elder of whom was soon to suffer a near-fatal car crash, which kept David in a state of constant anxiety for many months. He continued to work, however, finding in movies an escape from areas of his private life that he really could not or would not face too closely. He even occasionally managed to stumble into a good film, and the next of these was *Murder by Death*, Neil Simon's parody of 1930s Hollywood detective movies. It had in its favour a magnificent cast: Truman Capote played the mad crime writer who summons a group of celebrated private eyes (Peter Falk as Sam Spade, Peter Sellers as Charlie Chan, James Coco as Hercule Poirot, Elsa Lanchester as Miss Marple, and David and Maggie Smith as the couple from the *Thin Man* series) to a haunted mansion where Alec Guinness is the blind butler. The result was essentially a comic *Sleuth*, which worked not so much on its own merits as because of its loving references to classics of the same genre across thirty years. Sellers himself was later to dismiss the film as 'the epitome of eight-millimetre home moviemaking', but this is unfair to a script that might at moments not have disgraced Tom Stoppard ('No, Mum,' says Guinness, 'the name is not

Benson, Mum, it's Bensonmum'), and Niven and Maggie Smith made a wonderfully languid, elegant couple. In these last few years of David's life they were to make two more films together (*Death on the Nile* and *Better Late Than Never*) and she remembered with affection the large bunch of flowers and the bottle of champagne with which he greeted her on those subsequent locations.

Like *Beat The Devil*, a 1953 Humphrey Bogart–John Huston picture which had also involved Truman Capote, though as a screenwriter, *Murder by Death* was best loved and understood by those who had wasted large parts of their lives in darkened cinemas watching bad movies, and like that earlier film it opened to a certain amount of knowing critical enthusiasm, and an equal amount of public irritation at the in-jokes.

David followed it with another Disney comedy, this one fractionally better than the last. *Candleshoe* had him playing three roles, as chauffeur, friend and gardener to old Lady Candleshoe (Helen Hayes), in a plot which largely concerned Jodie Foster masquerading as the heiress to a missing fortune.

If *Candleshoe* was a disappointment, David could at least continue to bask in his success as an author. *Bring on the Empty Horses*, published in 1975, did not attract quite the same class of amazed and delighted reviews as *The Moon's A Balloon* four years earlier simply because critics now knew what to expect. This was really just a volume two, with the author himself fading quietly into the background and allowing various superstars from Fred Astaire and Humphrey Bogart through Errol Flynn and Cary Grant to Spencer Tracy and Loretta Young to take over the spotlight as Niven narrated selected highlights of their lives, much after the fashion of a man presenting a *Hollywood Greats* programme on television. It did, however, attract a massive paperback deal, heavy newspaper and magazine serialization on both sides of the Atlantic, and millions of people into bookshops.

David even found himself reading his books aloud on

BBC radio: Rosemary Hart, the producer and *Kaleido-scope* editor, journeyed to Cap Ferrat and recorded him in his garden, being only slightly surprised when he broke off in mid-paragraph with the news that he had to take one of his daughters to the dentist. After he had got into his car, Rosemary asked the houseman where the Nivens' dentist was to be found. 'Geneva,' was the reply. David was, however, back at the micophone early next morning.

As soon as that was over, Niven decided that his next book (for which a huge advance was already on offer) would be a novel. Originally entitled *Make It Smaller and Move It To The Left*, this seemed to have a variable plot which at one stage concerned several actors trapped in a lighthouse. Gradually, though, it settled down into a love story of the Second World War dedicated to his old Phantom unit (the first of his autobiographies had been dedicated to an entirely mythical Greek actress, and the second to all the people he'd forgotten to mention in it), though Hjordis took the view that war novels were boring.

'She has now', David told an *Express* reporter, 'taken to wearing a gold medallion round her neck that states, "I am allergic to penicillin and sometimes to my husband too," but I'm going ahead with the novel unless the publishers find it very boring. I write everything out in long-hand, you know: I started off trying to dictate into a machine but the sound of my own voice bored me rigid. Then I hired a lady from Nice but she couldn't bear the four-letter words, so then I got another lady who laughed at all my jokes until I began acting out all the scenes for her and that wouldn't do at all. So now I just write it all out in the girls' school notebooks and then the wonderful secretary of the manager of the Connaught Hotel types it out in her spare time.'

Talking to David one night while he was in England to dub some more commentaries on to wildlife films, one of his more distinguished jobs at this time, I asked him why he thought his two autobiographies had done so much better than those of other actors. 'Because I didn't use a ghost or a journalist or anything like that. Most actors' books are really written by journalists, who were only on the outside of the stockades peering in, whereas I was right in there with the best of them. Dietrich, you know, would only grant one interview for every 500 or so requests, and then after it was written it had to be handed back over the fence to her for correction, so the papers at that time only got what actors saw fit to give them. At least my stories are all from the inside looking out. Like the one about Alice Terry who, when she got a script in the post, used to ask only two things: "Do I get wet or have to ride a horse?" If the answer to both was in the negative, she'd do the film, but only until she had made enough money to spend the rest of her life eating cream cakes in the San Fernando Valley, which was what she most wanted to do. My trouble now is that I keep taking these huge advances for books, spending the money and then not having the remotest idea what to write about next.'

To delay the moment when he would have to start seriously rhinking about the novel that eventually became *Go Slowly, Come Back Quickly*, David signed for one of the all-star Agatha Christie thrillers that came to be made through the late 1970s, with first of all Albert Finney and then Peter Ustinov as Hercule Poirot. *Death on the Nile* was not the starriest of these, but it did feature Ustinov and Niven in a likeable double-act as the Belgian detective and his English military sidekick as well as Mia Farrow, Maggie Smith and Bette Davis who, as Ustinov recalls, really put the fear of God into the others.

'David and I were still very good friends but there was something infinitely touching about him, because it was just the time when he learnt of Kristina's car crash and that worried him terribly and made him for the first time seem very frail, though in this suddenly old man one could still see the boy he had always been. He was always dashing back to see her in hospital and praying that she would pull through, and the filming wasn't altogether easy. One night I remember we were both told that the next morning at

8 am we had to shoot a whole new scene with Miss Davis, of whom we were both terrified; so we stayed up most of the night learning the lines because she had this reputation for formidable rage if any actor in a scene with her didn't know every single word perfectly. The next morning I woke up at six, and there was David looking ashen, not having slept but still not having managed to learn his lines. Together we stumbled on to the set looking terrible and there was Miss Davis looking not a lot better and saying, "I've been lying awake all night trying to learn this bloody script because they said you were both such professionals." After that it was all fine.'

As Kristina slowly started to recover, David felt confident enough to go off on another location shoot, this one for his own son David who had now become a producer and was setting up with Jack Weiner an adventure caper set in a Greek prisoner-of-war camp on Rhodes in 1944. 'That really all began', says Roger Moore, who starred in *Escape to Athena* with Niven, Telly Savalas, Stefanie Powers and Claudia Cardinale, 'because one day I was having lunch with David Jr in Hollywood and I said, "Look, you call yourself a producer and you haven't given your father or me one single bloody job yet."'

'No special favours asked or given,' said David Jr of the working relationship with his father which they were to carry over into *Better Late Than Never* two years later. 'I'd often been with him on film sets in the past, of course; indeed he once took me on to the floor when he was shooting a scene in *Casino Royale* with a lot of nude girls in a bath, because he said he wanted me to understand how arduous an actor's life could be. But on *Athena* he was always the first one on the set in the morning, knowing all his lines, determined not to let me down. At night we'd go to the casino and he'd play for hours on 1-shilling bets while Roger and Telly and I lost rather more than that. But we had a lot of fun on that picture; I just wish it had been more successful.'

As if aware that time or the offers might be running out,

or perhaps just because he could never turn down a job, David now made four more films in rapid succession. For the first of these, *A Nightingale Sang in Berkley Square*, he was cast as the criminal mastermind behind a $30 million Mayfair bank job. From that he went on to a six-hour tele-film based on the wartime exploits of Sir William Stephenson (*A Man Called Intrepid*) who had used Korda, Coward and Niven himself on occasional courier missions for the secret service. With David on that film was Michael York whose photographer wife Patricia recalls 'the way that David suddenly seemed to have aged so terribly, I think perhaps as a result of Kristina's accident. We'd seen him a few times before this in Monaco looking marvellous but now, although he still sparkled on the set, when I tried to do some stills of him for publicity shots, which I'd been asked by the television company to get, I had to throw dozens of them away. No matter what light I got him in, he suddenly started looking very old and fragile.'

David was approaching seventy, and clearly the strain of the last few years was beginning to show. During the 1970s he had published two long books, undergone arduous sales and lecture tours to promote them, made a dozen movies and lived through weeks at the hospital bedside of his adopted daughter. His sixties had been both physically and emotionally exhausting, and there was still no sign of any real relaxation.

From *Intrepid* he went straight into *Rough Cut*, an all-too-accurately-titled Burt Reynolds thriller in which he played a Scotland Yard detective trying to entrap a jewel thief known, presumably in deference to David's own earlier work, as 'an American Raffles in London'. Niven got along well enough with Reynolds and their director, Don Siegel, but the film ended in a massive lawsuit brought by David against the producer David Merrick. Niven had never sued a producer (or indeed anyone) in his entire life, and wasn't happy to be starting at the age of seventy; but his lawyers claimed that he had not been given the same poster publicity as Burt Reynolds and Lesley-Anne

Down, nor had he received £40,000 owing to him. The suit was eventually settled out of court, though for rather less than the $2 million David had originally claimed for being allegedly shortchanged by Merrick on both pay and billing. The settlement was nevertheless, David proudly noted, 'well into six figures'.

Late in 1979 he embarked on the last film that he would make before his final illness was diagnosed. This was to be, and not only in retrospect, a nostalgic occasion reuniting him with Gregory Peck from *Navarone*, Trevor Howard from *The Way Ahead*, Roger Moore from *Escape to Athena* and Patrick MacNee from *The Elusive Pimpernel* for positively the last stand of a wartime territorial unit known as the Calcutta Light Horse. In many respects, *The Sea Wolves* was also to be David's last stand.

Chapter Twenty-Nine

1979–1981

'I think I might be getting toward the last reel.'

As the Hollywood biography trade which he himself had done so much to stimulate in the 1970s began to flood the market with filmbooks of one kind or another, David found that quite a lot of the spare time he used to devote to writing eccentric or indignant letters to *The Times* now had to be spent refuting other people's stories. No, he had not been a spy for Stephenson's 'Intrepid' unit during the war, even though he had known the man and filmed his life story recently for television; no, Errol Flynn had never been a Nazi (as at least one biography was now claiming) and no, he himself had never had a homosexual affair with Errol (as another gossip had suggested). Moreover, he had not yet himself suffered either a heart attack or a stroke, despite one American press report. 'I have', said David in a splendidly typical reply, 'today consulted my expert Swiss doctor, and his considered view is that I am very possibly still alive.'

He was not only alive but fighting in a film that was later to be subtitled by at least one London critic 'Golden Oldies Go To War'. *The Sea Wolves* had been scripted by Reginald Rose from a James Leasor story about a bunch of irregular soldiers who in 1942 rallied to sabotage a German attempt to broadcast shipping information from the supposedly neutral harbour of Goa. Like *Navarone*, though in my view very much better written and played, this was a war film based on a great deal of nostalgia and the notion that elderly men going to war was somehow more touching and also often a lot more effective then raw young recruits going over the top. This was, if anything, 'the Clean Dozen'.

In Gregory Peck's view, 'David was chipper as always on Goa. He didn't much like his part, but he made it look a lot better than it was. That was what he was paid to do. The thing was that he'd begun, religiously, to take long fast walks every day, late in the afternoon, after work . . . he had begun his valiant fight, his refusal to accept muscular weakness, and it was to last for three years. Never has a man fought a losing battle with such courage and such an outrageous sense of humour about the thing that was to bring an end to his life – the life that had been lived with such vigour and such a manly appetite for everything that was beautiful, excellent, graceful and funny.'

Niven had as yet no idea of the nature of the muscle-wasting disease that had already started to kill him. Motor neurone disease was still largely undiagnosed in many instances, and only just beginning to become familiar in America as 'Lou Gehrig's disease' because the base baller played in a film by Gary Cooper had been thus far its most famous victim. All Niven knew was that his arm and leg muscles would occasionally begin to ache unexpectedly, walking or swimming become suddenly exhausting, and his voice, late at night, sometimes begin to develop a very faint slur. But he was, after all, just marking his seventieth birthday and *The Sea Wolves* was an exhausting picture to make. Perhaps there was no more to it than that.

On that last location, he seemed for most of the time to be his usual cheery self. John Standing, the grandson of Sir Guy Standing (and the actor who, I reckon, should be asked to play Niven if ever they film his remarkable life story, so close is the resemblance if not in looks then certainly in character, attitude and performance), was also on that film.

'The thing that people forget about David', he recalls, 'is that apart from all the jokes and the stories, he was the most thoughtful and kindly actor I have ever worked with. I had hardly anything to do on that film, but we had known each other vaguely over the years and he took an almost paternal attitude towards me, coming over as soon as I arrived and offering to lend me his car and all of that. He was the last of that line, the last actor to have made it in Hollywood in the years when the British were automatically cast as the heroes instead of the heavies or the character men, but he still had a very strong sense of the pecking order, knew that he was still second in billing to Greg Peck and was always respectful of that. David was very underrated as an actor because he always underplayed everything to the point where it looked as though he wasn't acting at all, so nobody gave him the credit that he deserved. Considering what he did for the image of Englishmen on the screen across half a century, they should have given him a knighthood.'

In Roger Moore's recollection, *The Sea Wolves* was originally set up as a kind of follow-on to *The Wild Geese* which he had just made for the same producer (Euan Lloyd) and director (Andrew McLaglen) and screenwriter, with the Richards Harris and Burton. 'But there seemed an awful kind of sameness about just doing that sort of ageing guerrilla story again on a different location, so then they went off on a different tack and approached Gregory Peck and he was the one who wondered whether there might be a job in it for Niv, so that was how we all came to be on Goa together. But that was also the first time that I knew there was something wrong with David.' He and Patrick MacNee would go off every afternoon after the shooting for long walks across the beach and one evening he came back and said to Moore, 'You know, it's a funny thing but I can't get my bloody heel off the ground properly.' Nobody took it very seriously; they all thought it was a pinched nerve. Moore remembers, 'We told him to exercise it and sure enough in a day or two it was fine again. But that I'm sure was not a pinched nerve; it was the start of the disease that was to kill him.'

Yet for Faith Brook, cast as Niven's wife in that film and herself of course the daughter of one of the founding fathers of the English colony in Hollywood, Clive Brook, there was as yet no sign that he was in any health trouble: 'I was struck as always by his tremendous charm; not a great deal of talent there, it seemed to me, but enough charm to make you forget that. He took so much trouble to make me feel welcome on the location and spent a lot of time with me, at least until the Maharajah of Jaipur's family arrived for a visit; then, of course, he was off with them. You always had that faint feeling with David that he was looking over your shoulder, wherever you were, to see if anybody more exciting might be coming along; but even that one could forgive, because he took such trouble to be hospitable. He was also still a diehard professional: I saw him get off a plane one morning at six in Delhi and in make-up and costume on the set an hour or so later. He remained wonderfully funny: one afternoon we were at some sort of official reception and both exhausted, so he took me up to our hostess, who was an extremely grand Indian lady, and said, "We're both very tired now, and as we are playing husband and wife we are going off to bed; that's how it is in showbusiness."'

For Patrick MacNee, also on that film, the memories are of long walks along the Goa beach with David talking about his novel and never once mentioning the illness, though many people on the set now had an idea that there was something wrong. Roger Moore jokingly suggested to MacNee that he and David must be having an affair because they spent so much time together, but it was really just that they both had daughters who had recently been in hospital for long periods of time and David wanted to talk to someone who would understand. He also spoke often about the novel, which he had now decided to call

Go Slowly, Come Back Quickly because, he told MacNee, he had once been on Grenada during a terrible hurricane (which in fact forms the climax of the story) and heard a little black girl say that as a kind of goodbye to him. Later he wrote Patrick a number of letters, one of which said that he was finding 'long walks, long talks and long drinks' more and more difficult to deal with, but that if he never said another word he'd still be ahead, having talked non-stop for seven entire decades. 'Later still,' recalled MacNee, 'he sent me a copy of the novel, because he named the milkman in it after me, and on the title page he added, "Dear Pat, you've already suffered through all of this on Goa, so just give the book to someone you really loathe for Christmas!" Oh, but he was the most lovely man; every time I walk along a beach now I still find myself thinking about him.'

For those of us who have always believed, with John Mortimer, that Niven's life was essentially 'Wodehouse with tears', these last three years were the ones when you really caught a glimpse of the tears. Indeed, one of the muscle-wasting effects of motor neurone disease was an inability to control the tear ducts, so that David would often appear to be crying with laughter at the mildest of jokes. This was still a very intermittent problem, however, and for a while after *The Sea Wolves* he seemed to be his old self, back at the writing table in the garden of Lo Scoglietto working away on the novel.

Quite apart from his health, there was another problem: the novel, David suddenly realized, was not going to be a very good book. Thirty years earlier he had managed almost off the cuff to write a light and expert comic novel when there was almost nothing riding on it and those few people who did read it were just surprised that the actor could write at all. Now he had achieved two of the biggest non-fiction best-sellers of the 1970s and the stakes were therefore a great deal higher. David was still with Hamish Hamilton in Britain, but in America he had moved from Putnam to Doubleday, where his friend Bill Buckley was

published. Doubleday were keen to have a two-novel
contract and, after much negotiating, George Greenfield
managed to get them to increase the advance to $1,000,050
– the 'extra' $50 was because David said he always wanted
to be able to tell his friends that he'd got more than a
million out of them.

In fact, he never lived to write the second book of that
contract, though a fragment of about a hundred pages
concerning a terrorist plot does exist. But even with the
first David was only too aware that what he was delivering
to his publishers was simply not worth that kind of money.
In the first, early novel, and the two subsequent autobiographies, he had used up virtually his entire fund of good
stories, and he was not now or ever a creative writer. What
he had written so far had always been filtered out of an
imaginative memory, and although he managed to build
into this last book a few untold Army and Hollywood
anecdotes, they were few and far between. He did not
need literary critics to tell him a year later that *Go Slowly,
Come Back Quickly* was not quite good enough to justify
its share of the $1 million.

On the other hand, he wasn't about to hand back the
money, which he still felt he needed, nor was he about
to give up on something he had been trying to write
intermittently on many film locations over the past five
years; he simply had to get it finished, and that took him
most of the rest of 1980. That winter he was still able to
ski around Gstaad, and for once without hiding from the
cameras since (with, for once, no film to go to) he was
under no instructions from any insurance company to keep
his arms and legs unbroken. Hedy Olden, who owns and
manages the hotel in Gstaad where Niven most often
dropped in for lunch or an après-ski cognac on the way
back down the mountain to his chalet in Château d'Oex,
remembers this as the last really good time of his life.

'He was passionate about his skiing, took it really
seriously – unlike many of the stars who come here just to
be seen in the right magazines. David was always charming,

always a gentleman, but there were moments now when he would surprise me. He would suddenly stop in the middle of a conversation and say, "Am I speaking well?" or "Am I limping?" and at that time I could never understand what he was worried about because he seemed perfectly fine to me, always in total control. One night, I remember, he and Ustinov and Rainier all came to my restaurant and started playing the piano and drums and bass like a jazz group. I think he was always happiest in the mountains, and certainly he was a creature of great habit. One winter he came in here every day for lunch and always ordered the same curry. I don't think he liked change. He also didn't much like the big parties up at the palace, or the way that Burton used to come here and fall over drunk. He was a very sober, quiet man and, unlike Sellers, very open. You always knew where you were with David, whereas with Sellers and Burton you never had the remotest idea what was really going on inside their heads.'

Early in 1981, David went back to Hollywood for what was to prove his last public appearance there. He had agreed to act as the master of ceremonies for a network television gala at which Fred Astaire, one of the oldest of his Californian friends, would receive the life achievement award of the American Film Institute. Looking tired but still bronzed from the Gstaad sunshine, David reminded the audience of his first meeting with Fred back in 1934: 'I arrived with a letter of introduction from a mutual friend of ours, a London bookmaker, and one evening after a hot game of tennis I decided to present it. So I crossed the street to the Astaire house. Unfortunately, I had forgotten to put my shirt on. Fred's wife opened the door, sniffed at me like a bird dog, and shut it again very quickly indeed. Then I heard her say, "Fred, come quickly. There's a perfectly dreadful, half-naked man in the garden smelling horrible."'

Immediately after those celebrations David returned to Lo Scoglietto, and to a film he had promised to make for his son: originally shot as *Ménage à Trois*, and given a

British television release after his death as *Better Late Than Never*, this has the melancholy distinction of being the last film in which David's own voice is heard. He and Art Carney (though Bob Hope was the original casting) played a couple of seventy-year-olds trying to work out which of them might be grandfather to a little orphan now unexpectedly worth several million dollars, and as Niven was meant to be an old song-and-dance man eking out a tenth-rate living in a tacky Riviera nightclub, he actually sang for the first time ever on screen, part of the 'Marvellous Party' number written and made famous by his old friend Noël Coward. But this was not, as the director Bryan Forbes recalls, an easy film.

'We were shooting very near his home on Cap Ferrat, and one morning we were doing a beach scene when he suddenly said, "Forbesy I, er, can't run any more. My legs won't work," and I thought well, it's very hard anyway to run in the sand, so we did the shot a different way and that was that. But then he found it very hard to get his mouth round certain words when we were dubbing, and that brought back to me terrible memories of Jack Hawkins losing his voice at the end of his career. One night towards the very end of the filming we were walking along the beach and he suddenly said, "I think I might be getting towards the last reel," but I think he also felt that if he could just keep working, he might be able to fight it off. Also he clearly didn't want to let his son down.'

The part of the lawyer in that film was originally intended for Sir Ralph Richardson, but when he fell out it went instead to the actor Lionel Jeffries. 'I didn't know how ill David was,' he says, 'though I did notice that he wasn't very keen to mix with any of us socially. He used to go straight home after the shooting every night. Once we were doing a crowd scene, and he went around afterwards shaking every extra by the hand, which impressed me a lot because he didn't know I was watching and I thought that was a sign of true stardom. Another time we were doing a scene in a massage parlour, because Forbesy thought that might enliven it a bit, and David convinced me we would have to work in the nude which so terrified me that I couldn't remember a single line until he flashed open his towelling robe and showed me a sparkling pair of Y-fronts. I was all right after that. Then on the very last night we had a little party on the set and David arrived very late, about eleven o'clock, but looking immaculate and he came round every table shaking hands and saying goodbye and when he got to our table he just took me in his arms and said, "Goodbye, chum," and then everyone stood up and applauded him as he left. It was really very moving, not just sentimental.'

'The terrible thing was', says David Niven Jr, 'that Daddy's illness came at the moment when he was really happiest with his career. The success that he got from the books meant so much more to him than anything except possibly the Oscar, because the books were something that he had at last done all alone. They were just him and a pen and paper, and I think they gave him a whole new lease of life. But then suddenly one day when we were making *Ménage à Trois*, Bryan came over to me and said, "Have you noticed that David's voice is getting a little shaky?" and I said that I hadn't and so we looked at a couple of scenes and I thought well, let's not worry now, we can fix that when we do the final dubbing. But his voice got progressively worse during the filming. I don't mean a drastic change, but every day, as he got a little more tired, the voice would start to slur. I think at that time it was only noticeable on a microphone, though, and he certainly had no idea that he was really seriously ill until months later.'

Within weeks of finishing *Ménage à Trois*, David had agreed to go into a long and arduous promotional tour in England and across America for the novel; he knew that *Go Slowly, Come Back Quickly* was going to be much harder than the autobiographies to sell, given that fiction is almost always more tricky than semi-fact to get across bookshop counters in hardback, and he therefore felt that

in return for his $1 million the least he could do would be
to go out and sell as forcefully as his now shaky health
would permit. The promotion was due to start in London
with a solo fifty-minute appearance on the BBC1 *Michael
Parkinson Show* for 3 October 1981, and to those watching
it became immediately apparent that there was something
very wrong indeed.

Niven's previous appearances on *Parkinson* over the
past five years had been among the highlights of what is
still generally reckoned to have been the best of the BBC's
many attempts at a celebrity-interview show: long, relaxed,
rambling chats about the golden days of Hollywood and
the sometimes less golden days that had been endured on
the way there. But now, David's speech was distinctly
slurred. He kept clearing his throat and apologizing for 'a
frog in the throat', but many viewers actually rang in
suggesting that he'd had several drinks too many before
the programme.

To anyone who knew David even remotely, that was
out of the question: he took as much care and trouble over
a television interview as he did over any other screen
appearance, and as the master salesman of himself he was
painfully aware of the importance of this one in getting
the novel sales off to a reasonable start before the reviews
could do too much damage. After the show he seemed
aware that something might have been a little wrong, but
uncertain precisely what or how far it had been detectable
beyond the studio. He was very soon to find out: when he
got back that night to his usual room at the Connaught, a
woman staying a few doors down the corridor but totally
unknown to him had slipped a note under his door. She
had been, she said, trained as a nurse, and watching the
Parkinson show that night she had been extremely alarmed
by Niven's condition. Had he perhaps suffered a mild
stroke without fully realizing it?

This was very different from having his son or his last
director detect a slight slur on the soundtrack of a film;
this was a total stranger noticing on television that he was

a very sick man. Niven rang George Greenfield, who admitted that he too had noticed that something was wrong and that he had even slurred the punchlines of some of his own best stories. Greenfield suggested that David should see a doctor as soon as possible.

David had, however, promised not only Hamish Hamilton but also Sam Vaughan at Doubleday that he would do all he could to push the book, and was indeed due in New York later that same week. He arrived there looking terrible, and one of the first things he told Vaughan was the story of the note in the Connaught which had obviously worried him very much. Doubleday had a nationwide tour set up which they offered to cancel, but David would not hear of it. 'I've taken your money,' he said, 'and I shall now go out and sell the book.' Though Vaughan insisted that David's life was really rather more important than any novel, Niven did not seem to accept that there was any real danger. He said that as soon as the tour was over he would go for a holiday with the Loel Guinnesses in Mexico and the Buckleys in Connecticut.

By now, friends in London had sent a videotape of the *Parkinson* show to Jamie Niven in New York, who was also very disturbed by what he saw: 'I knew my father had never been really drunk in his life, and certainly not on a live television show, but that was how he sounded so I called him up and said I was very worried and he said, well, so was he; he thought maybe he might have suffered some sort of stroke, and he said that after this cross-country book tour was over he'd stop in at the Mayo Clinic and have some tests.'

The moment he received the result of those tests, David called his son from the clinic. 'The good news', he said, 'is that I didn't have a stroke. The bad news is that I've got amyotrophic lateral sclerosis. I am going to lose my voice, my ability to communicate, the use of my hands and legs, and then I am going to die. Maybe in weeks, maybe in months, maybe in years.' David Niven was seventy-one, and had just eighteen months to live.

Chapter Thirty

1981–1983

'Don't stretch the elastic too far, old chum: it snaps.'

On the plane back to New York from the Mayo Clinic in Minneapolis, David found himself seated next to the NBC news anchorman, Tom Brokaw. Half-way through the flight, after running through the latest repertoire of his stories as usual, Niven suddenly broke off and told Brokaw that he was soon going to die and that there was, in the view of the Mayo Clinic, nothing that even American medical science could do to save him. Brokaw, one of the best and also mercifully most sensitive television newsmen in the business, decided never to break the story and by that decision gave David, in the opinion of his younger son, twelve full months before the European media began to make prying enquiries after his health.

By now the reviews were coming in on *Go Slowly, Come Back Quickly* and, as David had feared, they were not good. 'Skittish in pace, uncertain in tone, a disappointing novel only occasionally heightened by the author's wit and charm,' was the opinion of Mel Watkins of the *New York Times*, and his views were echoed by literary critics on both sides of the Atlantic who were not prepared to make the allowances that their more showbusiness-oriented colleagues had made for the prose style of *The Moon's A Balloon* or *Bring on the Empty Horses*.

David had rather more to worry about than a few bad

book reviews. His final promotional tour had totally exhausted him, and when he got back to Connecticut to stay with the Buckleys there was, as Bill noted in his diary, real cause for concern: 'He wasn't in full control of his speaking voice . . . he'd had clear difficulty in enunciation and was so worried about it that he reduced his liquor consumption from his normal three glasses of wine per day to a single glass.'

Also staying with the Buckleys for that weekend was the publisher Sam Vaughan, who says: 'I remember David sitting by the fireplace on that grey, cold day and I was very glad to see him in that warm envelope of a place at last . . . Bill said that people were only to be allowed to talk about their health for thirteen minutes and after that we all went out for a sail, freezing but happy until we got back to the house and I noticed that David's hands had locked into a sort of claw-like position and he couldn't quite straighten them out. In the midst of all the warmth and happiness there were sudden, jarring moments like that.'

Back in London to finish the sales tour there, David still managed to rally himself to the point where even his old publicist friend, Theo Cowan, noticed nothing more than a certain exhaustion at the end of book-signing sessions: 'David was still breezing in and out of bookshops and radio stations as though he hadn't a care in the world. You never had to send cars for Niven or make special arrangements for him. He always travelled very light, in life and on the screen: he was never a man weighed down by a heavy suitcase. A raincoat maybe, but that would be that. He had no illusions about himself as a great actor or indeed a great author: but he was wonderful on those bookselling tours and I think up until the last he really enjoyed them, loved seeing five hundred people queued up in a bookshop for his autograph even if some of them hadn't bought his book at all. It reminded him that all those films had given him a very loyal following. David was like a garage mechanic in his attitude to films and filming: if they brought

him a Rolls-Royce of a movie, he'd fix that with an appearance. If they brought him a beaten-up old wreck, he'd try
to fix that too. He wasn't an actor like Olivier or indeed a
novelist like Dirk Bogarde: he was just a wonderfully
gifted amateur, like one of those amateur cricketers you
sometimes see scoring a century and then going back to
whatever it is they really do for a living. And that meant
he could mix with anybody anywhere: whether it was Sam
Spiegel or Sam Spade he ran into in a restaurant, David
would carry on more or less the same conversation. Nobody could have done those book tours the way he did
them: that old Goldwyn Studio training in how to handle
the press was very valuable, but even more importantly he
always had good manners and good taste. That's not a
combination you find very often among star actors. And
there was another side to David's character: when Peter
Sellers died in 1980, he made a remarkable speech at the
memorial service about how an actor is more than just
what he appears to be on the screen, and should never be
taken at face value. That was very true of Niven, too.'

Now it was very nearly all over, and in these last few
months of David's life his already weakening condition
was made worse by two violent deaths among the inner
circle of his old Hollywood friends. The first of these was
Natalie Wood, Robert Wagner's wife, who drowned in a
California boating accident in the November of 1981.
David was on the phone to Wagner straight away and,
doubtless remembering his own experience with the sudden death of Primmie, he was able to help him through
it all. He advised Wagner not to make any immediate
decisions, not to hide from what had happened, but
just very gradually to try to come to terms with it. That
Christmas, even though he was now far from well, he
found Wagner a house in Gstaad and stocked it up with
food, drink and great logs for the fire, which he carried up
himself. 'Then,' as Wagner recalls, 'because my daughters
and I arrived there in a terrible snowstorm, he waited
down the bottom of the road for two or three hours to

guide us and show us the way up the hill. And when we finally got there he just held me in his arms and we talked for hours about Natalie and Primmie, and what had happened to them, and he taught me that Christmas how to deal with a tragedy like the one we had both known.'

By the spring of 1982, with all the Mayo tests confirmed, David turned briefly to fringe medicine in the hope of some sort of solution, even sitting in baths of ice watching, he said, 'while my oldest friend in the world shrivelled up before my eyes like a little acorn'. Even now his ear for a good story did not desert him. An old acquaintance in Château d'Oex called out from a passing car one morning to ask how he was.

'Well,' replied David, 'I've got motor neurone disease.' 'Oh yes?' said the other man blithely. 'I've just bought a new Mercedes myself.' And with that he drove it away.

In these last few months of his life, David began to see more and more of an old English friend and Swiss neighbour, the writer and critic Alastair Forbes. 'David was a great romantic,' he recalls. 'I think that was what really kept his second marriage going through its most difficult times. He couldn't bear the idea that it might fail. He dearly enjoyed the thought of being a married man, even if in reality it wasn't always working out very well. He was under a lot of strain towards the end, and not all of it physical. We'd been friends across many years because one of the first people he ever tried to borrow money from in America was one of my richer brothers-in-law, and then I'd known him in his happiest years with Primmie, and again towards the end in Switzerland where he'd always had this tremendous determination to stay in training because he thought that was the way he got work. I used to say, "Riding in the 3.30 again at Leicester, are you?" because he so often had that look of a drawn jockey. He was always popping into saunas, determined to stay thin and fit and young. Some people even thought that was maybe how he had lowered his resistance to the motor neurone disease.'

Forbes knew little of David's Hollywood life, but in the later years Niven seemed to like the fact that his friend had kept in touch with an earlier English world he had long left behind, and they would talk about people they had known at Sandhurst or in the war. As Alastair Forbes observes, 'David was for a large part of the world the acceptable face of Britain, and the fact that he never got a knighthood is nothing short of a national disgrace. Quite a number of us tried to do something about that in these last few months of his life, but to no avail.'

The lack of any official enthusiasm for the idea, wrongly attributed after David's death to some sort of imaginary 'feud' between him and Prince Philip, was perhaps for much the same reason that Downing Street never gave a knighthood to such contemporaries of Niven as James Mason or (at the time of writing) Rex Harrison. English actors who have spent a large part of their lives living and working abroad do not usually rank high on honours lists unless, like Coward and Chaplin, their achievements have been so varied and considerable that the denial of that knighthood becomes a major, instead of merely a minor, oversight.

Even now, only a year or so away from his death and already in considerable pain, David never lost his determination to work, nor his insecurity about money. On his two autobiographies plus the novel alone he had already made just over £2 million, counting all the foreign and paperback rights, and his Swiss tax status meant that he could bank a considerable proportion of that. But he had promised Doubleday another novel as part of the last contract, and so he was determined to continue with that even though some days just holding a pencil became a major achievement. He was also keeping a file of stories that he'd somehow forgotten to include in the autobiographies, like the one about his Malta CO who had advised him never to leave the Army, and who a decade later was wandering through Leicester Square vaguely wondering to an ADC whatever had become of young Niven while above them blazed his name in neon letters as the star of *The Dawn Patrol*.

Yet years of economic unease in Hollywood were not to be obliterated by the sudden arrival of a couple of million pounds. David was a traditional figure, and tradition dictated that he never had enough money. When, therefore, it was suggested that he might soon need a full-time nurse, he quite seriously began to ask whether relatives thought he could afford such a luxury. He also had every intention of going ahead with another film, as though if he kept his head down and continued working, the illness might just give up and go away of its own accord.

'You have to remember', says Jamie, 'that motor neurone disease is psychologically terrifying because your mind stays fine while your body just melts away and you know there's nothing you can do about it. Every day now became an effort, and I was very much opposed to his doing those last *Pink Panther* films, but he'd committed to them and I don't think he realized quite how rapidly he was going down.'

Filmed near Niven's Cap Ferrat home in the summer of 1982, *The Curse of the Pink Panther* and *The Trail of the Pink Panther* were a curious (and some of us thought distinctly macabre) effort by Blake Edwards to cobble together two more Clouseau comedies a couple of years after Peter Sellers's death by cutting together unused footage from the earlier *Panthers* with new material for which such survivors of the very first in the series as Niven, Robert Wagner, Capucine and Herbert Lom were once again assembled, as well as one or two new-comers like the English actress Joanna Lumley.

'They'd hired some enormous villa on Cap Ferrat,' she remembers, 'and David was sitting by a swimming pool and I was playing a French reporter who had to interview him as the character he'd played in the very first film of the series almost twenty years earlier. But he was now really very ill, and there were all these Californian film people standing around saying wasn't he wunnerful and brave with all of that overbearing showbusiness sympathy about disease, and I could see that he really just wanted to be left alone. The first thing he told me was that he had to be terribly careful not to think about anything very funny, otherwise he just got hysterics and then couldn't stop laughing or crying. So of course the next thing he did was describe all these awful tests they had made him do in hospital, and soon there were tears of laughter pouring down his face at the memory of it all. He was like a child in that you had to tiptoe away from him when he started to get tired, otherwise he would just go on talking and wear himself out. Niven was a very loyal man. Instead of saying, "Look, I am really very ill and very tired, and I don't want to be in these awful little films," he went through with it because of his friendship with the director and his memory of the success they'd had together at the beginning of the series. Even now, he remained the most marvellous storyteller because he had that perfect grace which allowed him to let you into terrible Hollywood secrets as though you knew all the people involved anyway. He somehow elevated his listeners to his own social and professional level without ever patronizing them. And there was something infinitely touching about this very English man fighting for his life in the midst of a very phoney film environment. A few weeks after the filming ended, I had a letter from him in which he said that he was still managing to swim and even snorkel a little, but that he had taken to eating all alone because "it's better for all and I don't choke when spoken to". He also noted down the time it had taken him to write by hand the first four lines of the letter: eight minutes and thirty-three seconds.'

Soon even letter-writing at that pace would become an impossibility. 'My right arm', he told John Mortimer sadly a few weeks later, 'has now gone over to the enemy.' Fifty years on from Sandhurst, his metaphors were still those of a military man.

When they began to do the final edit on these *Pink*

Panthers, Blake Edwards decided that Niven's voice on the soundtrack was now totally unusable, and that he would need to have it dubbed by an expert mimic, the comedian Rich Little. 'I spent hours and days listening to the recordings that David had made of his own books on tape,' says Little, 'and I was never told how seriously ill he was, just that he had this problem with his voice. Unfortunately, however, one morning when I had the Niven tapes on, a Toronto radio reporter called me for an interview and he heard this voice in the background and recognized it, so I told him I was teaching myself to sound like Niven for a dubbing job, because nobody had yet told me to keep it a secret.'

Sadly, nobody had thought of telling Niven he was being dubbed either, so the first he knew of the change of voice was an item in a gossip column and it is not difficult to estimate the effect of that story. Here was an actor who, across fifty years and almost a hundred films, had prided himself on his professionalism finding that one of the major tools of his trade now had to be replaced in a dubbing theatre by a stranger. The news depressed him badly enough; what depressed him even more was the way he'd had to find out about it, though that was no fault of Mr Little. 'I don't know,' wrote Alan Brien for the *Sunday Times* when *The Trail of the Pink Panther* opened in London in December 1982, 'which is more depressing: the sight of a young Peter Sellers at the beginning of this film, or the sight of an old David Niven at the end of it.'

By now, there was no longer much chance that Niven's debilitating illness could be kept out of the press. The story of the Rich Little dubbing, and indeed the sight of Niven's cadaverous face in that last film, alerted even the most casual observer to the fact that here was a very sick man, and by the autumn of 1982 the gossip columnists had found another thread of the story. In that September, less than a year after the Natalie Wood drowning, another old and staunch Niven friend, Princess Grace of Monaco, was killed in a car smash and David did not attend the funeral, aware that if he did go the weakness of his own muscles would turn his tears to hysteria.

His absence from so public an occasion was of course noticed and, to make matters worse, a month or so earlier Princess Grace had herself given an interview in which she had said that she thought David was suffering from some sort of minor stroke. 'If I'd known she was going to give me a medical,' noted David ruefully, 'I'd have tried to enjoy it more.' For a while the family attempted to contain the damage, and a press report was issued to the effect that David was now 'suffering from exhaustion'. But, as the months went by, there seemed little point in trying to keep secret what so many people already knew, especially as the rumours were by now getting out of hand. In December 1982 Hjordis therefore put out a short press release to the effect that her husband was suffering 'a muscular disorder, but it is not cancer or a heart attack as many people have supposed'.

'My father', said Jamie later, 'behaved throughout that last winter with incredible bravery, because it would have been so easy to lose control. Every day, in every way, his life got more and more difficult: I think even cancer would have been preferable to that wasting of the muscles. He was beginning now, understandably, to look back at his life and I once asked him why he was still so concerned about money when, since 1960, he had really been a very rich man, and he just said I had never known what it was like to be poor.

'I asked him another time if he had any real regrets, and he said not about the things he'd done, but maybe about the things he hadn't done. There were some relationships quite close to home which he felt hadn't worked out as well as they should have, and he also felt that perhaps towards the end he should have lived in a more real world than the one contained by the walls of a villa on Cap Ferrat or a chalet in Switzerland. A lot of his friends had been older than he was, and as they died off there were places he would no longer go back to because they reminded him of happier times. As my father got sicker, I felt our relationship was reversing: some of his fears were now childlike and I was the one who had to allay them. He worried about what was going to happen to Hjordis and the girls after he died.'

For Hjordis, too, these were difficult times. 'For a man like David,' she said, 'who so loved to swim and walk and ski and sail and talk, gradually to find all those pleasures denied him was unbearable. The frustration of trying to say or write something and then finding that he just couldn't communicate, together with the wasting of the body, made it the most cruel illness.' He was still trying to work on the second novel but it was very hard for him. Old friends would call to see him and Hjordis would have to warn them not to show how shocked they were by his condition.

By Christmas it was clear that the disease was accelerating fast. The French actress Capucine, who had been with him in the first and last of the *Panther* films, went up to Château d'Oex and then found herself weeping all the way back in the train to Lausanne, having realized that she would never see him again. For his son David, 'the problem was that you really couldn't understand too much of what he was saying. Just sitting there, seeing someone you love in pain, is traumatic enough; but the fact that he couldn't really express himself, so that you'd get maybe one word out of ten and then he'd say, "Fuck it!" and start out all over again trying to make you understand, that was what really destroyed me. I began to hope that it would end soon, so that his suffering would be over.'

Others felt much the same; for a man who had taken so much trouble to make his family and friends laugh now to be so often so close to tears was infinitely depressing. When he got back to Cap Ferrat from that last Christmas at Château d'Oex, a couple of French photographers with telephoto lenses stole shots of him in the garden of Lo Scoglietto and one of the more despicable English tabloid dailies ran a photograph of David's cadaverous body, an act of such stunning tastelessness even by their own standards that they were rapidly hauled before the Press Council by some of their own readers. Roderick Mann, in Cannes later that spring for the film festival, was told by Roger Moore that he really ought to go and see his old friend for what might well be the last time: 'Roger said I should bite the bullet and go, so I went up to the villa but it was horrendous because I literally couldn't understand a word David was saying, and he seemed to have shrivelled inside his clothes. We sat in the garden and just looked at each other and he was still smiling and the brain had stayed active but nothing else. It was desperately sad and very grim, and when I left he stood in the drive waving right until my car was out of sight.'

'Some people, like Richard Burton, who went to see him in those last few months,' says John Mortimer, 'used to shout at him as though he were deaf because he couldn't speak, and that really drove him wild. The everyday struggle of just eating and swallowing and trying to talk really obsessed him, but I think he still had the hope that someone would find a miracle cure. He wasn't about to give up without a struggle, even now.'

In his last few winters at the chalet in Château d'Oex, David had begun to see a lot of a local English physiotherapist, David Bolton, whom he had first met back in 1974. Bolton recalls: 'David was one of my first patients when I started practising in Gstaad. Whenever he had a minor skiing or back problem he'd come to me, and so naturally enough after he'd had the diagnosis from the Mayo Clinic he came to tell me and just for a minute seemed utterly destroyed by the news. But then he pulled himself together and went back into battle, the same old Niven, though we both knew now that it was terminal. But neither of us ever talked about how long he was going to last: we both knew that it was just a matter of making what time was left as comfortable as possible for him. The loss of the voice was what most upset him, because of course that meant the end of his career as an actor; then he only had the writing, and that was slow going because he could hardly hold a pen. All the time I was giving him routine physiotherapy, trying to keep the muscles supple after they'd stopped being active, breathing exercises, all the usual things, but I think the conversations were doing as much good as anything because I learnt to understand him fairly early on: I could lip-read and follow his gestures. He made very brave attempts to keep up with the exercises right to the last: he knew he was in a fight for survival.'

In that fight with what David was now calling 'my Gandhi body', one of his other great allies was the Irish nurse Kathleen Matthewson, who came to look after him about nine months before his death. David told her that as a child he had once had a nurse called Miss Matthewson: 'A Matthewson helped me into this world,' he added, 'and a Matthewson will help me out of it.' But not before he was good and ready. Originally Kathleen was only meant to be with him for about three weeks, but then he asked her to stay and she was with him right up to the end.

At the end of February 1983, just before his seventy-third birthday, David made his last journey from Cap Ferrat to London, there to spend ten days having medical treatment at the Wellington Hospital in St John's Wood. The visit attracted considerable press attention even though David had been booked in under a false name, but both he and Hjordis grinned bravely for the waiting cameras and it was then announced that he was going home to France 'to recover and work on his new novel'. In fact, there was to be no more work on the novel, and no chance of any real recovery.

'A few weeks later,' Hjordis recalls, 'David kept saying that he wanted to leave Cap Ferrat and go back to the chalet, back to Château d'Oex, but that he wanted me to stay and have a rest from him for a while. The air was very clear up there, and he thought the change might be good for him. I was then going to join him there a few days later.'

When Hjordis did go to Château d'Oex, it was for David's funeral. He had arrived at the chalet with Kathleen in the middle of July, and at first the change of air did seem to be doing him some good. 'He insisted we should travel by a scheduled Swissair flight,' she says, 'instead of a charter plane, and he was amazing: his weight was now down to about 54 kilos from his usual 72, but he sipped a little diluted wine on the flight and even chatted with the stewardess. Then when we arrived in Château d'Oex, Gunther Sachs had his house opened up near by so David could use the indoor pool, and every day he would swim and walk a little and seemed so much better than he had in France. There it used to take him more than half an hour just to get a glass of water down and all his food had to go through a blender, but suddenly one morning at the chalet he said he thought he'd like to start having toast again for breakfast. He really was a different man, much more relaxed than he had been in France; I think he knew now that he really was dying, and he just wanted to enjoy his last few days in the place he loved best.'

With Hjordis still on Cap Ferrat, his sons working in America and Kristina in Geneva, Fiona was the only member of his immediate family with him at the chalet during these last few days, though a nephew of Hjordis was also staying there when, on Wednesday 27 July, as Kathleen recalls: 'David went to swim in the morning and then meant to go in the evening again but couldn't because he was exhausted, having failed to sleep in the afternoon because of the heat. That night his sleeping tablet didn't work so I sat up chatting to him until about two in the morning; he was talking now about Primmie and his first marriage and his early days in the Army. Then he did manage to sleep, and the next day I called his doctor, who said that he was deteriorating very rapidly and that there was really nothing he could do unless David went into hospital again. But he desperately didn't want to do that, and so I called his sons in America and they agreed that he should be allowed to stay peacefully at home. On the Thursday he couldn't speak a word, but he was still writing me little notes and David Bolton brought him some oxygen to clear his chest. That night I stayed up again with him until about three in the morning, when he told me to go and get some sleep, but I didn't, and he suddenly began talking again about Primmie and how he had first met her in the war and how happy they had been together and how different his life would have been if she had not been killed. Then he said I really had to get some sleep, but to look in on him and if he was OK he'd have his thumb up. About seven the next morning, the Friday, I looked in and his thumb was up so I went downstairs to make myself some coffee and just as I got to the bottom of the stairs I heard a sort of noise, as though he'd been trying to get out of bed, and when I got back into his room he had the oxygen mask off and gave me a big smile and held my hand and away he went. As quickly as that.'

Kathleen immediately called his doctor, who also called the police, according to local Swiss custom; she then phoned David Bolton and together with Fiona they started to alert the family and a few close friends. But with Hjordis still on Cap Ferrat and the boys in America it was in fact two old friends, Roger Moore and Alastair Forbes who, together with Fiona, Kathleen Matthewson and David Bolton, made the funeral arrangements for the following Tuesday and began fending off the inevitable arrival in Château d'Oex of the world press. As there is an English church there, one where both the girls had been baptized and where David himself had once gone to pray for Kristina's recovery after her car crash, that seemed the most natural place to bury him, in the midst of the skiing country he had always loved best.

Tributes to David were now pouring in from all over the world, and at the Château d'Oex funeral on 3 August 1983, Yehudi Menuhin played Mendelssohn to a congregation which included Prince Rainier, Audrey Hepburn and the British ambassador representing not only the British government but also the royal family. Later, memorial services were led in Hollywood by Gregory Peck and Peter

Ustinov, and in London by Laurence Olivier and John Mortimer, who also now heads with Anthony Quayle the appeal fund set up in David's name to combat the disease which killed him.

David Niven left a fortune roughly estimated at $5 million, most of it to Hjordis and his two adopted daughters in a trust fund administered by his two sons who also benefit by it. He also left what his *Times* obituary called 'the memory of an archetypal English gentleman: witty, debonair, immaculate in dress and behaviour, but with mischief lurking never far from the surface', and the memory of a small gathering of family and friends on that Swiss hillside in the August sunshine while the local Lutheran vicar read lines of Hilaire Belloc that seemed perfectly applicable to the life and times of the man they were mourning:

> From quiet homes and first beginning
> Out to the undiscovered end,
> There's nothing worth the wear of winning,
> But laughter and the love of friends.

APPENDIX

BOOKS

1951 *Round the Rugged Rocks* (novel)
1971 *The Moon's A Balloon* (memoirs)
1975 *Bring on the Empty Horses* (memoirs)
1981 *Go Slowly, Come Back Quickly* (novel)

FILMS

1932 (debut) *All The Winners* (London Film Company) with Allan Jeayes, Muriel George. Dir: Bunty Watts.

1934 *Without Regret* (Paramount) with Elissa Landi, Paul Cavanagh, Frances Drake. Dir: Harold Young.
Barbary Coast (Goldwyn-UA) with Miriam Hopkins, Edward G. Robinson, Joel McCrea. Dir: Howard Hawks.

1935 *A Feather in Her Hat* (Columbia) with Pauline Lord, Basil Rathbone, Louis Hayward. Dir: Alfred Santell.
Splendour (Goldwyn-UA) with Miriam Hopkins, Joel McCrea, Paul Cavanagh. Dir: Elliot Nugent.

1936 *Rose Marie* (MGM) with Jeanette MacDonald, Nelson Eddy, Reginald Owen, James Stewart. Dir: W. S. Van Dyke.
Palm Springs (Paramount) with Frances Langford, Guy Standing, Spring Byington. Dir: Aubrey Scotto (US title: *Palm Springs Affair*).
Thank You, Jeeves (Twentieth Century-Fox) with Arthur Treacher, Virginia Fields. Dir: Arthur Greville.
Dodsworth (Goldwyn-UA) with Walter Huston,

Ruth Chatterton, Paul Lukas, Mary Astor. Dir: William Wyler.

The Charge of the Light Brigade (Warner Brothers) with Errol Flynn, Olivia de Havilland, Nigel Bruce. Dir: Michael Curtiz.

Beloved Enemy (Goldwyn-UA) with Merle Oberon, Brian Aherne, Jerome Cowan. Dir: H. C. Potter.

1937 *We Have Our Moments* (Universal) with Sally Eilers, James Dunn, Mischa Auer. Dir: Alfred L. Werker.

The Prisoner of Zenda (Selznick-UA) with Ronald Colman, Madeleine Carroll, Douglas Fairbanks Jr, Mary Astor, C. Aubrey Smith, Raymond Massey. Dir: John Cromwell and W. S. Van Dyke.

Dinner at the Ritz (New World-Fox) with Annabella, Paul Lukas, Romney Brent. Dir: Harold Schuster.

1938 *Bluebeard's Eighth Wife* (Paramount) with Claudette Colbert, Gary Cooper. Dir: Ernst Lubitsch.

Four Men and a Prayer (Twentieth Century-Fox) with Loretta Young, Richard Greene, George Sanders, C. Aubrey Smith. Dir: John Ford.

Three Blind Mice (Twentieth Century-Fox) with Loretta Young, Joel McCrea, Marjorie Weaver. Dir: William A. Seiter.

The Dawn Patrol (Warner Brothers) with Errol Flynn, Basil Rathbone, Donald Crisp. Dir: Edmund Golding.

1939 *Wuthering Heights* (Goldwyn-UA) with Merle Oberon, Laurence Olivier, Geraldine Fitzgerald, Flora Robson, Hugh Williams. Dir: William Wyler.

Bachelor Mother (RKO) with Ginger Rogers, Charles Coburn, E. E. Clive. Dir: Garson Kanin.

Eternally Yours (United Artists) with Loretta Young, Hugh Herbert, Billie Burke. Dir: Tay Garnett.

The Real Glory (Goldwyn-UA) with Gary Cooper, Andrea Leeds, Reginald Owen. Dir: Henry Hathaway.

Raffles (Goldwyn-UA) with Olivia de Havilland,

May Whitty, E. E. Clive. Dir: Sam Wood and William Wyler.

1942 *The First of the Few* (British Aviation Pictures) with Leslie Howard, Rosamund John, Roland Culver. Dir: Leslie Howard US title: *Spitfire*).

1944 *The Way Ahead* (Two Cities) with Raymond Huntley, William Hartnell, Stanley Holloway, Peter Ustinov. Dir: Carol Reed.

1945 *A Matter of Life and Death* (J. Arthur Rank) with Roger Livesey, Raymond Massey, Kim Hunter, Marius Goring, Richard Attenborough. Dir: Michael Powell and Emeric Pressburger (US title: *Stairway to Heaven*).

1946 *The Perfect Marriage* (Paramount) with Loretta Young, Eddie Albert, Zasu Pitts. Dir: Lewis Allen. *Magnificent Doll* (Universal) with Ginger Rogers, Burgess Meredith, Horace McNally. Dir: Frank Borzage.

1947 *The Other Love* (Enterprise) with Barbara Stanwyck, Richard Conte, Gilbert Roland. Dir: André de Toth.
The Bishop's Wife (Goldwyn) with Cary Grant, Loretta Young, Gladys Cooper. Dir: Henry Koster.

1948 *Bonnie Prince Charlie* (London Films) with Margaret Leighton, Jack Hawkins, Judy Campbell. Dir: Anthony Kimmins.
Enchantment (Goldwyn) with Teresa Wright, Evelyn Keyes, Farley Granger, Leo G. Carroll. Dir: Irving Reis.

1949 *A Kiss in the Dark* (Warner Brothers) with Jane Wyman, Broderick Crawford, Maria Ouspenskaya. Dir: Delmer Davies.
A Kiss for Corliss (Strand) with Shirley Temple, Tom Tully, Virginia Welles. Dir: Richard Wallace.
The Elusive Pimpernel (London Films) with Margaret Leighton, Cyril Cusack, Jack Hawkins. Dir: Michael Powell and Emeric Pressburger (US title: *The Fighting Pimpernel*).

1950 *The Toast of New Orleans* (MGM) with Kathryn Grayson, Mario Lanza, J. Carrol Naish. Dir: Norman Taurog.
Happy Go Lovely (Associated British) with Vera Ellen, Cesar Romero, Bobby Howes. Dir: Bruce Humberstone.

1951 *Soldiers Three* (MGM) with Stewart Granger, Walter Pidgeon, Robert Newton. Dir: Tay Garnett.
The Lady Says No (Stillman Productions) with Joan Caulfield, James Robertson Justice. Dir: Frank Ross.
Appointment With Venus (British Films) with Glynis Johns, Barry Jones, Kenneth More. Dir: Ralph Thomas (US title: *Island Rescue*).

1953 *The Moon is Blue* (Preminger Productions) with William Holden, Maggie McNamara. Dir: Otto Preminger.
The Love Lottery (Ealing) with Peggy Cummins, Anne Vernon, Herbert Lom. Dir: Charles Crichton.

1954 *Happy Ever After* (Associated British) with Yvonne de Carlo, Barry Fitzgerald, George Cole. Dir: Mario Zampi (US title: *Tonight's the Night*).
Carrington VC (Romulus) with Margaret Leighton, Noelle Middleton, Laurence Naismith. Dir: Anthony Asquith (US title: *Court Martial*).

1955 *The King's Thief* (MGM) with Ann Blyth, Edmund Purdom, George Sanders, Roger Moore. Dir: Robert Z. Leonard.

1956 *The Birds and the Bees* (Gomalco Productions) with George Gobel, Mitzi Gaynor. Dir: Norman Taurog.
Around the World in Eighty Days (London Films-Todd AO) with Cantinflas, Shirley MacLaine, Robert Newton, Charles Boyer, Ronald Colman, John Gielgud, Noël Coward, Robert Morley, Marlene Dietrich, Fernandel, Hermione Gingold, Trevor Howard, Buster Keaton, Frank Sinatra, John Mills, etc. Dir: Michael Anderson.
The Little Hut (MGM) with Ava Gardner, Stewart

Granger, Walter Chiari, Finlay Currie. Dir: Mark Robson.

The Silken Affair (Dragon Films) with Genevieve Page, Ronald Squire, Wilfrid Hyde-White. Dir: Roy Kellino.

1957 *Oh Men! Oh Women!* (Twentieth Century-Fox) with Dan Dailey, Ginger Rogers, Tony Randall. Dir: Nunnally Johnson.

My Man Godfrey (Universal) with June Allyson, Eva Gabor, Jessie Royce Landis. Dir: Henry Koster.

Bonjour Tristesse (Wheel Productions) with Deborah Kerr, Jean Seberg, Juliette Greco. Dir: Otto Preminger.

1958 *Separate Tables* (Clifton Productions) with Deborah Kerr, Rita Hayworth, Burt Lancaster, Wendy Hiller, Gladys Cooper, Cathleen Nesbitt, Felix Aylmer. Dir: Delbert Mann.

1959 *Ask Any Girl* (Euterpe Productions) with Shirley MacLaine, Gig Young, Rod Taylor. Dir: Charles Walters.

Happy Anniversary (Fileds Productions) with Mitzi Gaynor, Carl Reiner, Patty Duke. Dir: David Miller.

1960 *Please Don't Eat the Daisies* (Euterpe Productions) with Doris Day, Janis Paige, Richard Haydn. Dir: Charles Walters.

1961 *The Guns of Navarone* (Open Road) with Gregory Peck, Anthony Quinn, Stanley Baker, Anthony Quayle, Irene Papas, Gia Scala. Dir: J. Lee Thompson.

The Best of Enemies (de Laurentiis) with Alberto Sordi, Michael Wilding. Dir: Guy Hamilton (Italian title: *I Due Nemici*).

1962 *The Captive City* (Maxima Film) with Ben Gazzara, Michael Craig, Martin Balsam. Dir: Joseph Anthony (US title: *The Conquered City*; Italian title: *La Città Prigioniera*).

The Shortest Day (Titanus) with Marcello Mastroianni, Stewart Granger. Dir: Sergio Corbucci (Italian title: *Il Giorno Più Corto*).

The Road to Hong Kong (United Artists) with Bob Hope, Bing Crosby, Dorothy Lamour, Joan Collins, Robert Morley. Dir: Norman Panama.

Guns of Darkness (Cavalcade-Concorde) with Leslie Caron, James Robertson Justice. Dir: Anthony Asquith.

1963 *55 Days at Peking* (Bronston Productions) with Charlton Heston, Ava Gardner, Robert Helpmann, Flora Robson, Leo Genn. Dir: Nicholas Ray.

1964 *The Pink Panther* (Mirisch) with Peter Sellers, Robert Wagner, Capucine, Claudia Cardinale. Dir: Blake Edwards.

Bedtime Story (Lankershim-Pennebaker) with Marlon Brando, Shirley Jones. Dir: Ralph Lavy.

1965 *Lady L* (MGM) with Sophia Loren, Paul Newman, Claude Dauphin, Philippe Noiret. Dir: Peter Ustinov.

Where the Spies Are (Val Guest) with Françoise Dorleac, Cyril Cusack, Nigel Davenport. Dir: Val Guest.

1966 *Eye of the Devil* (Filmways) with Deborah Kerr, Donald Pleasance, Flora Robson. Dir: J. Lee Thompson.

1967 *Casino Royale* (Famous Artists) with Peter Sellers, Ursula Andress, Orson Welles, Woody Allen, Deborah Kerr, William Holden, Charles Boyer. Dir: John Huston, Ken Hughes, etc.

1968 *The Extraordinary Seaman* (Frankenheimer) with Faye Dunaway, Alan Alda, Mickey Rooney. Dir: John Frankenheimer.

Prudence and the Pill (Twentieth Century-Fox) with Deborah Kerr, Robert Coote, Edith Evans, Judy Geeson, Keith Michell. Dir: Fielder Cook and Ronald Neame.

The Impossible Years (Marten Productions) with Lola Albright, Christina Ferrare. Dir: Michael Gordon.

1969 *Before Winter Comes* (Windward) with Topol, Anna Karina, John Hurt, Anthony Quayle. Dir: J. Lee Thompson.

The Brain (Gaumont International) with Jean-Paul Belmondo, Bourvil, Eli Wallach. Dir: Gérard Oury (French title: *Le Cerveau*).

1970 *The Statue* (Shaftel Productions) with Virna Lisi, Robert Vaughn, John Cleese. Dir: Rod Amateau.

1972 *King, Queen, Knave* (Maran-Wolper) with Gina Lollobrigida, John Moulder Brown. Dir: Jerzy Skolimowski (German title: *Herzbube*).

1973 *Vampira* (World Films) with Teresa Graves, Peter Bayliss, Jennie Linden, Nicky Henson. Dir: Clive Donner.

1974 *Paper Tiger* (MacLean Films) with Toshiro Mifune, Hardy Kruger, Ivan Desny. Dir: Ken Annakin.

1975 *No Deposit, No Return* (Disney) with Barbara Felden, Kim Richards, Darren McGavin. Dir: Norman Tokar.

1976 *Murder by Death* (Columbia) with Truman Capote, Maggie Smith, Alec Guinness, Peter Sellers, Peter Falk, Elsa Lanchester, Estelle Winwood. Dir: Robert Moore.

1977 *Candleshoe* (Disney) with Jodie Foster, Leo McKern, Helen Hayes. Dir: Norman Tokar.

1978 *Death on the Nile* (EMI) with Peter Ustinov, Bette Davis, Mia Farrow, Maggie Smith. Dir: John Guillermin.

1979 *Escape to Athena* (ITC) with Roger Moore, Telly Savalas, Stefanie Powers, Claudia Cardinale. Dir: George Pan Cosmatos.

A Nightingale Sang in Berkeley Square (Fisz Productions) with Oliver Tobias, Gloria Grahame, Joss Ackland, George Baker. Dir: Ralph Thomas.

1980 *Rough Cut* (Paramount) with Burt Reynolds, Lesley-Anne Down, Patrick Magee. Dir: Don Siegel.

The Sea Wolves (Uniprom International) with Gregory Peck, Roger Moore, Trevor Howard, Patrick MacNee, John Standing. Dir: Andrew V. MacLaglen.

1981 *Better Late Than Never* (Golden Harvest) with Maggie Smith, Art Carney, Lionel Jeffries. Dir: Bryan Forbes (Working title: *Ménage à Trois*).

1982 *The Trail of the Pink Panther* and *The Curse of the Pink Panther* (MGM-UA) with Robert Wagner, Joanna Lumley, Capucine, Richard Mulligan. Dir: Blake Edwards.

STAGE

1936 *Wedding* (Pasadena Playhouse, California)
1951 *Nina* with Gloria Swanson, Alan Webb (Broadway and tour)
1953 *The Moon is Blue* (San Francisco)

TELEVISION AND RADIO

Throughout the late 1930s David Niven made frequent appearances in American radio dramas including the first American production of Coward's *Cavalcade* with Herbert Marshall and Madeleine Carroll in 1936. He also hosted the 1939 tribute by the British acting colony in Hollywood to King George VI and Queen Elizabeth during their state visit to the USA. During the Second World War he was a regular member of the panel for a transatlantic BBC discussion programme, and early in the 1950s began appearing in live television dramas from New York. In later years his major television roles included many plays for his Four-Star Playhouse production company as well as three seasons of *The Rogues* (1963–5). He starred in *The Petrified Forest* (1952), *Girls in their Summer Dresses* (1954), *The Bluffers* (1974), *The Canterville Ghost* (1975) and *A Man Called Intrepid* (1979), and did the commentary for two series of wildlife documentaries for American and

British television. He also made appearances in several whisky and coffee advertisements and one Japanese deodorant commercial.

Index